SPIRITUAL ABUSE AND HEALTHY ACCOMPANIMENT

Spiritual Abuse and Healthy Accompaniment

Insights from Psychology and Theology

THEOLOGY AT THE FRONTIERS

Katharina Anna Fuchs
Stefania De Vito

Paulist Press
New York / Mahwah, NJ

Cover image by DavidZydd/iStock.com
Cover design by Dawn Massa, Lightly Salted Graphics
Book design by Lynn Else

Library of Congress Cataloging-in-Publication Data available upon request.

ISBN 978-0-8091-5764-8 (paperback)
ISBN 978-0-8091-8930-4 (ebook)

Published by Paulist Press
997 Macarthur Boulevard
Mahwah, NJ 07430
www.paulistpress.com

Printed and bound in the
United States of America

To those who were touched by the love of Jesus
through the wounds on the cross,
who saw the light in them and made them slits of light.
And to all the wounded on their journey,
struggling to find the strength to imagine a brighter future,
despite the challenges they are facing.

Contents

Preface

As the authors were in the process of correcting the final proofs of this volume, the Dicastery for the Doctrine of the Faith and the Dicastery for Legislative Texts set up a working group to define the crime of spiritual abuse and to arrive at a more appropriate definition in matters relating to spirituality and alleged supernatural phenomena.[1] This shows the need for and the challenges of facing the issue of spiritual abuse. We hope that our book can make a concrete and proactive contribution to this sensitive issue. Indeed, identifying and exposing abusive behavior of diverse kinds is a key sign of the times. Among the Christian Churches, and not least the Catholic Church, this has become increasingly evident over the last thirty years. Recent years have witnessed numerous accusations against priests, men and women religious, and laity of the Catholic Church who, in "the name of God," physically or sexually abused minors and (vulnerable) adults or covered up these crimes. Many faithful have turned away from the Church, questioning the experience of faith they have received and showing anger, resentment, and a loss of trust toward Christian leaders as well as the Christian community as a whole.

Addressing this problem requires that Christians recognize that the Church is undergoing not only an institutional crisis but also an anthropological one. In-depth reflection about what theories of the human person—what anthropology—have been operative in its institutional practices is required. The Church also increasingly recognizes that reflecting on this matter cannot be achieved by any one discipline but must be addressed by the collaboration of several areas of expertise.

In Catholic circles, some of the clearest and most positive responses to the abuse crisis have emerged in documents produced to guide the formation of young men for the priesthood. This need not come as a surprise because abuse perpetrated by priests has caused the most scandal.[2]

Abuse in the Church is a symptom of a generalized anthropological crisis marked by a loss of identity from anthropological as well as spiritual and psychological points of view. This results in an inability to recognize ethical values and meanings on which to act and make responsible choices,[3] leading to widespread consumerism, the dissipation of human relationships based on mutual recognition, the consumption of spiritual values, selfishness, loneliness,[4] idolatry, and a culture of waste. Pope Francis says, "The current socio-cultural context is progressively eroding awareness of what makes human life precious."[5]

A Fruitful Collaboration

This volume is the result of a fruitful collaboration between two laywomen, a psychologist and a biblical theologian, who deal daily with the formation and the accompaniment of fellow Christians. From the beginning, our perspectives and sensibilities were extremely different, albeit both valid and meaningful, but they needed to converge. One of the first convergences was to use the term *spiritual accompaniment* instead of the terms *spiritual direction* or *spiritual guidance*. As you will see throughout the volume, linguistic transformations are not a matter of semantics. They are the tangible sense of an anthropological and theological renewal. Furthermore, the terms *direction* or *guidance* have a different connotation and may create a false expectation in those who ask for it, namely, that they will be directed on or toward the right way and receive the solution for their problems. Indeed, as stated by Pope Francis, spiritual accompaniment is

> looking at oneself in the mirror with the help of another, this helps a great deal because the other tells you the truth—when he or she is truthful—and in this way helps you. God's grace in us always works on our nature.…First of all, it is important to make ourselves known, without fear of sharing

> the most fragile aspects, where we find ourselves to be more sensitive, weak, or afraid of being judged. Making oneself known, manifesting oneself to a person who accompanies us on the journey of life. Not who decides for us, no: but who accompanies us.[6]

Katharina Anna Fuchs is a trained psychologist and a native of Germany who has chosen Rome, Italy, as her second hometown. She studied at the Catholic University of Eichstaett-Ingolstadt in Germany, the Pontifical Gregorian University in Rome, Italy, and the University of Glasgow in Scotland. She works as a tenured full professor (*professore straordinario*) at the Institute of Psychology of the Pontifical Gregorian University.

Furthermore, she teaches at the S. Peter Favre Centre of the Gregorian University, a center specializing in the formation of future formators to priesthood and religious life. She has more than twelve years of experience working in the field of the prevention of sexual abuse. Over the past six years, she has also been working on other forms of abuse and their prevention, especially spiritual abuse and the abuse of conscience. Over the years, she became more aware that sexual abuse is just one piece of many related aspects of abuse that are found within the Catholic Church but also in other Churches (for example, Protestant Churches) and in society at large. Coming to understand better the role of power, trust, manipulation, and vulnerability, she recognized the urgent need for an interdisciplinary and intercultural treatment of these issues.

Stefania De Vito is an Italian Catholic biblical scholar and a trained family counselor who grew up in southern Italy in an area plagued by economic, educational, and religious problems. She earned a bachelor's degree in philosophy and a doctorate in biblical theology at the Gregorian University in Rome. Currently, she is professor of biblical culture at Lumsa University in Rome and engages in formation and spirituality. Her experiences with The Spiritual Exercises of St. Ignatius were an essential part of her life journey and her desire to help others. In her pastoral work, she has gained an awareness that no one experience of God fits everyone, and even abused and traumatized people can experience deep and sincere faith. Their stories of faith and conversion generate new life in the Church and society.

Principal Questions

Faced with the crisis of abuse in the Church, we sought to offer a contribution to this issue from an explicitly Catholic perspective, indeed from one influenced by the tradition of Ignatian spirituality. By analyzing spiritual abuse in an interdisciplinary way—including through psychology, theology, and spirituality—this book seeks to answer several questions:

1. What is the boundary between a healthy spiritual accompaniment and an abusive one?
2. How can one avoid the proliferation of abuse in individual and communal spiritual journeys?
3. What is the appropriate relationship between psychology and theology in guiding reflection about these matters?
4. Might the explicitly religious reflection of a theological book like this be of assistance to psychologists as they consider what are the anthropological presuppositions that guide them?

Audience

A primary audience for this work is spiritual companions, retreat leaders, catechists, and formators working in dioceses, seminaries, or religious communities. Here the book can contribute to reflection on how to prevent spiritual abuse. A secondary audience is psychologists. We invite a deeper reflection on the anthropology of the human person that underlies the discipline. Is psychology open to the notion that the individual has a spiritual orientation? What is the nature of this spirituality? Might psychology need to accept that it has a necessary contribution to make to healthy spiritual accompaniment? Might psychology need to engage in interdisciplinary collaboration with theology on this matter? How are we to compare spiritual accompaniment and psychotherapy as professional practices?

Spiritual abuse and the spiritual journey involve all human dimensions: biological, cognitive, affective, psychic, and spiritual. The many survivors of spiritual abuse point to the existence of a deep desire for

God that had led those people on individual or communal journeys of faith that turned out to be abusive. For this reason, we wondered whether the traditional expressions of religion, rooted in a pure desire to know God, can help more secular thinkers draw up guidelines for a "healthy spiritual accompaniment" that can differentiate itself from anything resembling spiritual or mental abuse.

Within the Catholic Church, Pope Francis has exhorted Catholic thinkers to interdisciplinary collaboration at many levels. Addressing a conference relating psychotherapy to spiritual accompaniment, he stated,

> The world today is going through a profound anthropological crisis, a crisis of meaning to which the Church has the duty to respond appropriately and effectively.... Thus, in the face of the imperative to learn to say no to evil, to lift up those whose dignity is wounded or offended, and the urgent need to train people capable in turn of forging trainers with a solid anthropological background, the Church continues to expect from your Institute a quality service based on the knowledge of psychology with the contributions of theology and philosophy.[7]

Method: See-Judge-Act

What is the secret to such a fruitful dialogue? From our perspective, the answer is the employment of a method known in Roman Catholic circles as "see-judge-act." This method was first envisioned by a young priest, Joseph Cardijn, who would later become a cardinal and an active participant in Vatican II. His method was endorsed by Pope John XXIII in 1961, both as a method of relating pastoral action to theological reflection and as a basis for the interdisciplinary collaboration of academics. Pope John XXIII states:

> There are three stages which should normally be followed in the reduction of social principles into practice. First, one reviews the concrete situation; secondly, one forms a judgment on it in the light of these same principles; thirdly, one

> decides what in the circumstances can and should be done to implement these principles. These are the three stages that are usually expressed in the three terms: look, judge, act.[8]

The first stage, "to see," begins with a problem that is emerging from concrete situations. For the case of this present study, this implies gathering an accurate understanding of the phenomenon of spiritual abuse and attempting to see it through the eyes of wounded people. This first step should be characterized by an attitude of deep solidarity. The second movement, "to judge," should involve discernment in which one seeks to understand the situation—using all the academic disciplines necessary to do so—with an eye to identifying where one might be able to take effective action to ameliorate the situation. In our case this implied studying the phenomenon of spiritual abuse through the lens of gospel and Christian tradition, where faith and reason, past and present gather. The third movement, "to act," should involve acting in solidarity both with the community affected by spiritual and mental abuses and with the Christian community responsible for the formation and accompaniment of individuals in their care, helping them to avoid any hint of abusive behavior and to understand deeply what is involved in healthy accompaniment.[9] While our focus will be on processes of Christian, indeed Catholic, accompaniment, we hope that what we have to say will be helpful for others.

Further, we would like to develop an approach to spiritual accompaniment influenced by the tradition established by Saint Ignatius of Loyola who lived between 1491 and 1556 and founded the religious order the Society of Jesus, known as the Jesuits. "Ignatian spirituality" has its origins in *The Spiritual Exercises of St. Ignatius*. These spiritual practices do not presuppose that the individual being accompanied has "withdrawn from the world" and lives in a monastery. As a result, Ignatian spirituality was found useful for laypeople from its earliest emergence. Indeed, this spirituality is well suited for the modern person. It implies an ability to read and a certain freedom to choose between diverse forms of life, something less possible in premodern centuries. Its combination of engagement with practical affairs and an appeal to interior reflection makes it compatible with a see-judge-act process of institutional decision-making.

The ever-increasing cases of sexual, psychological, spiritual, and conscience abuse in the Catholic Church are "signs of the times" to be heeded. In truth, on one side, they scandalize and generate a flight from religious experience; on the other side, they testify to a deep longing for God. For this reason, it is urgent to challenge abusive behavior and to invite the Church to rethink the educational and formative processes not only of seminaries and houses of formation for men and women religious but also of young people and families.

Relational fragmentation and the loss of community identity can result from ignoring mutual care and acceptance.[10] So, the challenge of abuse calls not only the theologians, the canonical judges, spiritual fathers or mothers, and psychologists but also those living a baptismal vocation.[11] Says Pope Francis, "We are called to be guardians of one another, to strengthen the bonds of harmony and sharing."[12] Therefore, this book was born as an attempt at collaboration between psychology, theology, and spirituality in which the horizontal dimension implies and does not exclude a vertical dimension.

This book is divided into two sections. The first part, "What Is Spiritual Abuse?," defines spiritual abuse and examines its dynamics and consequences. Part 1 concludes with a psychological and theological evaluation of spiritual abuse. Part 2, "What Is Healthy Spiritual Accompaniment?," looks at the roles of both psychology and theology in accompaniment and outlines principles of spiritual accompaniment and ways of preventing abuse. It also discusses ways to help in healing spiritual abuse. The final reflection offers insights into a praxis of the kingdom of God in the face of the challenge of abuse. The importance of reflecting on the mission of the Church, wounded by the scourge of abuse, allows for the emergence of a cruciform praxis that starts from abuse as an experience of the cross, crosses the moors of a renewed theology of the cross, and arrives at an ecclesial praxis of the cross.

Pope Francis has characterized our historic moment as "Dark Clouds over a Fragmented World."[13] Perhaps the need has never been so great to create communities of humanly and spiritually mature people capable of being catalysts of redemptive transformation of such circumstances and promoters of genuine human progress.

Acknowledgments

The creation of this book is certainly the result of a valuable collaboration between the two authors. However, it is also a result of the passion, perseverance, and commitment of the people who have accompanied us on this journey in various capacities and moments. Our thanks therefore go to Fr. Gerard Whelan, SJ, who encouraged us to write together on this topic and who spent time engaged in dialogue with us. Further thanks go to Paul McMahon for his persistent confidence in this endeavor and to Mary Dern Walker, whose editorial mastery made the final layout of the volume possible. We thank her also for her patience in the linguistic revision process.

We want to express our gratitude to the people who have quietly accompanied us with their prayers, their presence, and their encouragement, especially our families. Last but not least, our special thanks go to those who have been wounded and abused, who have stood up and witnessed to us the ongoing creative and redemptive power of God the Father. Thank you for your sharing and for giving us the opportunity of listening to you.

Abbreviations

AL	*Amoris Laetitia*
APA	American Psychological Association
CCC	*Catechism of the Catholic Church*
DH	*Dignitatis Humanae*
EG	*Evangelii Gaudium*
Exx.	*The Spiritual Exercises of St. Ignatius*
GS	*Gaudium et Spes*
LG	*Lumen Gentium*
SNTM	Servizio Nazionale per la Tutela dei Minori e delle Persone Vulnerabili

PART 1

WHAT IS SPIRITUAL ABUSE?

1

Spiritual Abuse

What Are We Talking About?

HOW CAN ABUSE be spiritual? Some people may associate spiritual abuse with sects or cults. Still others may think of the sexual abuse that has erupted in the Roman Catholic Church (as well as in Protestant Churches to some extent). Still others speak out, urging Churches and society to face spiritual abuse as soon and as fast as possible to avoid further damage to the life, the faith, and the health of those affected over decades of not dealing adequately and immediately with cases of sexual abuse. We need to become aware of the central elements of spiritual abuse in order to understand its effects on the lives of victims as well as on their environment. Furthermore, a better understanding of spiritual abuse will have a strong impact on what measures need to be taken to prevent spiritual abuse in accompaniment and in community life. This includes knowing how to offer those who suffer or who have suffered spiritual abuse the care they need to start a process of healing—be it on an individual, a group, or a community level. From a theological point of view, it may help to recognize the fundamental aspects in the life of a believer that deserve to be dealt with in a new way.

Beyond the Sexual Abuse of Minors

The word *abuse* is most associated with child sexual abuse, be it in the Catholic Church or in the secular world. This is due to the various child sexual abuse scandals in the Catholic Church starting in Canada and the United States in the 1980s and 1990s followed by other English-speaking countries around the globe (Ireland, Australia, the United Kingdom). Over the past twenty years, child sexual abuse scandals have shattered the Catholic Church in European countries including Austria, Belgium, Germany, Poland, and, more recently, France, as well as in non-Western or non-European countries such as Chile in 2018.

Over the last years, the focus of sexual abuse has shifted to include, in addition, a group of adults that is particularly vulnerable or at risk of harm, called vulnerable persons, vulnerable adults, or adults at risk (of harm). These adults are aged eighteen or older but in need of special protection, care, or support because of disability or other types of mental or physical impairment, risk of abuse, exploitation, or neglect. Usually, they are unable to make, communicate, or implement informed decisions regarding their person. A uniform definition of vulnerable adults does not exist so far but varies from country to country and context to context.

For the Catholic Church, the definition of vulnerable adults was updated and extended by Pope Francis in his *motu proprio Vos Estis Lux Mundi* (2023). According to the *motu proprio*, the term *vulnerable person* refers to "any person in a state of infirmity, physical or mental deficiency, or deprivation of personal liberty which, in fact, even occasionally, limits their ability to understand or to want or otherwise resist the offence." The issue of whether "vulnerable people" can include seminarians, religious sisters, or other adults who are emotionally or spiritually dependent on clergy has come to the fore in the wake of the scandal over ex-Cardinal Theodore McCarrick, a once high-ranking American cleric who molested seminarians, and over revelations of priests and bishops around the world sexually preying on nuns or laywomen. With this in mind, Pope Francis approved changes in Book 6 of the Code of Canon Law to explicitly criminalize the sexual abuse of adults by priests who abuse their authority and to underline that laypeople who hold Church offices (such as school principals) also can be sanctioned for similar sex crimes. These examples of definitions and changes made over the last few years show clearly that adults can also be vulnerable, whether defined as vulnerable or not, and at risk of harm.[1]

The sexual abuse of minors and vulnerable adults involves much more than crossing sexual boundaries; trust and power are abused. The phenomenon of clericalism is seen as one of the main causes not only of sexual abuse but also of the abuse of power and conscience in the Catholic Church. The perspective can be extended to the problem of grace and sin that has run through the history of Christianity since its origins, as we shall see in the following chapters.

The overwhelming majority of research on sexual abuse that occurred and still occurs within religious settings has focused on the Roman Catholic Church, not on Protestant Christians. Yet, Protestant Christian Churches are the most prominent religious institutions in such countries as the United States of America in terms of the number of Churches and participants. Protestant Christian Churches seem to have been dragging their feet in many countries around the globe; nevertheless, awareness and sensitivity toward sexual abuse have grown over the last few years. Empirical research studies on sexual abuse in Protestant Christian Churches in the United States report 326 cases for the years from 1999 to 2014.[2] Another study identified seven hundred alleged predators within the Southern Baptist Convention over a period of twenty years.[3] The Southern Baptist Convention has started to move to prevent sexual abuse and cover-up, based on the #MeToo and #ChurchToo movements. In 2019 it voted to change its constitution to distance itself from Churches that cover up and fail to report sexual abuse. In addition, a committee was set up for the review of complaints about how cases were and are handled.[4]

Another source of abuse was the heavy-shepherding movement (discipleship movement) that emerged in the 1970s and 1980s within the charismatic-evangelical communities of the United States.[5] This movement was based on a system of personal shepherds to whom subordinates owed openness of conscience and blind obedience. The strictly hierarchical structure was supposed to serve the more rapid spiritual growth of the members and a greater missionary success of the movement. However, after a short period of rapid growth, fierce tensions and disputes emerged. Rigid authority structures that were biblically based were susceptible to abuse and left many members damaged and traumatized. All this caused a lasting sensitization of the U.S. evangelical-charismatic communities on the topic of abuse.[6]

In Germany, another country with a long history of Protestant Christians, the Evangelische Kirche Deutschlands[7] (the Evangelical Church in Germany) reported in 2019 over seven hundred complaints of sexual abuse committed by clerics or Church employees. At the beginning of 2024, the Evangelische Kirche Deutschlands presented the results of a three-year investigation on sexual abuse within the Protestant Church in Germany, extrapolating about 9,355 victims since 1946.[8]

The different organization of Protestant Christian Churches compared to the Catholic Church needs to be mentioned as one possible significant difference for the cover-up but also the discovery of sexual abuse. Contrary to the Roman Catholic Church on a global and national level, Protestant Christian Churches do not have hierarchical structures. "Consequently, instances of sexual abuse within Protestant Christianity might appear isolated when they could be part of a larger overall pattern of offender and offending behaviors."[9]

The Catholic Church has gone through a long-lasting and painful learning process in many countries about how to face the tragedy of sexual abuse of minors and vulnerable adults. It would be fatal if the mistakes of the past (such as systematically covering up abuse, not listening to those affected and not believing them, putting offender protection before victim protection, and more) were repeated. This also applies to spiritual abuse. There is no need to start from zero to understand and prevent spiritual abuse in the Catholic Church when the possibility and the need exist to build on prior experiences with the prevention of sexual abuse. Thus, the psychological and theological reflections developed so far are of great value; they help us to make progress in this challenge.

Defining Spiritual Abuse

Spiritual abuse is not easy to grasp due to both a lack of empirical studies and conceptual imprecision and ambiguity. A major difficulty linked to the issue of spiritual abuse is its understanding and, therefore, its definition and translation into diverse languages.[10] In the German-speaking world, the expression *geistlicher Missbrauch* has gained acceptance in recent years, although the terms *spiritual* and *religious* (*spiritueller Missbrauch* and *religiöser Missbrauch*) are used, emphasizing the reference to a Church or a religious community. One seldom hears or reads such words as *spiritueller Missbrauch*, the literal translation of *spiritual abuse*, whereas the French, Spanish, and Italian languages use the terms *abus spirituel, abuso espiritual,* and *abuso spirituale.* Out of these terms the question arises whether we are talking about the same thing when we talk about spiritual abuse in an international or multilinguistic context. Not necessarily. Therefore, agreeing on what is meant by *spiritual abuse* becomes more important than agreeing on a common term.

In the Anglophone world, the term *spiritual abuse* had already appeared in the 1960s in the United States and reappeared at the beginning of the 1990s through a then-groundbreaking work published by David Johnson and Jeff VanVonderen. Johnson and VanVonderen proposed a broad definition of spiritual abuse, defining it as "the mistreatment of a person who is in need of help, support, or greater spiritual empowerment, with the result of weakening, undermining, or decreasing that person's spiritual empowerment."[11]

German theologians have proposed several descriptions of spiritual abuse. Sr. Dr. Katharina Kluitmann, a German Franciscan sister, understands spiritual abuse as a collective term for various forms of emotional abuse and/or abuse of power that occur especially in the context of spiritual and/or religious life as well as in accompaniment (such as confession, spiritual accompaniment, and so on) and can affect both individuals and entire communities. As such, boundaries in a person's intimate sphere are violated and exceeded.[12] According to the German Jesuit Fr. Klaus Mertes, the term tries to grasp something that affects individuals and groups in which people claim to be able to tell other people what God wants for them. So, the abuse is spiritual and religious in the strict sense of the word, where religion and religious language are misused to gain spiritual power over people.[13] Still another way to define spiritual abuse is proposed by Dr. Doris Reisinger, a German theologian and philosopher who experienced spiritual and sexual abuse herself in the past as a former member of a religious community. She defines spiritual abuse as "a violation of spiritual self-determination." She adds that "the injury brings people into spiritual distress."[14]

Dr. Lisa Oakley and her colleague Justin Humphreys propose a comprehensive definition of spiritual abuse on the basis of their research and experience. They define spiritual abuse as:

> a form of emotional or psychological abuse, which is characterized by a systematic pattern of coercive and controlling behavior in a religious context and which can have a deeply damaging impact on those who experience it.[15]

They extend their definition by listing various aspects that spiritual abuse may include.

> This abuse may include: manipulation and exploitation, forced accountability, censorship of decision-making, requirements for secrecy and silence, coercion to conform, control through the use of sacred texts or teaching, requirement of obedience to the abuser, the suggestion that the abuser has a "divine" position, isolation as a means of punishment, as well as superiority and elitism.[16]

Based on the various definitions proposed so far, it becomes obvious that spiritual abuse is not easy to grasp and has a wide range of characteristics. This is why many people do not yet understand what lies at the core of a spiritually abusive experience. At the same time, the differing definitions underline the overlap and relationship with other forms of abuse (such as psychological abuse or the abuse of power).[17] Also, a link to narcissism has been observed because people with narcissistic personality structures like to take on leadership roles, as these guarantee them power and keep them at the center of attention.[18] Frequently, these narcissistic traits are combined with a high level of empathy.[19]

On the basis of Katharina Anna Fuchs's work experience in a intercultural and interdisciplinary context, the exchange with other experts working and researching in the field on an international and interdisciplinary level, and conversations with victims of various forms of spiritual abuse (in spiritual accompaniment, in communities, or in movements), Fuchs proposes the following definition:

> Spiritual abuse occurs in religious or spiritual contexts, by using power and trust to manipulate, instrumentalize, control, and oppress others through spiritual means and/or "in the name of God." On the part of those affected, this leads

> to a restriction of their spiritual freedom and growth to the point of damaging their faith and/or their relationship with God; on the part of those committing the abuse to a strengthening of their own person and position, which in turn serves them to satisfy their personal needs and achieve their personal goals.[20]

Central Elements of Spiritual Abuse

Frequently, spiritual fathers or mothers, spiritual companions, or founders of religious communities or new religious movements are seen or see themselves as the voice of God. This confusion can lay a foundation for spiritual abuse.[21] It may start from the accompanying person and is mostly presumptuous, narcissistic, and instrumentalizing. Or it starts as an attribution from the accompanied person and reflects exaggerated competence, attributions, or dependencies. Systematic patterns of controlling, intimidating, and manipulative behavior are typical. The following are examples of central and specific elements of spiritual abuse: the abuse of the Holy Scripture and other sacred texts to control the behavior of the other, the suggestion of God as an accomplice, the threat of negative spiritual consequences, and the idea that a spiritual companion has been "appointed" by God for this position and therefore cannot be questioned because the person acts "in God's name."[22] One could state that spiritual abuse combines the abuse of spiritual power with claims of unique access to the divine.[23]

ABUSIVE TEACHINGS

Abuse of the Holy Scriptures often takes the form of so-called abusive teachings. Abusive teachings interpret specific sentences or terms literally or take them out of context. Typical examples are biblical and other traditional texts that present women as subordinate to men and that therefore can be used to oppress women. For example, in 1 Corinthians 7:4 we read, "The wife does not have authority over her own body, but the husband does." This is only the first part of the whole sentence that continues, "likewise, the husband does not have authority over his own body, but the wife does." Taking only the first part, as is often done by manipulative or abusive persons or communities, this sentence allows men to do whatever they like with the body of a woman and "invites" them to abuse women physically and/or sexually. Similarly, Ephesians 5:22 states, "Wives be subject to your husbands as you are to the Lord." This sentence may again empower men over women and favor patriarchal structures. But it may go even further; in spiritually abusive relationships and situations, this sentence is often used to explain and justify the "divine power" of men who make themselves equal to the Lord and command women to obey men in the same way as they would obey God.[24]

Linked to a prominent topic in abusive relationships—what is a sin and what isn't—is a misogynistic interpretation of 1 Timothy 2:14: "And Adam was not deceived; but the woman was deceived and became a transgressor." Women are frequently seen as the source of sin and were/are treated like that by abusive male spiritual companions, priests, deacons, or religious, who "needed" to find out where this sin is hidden by examining the body of a woman. The competence to define sin gives the abuser an immense and often gender-specific power over those affected.[25]

In 1 Corinthians 15:33, another sentence has been used to permit the spiritual companion or founder or superior of a community to prescribe with whom the accompanied person or community members may stay in contact: "Bad company ruins good morals." In this way, an abuser may isolate the accompanied person or members from other people, including family, friends, colleagues, and the like.

Another example that will help to explain the abuse of the Holy Scripture can be found in Matthew 18:3: "Truly, I tell you, unless you change and become like children, you will never enter the kingdom of heaven." Literally interpreted, this demand on the part of Jesus may give the impression that he wants people to behave in a childish, nonautonomous, unresponsible way, according to the wish of their parents or caregivers, without questioning or contradicting. This sentence, taken out of context, often forms the basis for spiritual companions, founders or superiors to control others, to introduce themselves more and more into others' lives, and to tell them what to do, how to behave, and what to believe.

Other religious teachings that can be used to manipulate people include the Church's doctrine of the devil and associated exorcistic practices; ideas of hell that can be used to instill fear in people; atonement theology, which can be misused to present avoidable suffering as God's will and the challenge to endure it as godly; and forcing another person to live according to the life of the Virgin Mary or another figure of the Bible, to become like them. This may include suffering like they did; for instance, on the Feast of the Seven Sorrows of Mary, a woman could be expected to suffer painful things.[26]

These examples are only a few of the many ways biblical or other traditional texts can be used to abuse others spiritually—or even physically or sexually—by manipulating, controlling, and dominating their behavior and their way of thinking, perceiving, and discerning, even permitting and justifying other forms of abuse, especially against women.

It is vital to underline the distinction between texts and teachings on the one hand and their interpretation and misuse by individuals and communities on the other. In spiritually abusive contexts and relationships, complex texts and relations between single texts and verses are reduced to a few statements. This leads to foreshortening and black-and-white thinking. A manipulative or abusive interpretation and use of the texts or verses can stem from various reasons. A person who accompanies another spiritually or a group of people (for example, in a religious community or movement) deliberately misinterprets and explains texts to others in order to manipulate and later abuse them. But it could also be that such a misinterpretation or explanation happens unconsciously due to the lack of the necessary capacity and knowledge to understand and interpret texts correctly. A third reason could be spiritual immaturity on the part of the accompanying or leading person who may have only "absorbed" what his or her own spiritual companions had taught (mostly in very directive way) without really integrating and elaborating one's own personal spirituality and taking the chance to grow and to mature spiritually. Still another reason could lie in the fact that the accompanying person, founder, or superior has been abused spiritually or is living in a spiritually abusive context and has never received any other teaching or interpretation of those texts or verses other than a spiritually manipulative and abusive one.

IDEALIZATION AND IDOLATRY

Spiritual abuse in the Christian context may be particularly perfidious, as values, beliefs, promises, biblical quotations, rituals, and the like can first be idealized and later become idols. Idols make a part of the divine, which is invisible and intangible, visible and tangible. This creates the illusion that the invisible and incomprehensible God can be seen, understood, grasped, and ultimately controlled.[27] Abusive persons (idols) put themselves or are put into a divine position, but in reality, they impede the relationship between God and human beings. This may seem to promise security, but the idol restricts the space of personal freedom in which individuals stand before God on their own responsibility. In addition, concepts or ideas can also become ideals and afterward turn into idols. Once a concept or idea is idealized, it can become absolutized in a way that other interests, needs, and rights may be sacrificed for it. Objects (such as Christian symbols) as well as persons can be seen as ideals, too, and later become idols.[28] This can be observed in many fields of the secular world (actors, singers, influencers, athletes, politicians, and others) as well as of the ecclesial world (the pope, cardinals, bishops, priests, religious men and women, missionaries, and others).

Idols are bright, alluring, and promising. They do not live only from admiration; they also live from some kind of "sacrificial cult." People who devote themselves to an idol and see in that idol their only access to the divine or to God become more and more willing to make huge sacrifices for it, even to the point of giving up themselves.[29] This means that the admirers (the person in accompaniment or the members of a community or movement) become more and more "powerless," and their idol (the spiritual companion, the superior or founder of a community or movement) becomes more and more powerful. In other words, the spiritual companion might become the one who is almighty and knows the correct answers to questions regarding life and faith; therefore, submission to the spiritual companion becomes necessary to obtain eternal salvation. Other examples of excessive values and ideals include: a clearly defined purpose in life, such as the salvation of souls or the renewal of the Church; belonging to a "new family," to the "true Church" or to the "new original community"; wealth and reputation; or the certainty of being chosen and ultimately better than others.[30]

How Spiritual Abuse Relates to Other Forms of Abuse

Due to its different dimensions and shades, spiritual abuse is not always easy to recognize and identify, but it frequently exists alongside other forms of abuse.

SPIRITUAL NEGLECT

Abuse can be thought of as acts of commission, but acts of omission also exist, which include neglect and abandonment. Just as on a physical or emotional level one can experience abuse and neglect, the same is true on a spiritual level. Emotionally, a child needs affection, love, and closeness, and physically, the child needs something to eat, drink, and wear to grow and mature in a healthy way. Similarly, people have spiritual needs. Spiritual neglect is an act of omission in spiritual accompaniment or in the daily life of movements and communities.

Spiritual neglect means that the responsible spiritual companion does not respond appropriately to the spiritual or emotional needs of the persons being accompanied but leaves them to their own devices, even though the accompanying person has the necessary capacities and requisites to accompany them and to respond to their needs.[31] It is crucial to understand that in cases of neglect the person would be able to respond to the needs of the other(s) but does not care about those needs, does not really see them, or decides consciously not to respond appropriately. This denies individuals the right and the freedom to make their own choices; consequently, they are robbed of their spiritual and/or emotional freedom and remain in a "prison" of immaturity. For example, spiritual neglect frequently happens when someone is denied the sacraments because that person does not come to Church regularly. Also, advising a victim of sexual or physical abuse from the pulpit or the confessional to offer up their suffering to God is a form of spiritual neglect. Such interpretations of suffering will lead victims of abuse to more suffering in addition to what they have already endured. Furthermore, not caring about or responding to the spiritual needs of victims of spiritual abuse can be interpreted as form of spiritual neglect.[32]

SPIRITUAL BULLYING

Spiritual bullying happens when the leaders of a movement or community use their authority and power to dictate.[33] In cases of spiritual accompaniment, it means using the accompaniment to intimidate, to harass, and to embarrass people, to make them feel uncomfortable, or to exclude them. Such behaviors are often shown in public or in the presence of others by means of texts, images, or videos. As happens in cases of bullying in other contexts such as schools, spiritual bullying may also happen through the use of new technologies and social media in the form of cyberbullying. Spiritual bullying may also affect people who left a movement or community or stopped spiritual accompaniment, "and the spiritual leader himself wrote letters on backsliders and their fate and if you ever heard of anything bad happening to any backsliders, he would make a big deal out of it and this is what God does to those who leave."[34]

SPIRITUAL MANIPULATION AND CONTROL

Spiritual manipulation and control manifest themselves by using spiritual accompaniment, pastoral care, supervision, mentoring, coaching, and the like to control the person(s) being accompanied. Often personal information and private details are passed on to third persons without asking for permission or are used in a targeted manner to manipulate others. Spiritual manipulation makes people believe that they have taken a certain decision or made a certain choice freely and consciously. In reality, they were "guided" and manipulated with spiritual means; nevertheless, spiritual control or manipulation does not limit spiritual freedom and growth in the same way as spiritual abuse or spiritual neglect do.[35]

Reviewing the characteristics related to spiritual abuse shows clearly how subtle and difficult it is to identify single types of abuse when they happen. These difficulties are linked to the fact that each characteristic has many shades of meaning and often overlaps with another one, making it difficult to identify single characteristics of spiritual abuse.

SPIRITUAL ABUSE AND SEXUAL ABUSE

Spiritual abuse has various intersections with sexual abuse.[36] The basic dynamics of both forms of abuse are similar. In both cases, power and trust have been abused. In both cases, an asymmetrical relationship exists between the abusing person and the abused person. Also, the structures (such as patriarchal structures, a strong emphasis on hierarchies, and more) that encourage abuse are comparable. Closed systems harbor a high risk of sexual abuse and spiritual abuse too. Closed systems are organizations that have no relationships with their social environment; mostly they organize all processes internally and do not try to imitate other organizations in their environment, not even partially.[37] In both sexual and spiritual abuse, boundaries are violated, which leads to lower inhibition thresholds in other areas. It can therefore be concluded that spiritual abuse can be the "breeding ground" for sexual abuse.[38]

Some examples that illustrate the relation of spiritual and sexual abuse can be seen in the sacrament of confession.[39] A quotation taken from the book *Erzählen als Widerstand*[40] (*Telling as Resistance*) illustrates the relation between spiritual and sexual abuse well: "After the absolution, he explained to me that he also had to check my marital capacity in physical terms. I had to undress."[41] Another quite prominent case combining sexual and spiritual abuse in Germany, also narrated in the above-mentioned book, is the story of a young woman pregnant by a priest after he had abused her sexually. He coerced her into an abortion and sent her to an initiated friendly priest for the subsequent necessary confession. At first, she did not allow the abortion to be performed and sought help instead of absolution in confession. But the confessor told her that there was no other way, instrumentalizing the sacrament of confession to get her to have the abortion. She felt pressured and carried out the abortion directly.[42] This story is not a single case; similar stories happened quite often in the past with regard to sexual morality and have contributed to a confessional crisis in various countries[43] as well as to sexual abuse.

Other examples that today could be classified as cases of spiritual as well as sexual abuse are the Anabaptist Kingdom of Münster in the sixteenth century,[44] the *Colonia Dignidad* (German dignity colony) in Chile,[45] the Christ Community,[46] or the crimes committed by the Mexican priest Fr. Marcial Maciel, founder of the Catholic religious order Legionaries of Christ and the Regnum Christi movement.[47] A very prominent example of the combination of sexual and spiritual abuse is the case of the Chilean priest Fernando Karadima. This case shows clearly that more than sexual abuse by a priest was involved; this is about an abusive system, more specifically, a widely ramified spiritual abuse system that continued to exist even after the conviction of Karadima. Similarly shocking have been the outcome of a two-year investigation and a report of almost nine hundred pages on the sexual and spiritual abuse by Jean Vanier, the founder of L'Arche, and by his spiritual mentor, Fr. Thomas Philippe.[48] Already a previous report released by L'Arche Internationale in 2020 confirmed that Jean Vanier had been credibly accused of sexual abuse and lied about his knowledge of abuse by Fr. Thomas Philippe, the source of the twisted "mystic-sexual" beliefs and practices.[49] These examples illustrate that sexualized violence in communities and religious institutions often cannot be understood without knowing and understanding the issue and the context of spiritual abuse. Spiritual abuse alone can "destroy" people and have deeply damaging effects, as chapter 3 illustrates, even if it is not accompanied by sexual abuse or sexualized violence.[50] Sexual abuse in ecclesial or religious contexts is not necessarily linked with spiritual abuse, though it is in most cases, just as spiritual abuse may happen without any link to sexual abuse.[51]

SPIRITUAL ABUSE AND PSYCHOLOGICAL ABUSE

Psychological abuse involves various tactics that the abusing person uses to control, frighten, or isolate another person. In most cases, the abuser is a person known to the victim. If psychological abuse occurs in the context of domestic violence, the abuser is usually the romantic partner or spouse of the victim, but it may also be a parent or another family member. Psychological abuse also happens in working and business relationships where the abuser might be the superior or a partner. In addition, cases of psychological abuse are also known from caretaker-supervised relationships in which the caretaker abuses his or her position and the dependency of the supervised person.[52] Psychological abuse may happen in secular contexts as well as in ecclesial and religious ones.

The "faces" of psychological abuse are numerous and range from humiliating, criticizing, negating, controlling, accusing, blaming, denying, and isolating. The list is long, and even longer is the list of tactics that are used to make others feel ashamed, to destabilize and minimize their self-esteem, to neglect their emotional needs, to create dependency on the abuser, and to maximize the (perceived) power of the abuser.[53] Such tactics include verbal statements on the victim's competence or character that make the victim feel like a bad person or good for nothing. Frequently abusers embarrass their victims in public by making fun of them, exposing secrets, or commenting negatively on their appearance. Furthermore, they may dismiss or put down arguments, interests, people, or objects that are important or dear to their victims. In order to control their victims, abusers may threaten, monitor, observe, or spy on their activities, contacts, mail, or passwords. Sometimes they treat them like a child, including making decisions for them or giving them orders. This may lead to complete isolation of the affected persons through shutting down social contacts and creating distance between them and their family or friends. Often psychologically abusive people try to turn others against their victims, or they ask their victims for obedience and respect.

To accuse or blame a victim, abusers may use tactics that provoke conflicts and later state that the conflict was the victim's fault, provoking feelings of guilt or of indebtedness in the victim ("I think you owe me…"). All this culminates in the denial of the abuse or accusing the victim of abuse.[54] A very devious and violent form of psychological manipulation or abuse is so-called gaslighting that includes giving false information to a person with the intent of making the victim doubt his or her memory, perception, or mental health.[55]

Despite obvious similarities between psychological abuse and spiritual abuse, it is still possible, and necessary, to see spiritual abuse as a separate form of abuse and not just as a form of psychological abuse in a religious or spiritual context, as proposed by Lisa Oakley and her colleagues.[56] Such a view on and classification of spiritual abuse would neglect the religious or spiritual motivation of the abuse ("in the name of God") and its deeply damaging impacts on the relationship with God. Furthermore, this reductionist approach risks not adequately understanding the cornerstones of a spiritual journey and ignores the relevance of soteriology, staurology, and pneumatology in the life of a believer. For this reason, the issue of spiritual abuse deserves an interdisciplinary approach that ensures a proper balance between the psychological and theological perspectives.

SPIRITUAL ABUSE AND THE ABUSE OF CONSCIENCE

Abuse of conscience occurs when the accompanying person puts him- or herself in the place of the accompanied person's conscience, which in the context of the Catholic Church is "the most secret core and sanctuary" (*GS* 16). Abusing another's conscience violates the intimacy and freedom of the other person,[57] with the risk for the substitution or nullification of the conscience of the other person. In other parts of the world and in other contexts, the abuse of conscience is seen mostly as a synonym of spiritual abuse. However, in the Italian context, Pope Francis often talks about the abuse of conscience (*abuso di coscienza)* and defines it (together with the abuse of power) as the origin of every kind of abuse. He also states clearly that "we have been called to form consciences, not to claim to replace them" (*AL* 54). The term *abuso di coscienza* is a term mostly used in the Italian (ecclesial) context, and due to a lack of research and knowledge on the issue is also sometimes used as a synonym for spiritual abuse, seen as an extreme form of spiritual abuse, or identified as a form of abuse that can accompany other forms of abuse, such as psychological violence or spiritual abuse.

The National Service for the Protection of Minors of the Italian Episcopal Conference defines the abuse of conscience as "a form of violation of another's intimacy, consisting of inducing in the other person one's own way of judging and one's own criteria of discernment, or one's own moral (and penitential) sensitivity."[58] This definition sees the abuse of conscience as a form of abuse of power, as it does for spiritual abuse, but it also sees the abuse of conscience as distinct from spiritual abuse. This distinction is made based on the sensitivity that is touched. According to the proposal of the National Service, when the relationship with God is affected (spiritual sensitivity), it is spiritual abuse, whereas when the moral sensitivity (what one should do or should not do, what is right or what is wrong) is affected, it is an abuse of conscience.

Based on a predominantly ecclesial view of conscience that distinguishes three dimensions of conscience—an instrument of recognition of God's law (*GS* 16; *DH* 3), an act of judgment (*CCC* 1778), and a place of encounter with God—another definition of the abuse of conscience, focusing more on the moral charge and moral authority, has been proposed:

> Abuse of conscience are those acts occurring in the context of a relationship of spiritual direction or help in which the person giving guidance ascribes to himself divine authority—that is, identifies his advice with God's will—imposing himself on the identity, freedom and responsibility of the person being guided in an area concerning moral judgment.[59]

This way of understanding the abuse of conscience is strongly linked to spiritual abuse and the ecclesial context by defining it as a severe form of spiritual abuse that should not be seen—contrarily to the proposal of the National Service—as separate from spiritual abuse because the basic elements and dynamics are the same, but the moral component is added.[60]

These two slightly different points of view show how difficult it is to define and to deal with these two forms of abuse and how necessary future research on the issue is. Both definitions have a strongly ecclesial point of view on the abuse of conscience, which is understandable and appropriate in a Catholic context; nevertheless, it is vital not to forget or neglect that the abuse of conscience may also happen in nonecclesial, secular contexts, for example in therapeutic or medical relationships that are characterized by an asymmetry and by the trust that the client or patient has in the psychotherapist or the medical doctor. Furthermore, the abuse of conscience may also happen in other asymmetric relationships (e.g., in education or formation) that are based on trust. Another quite prominent context that should not be forgotten is social media and the fact that young people's consciences are often influenced or manipulated by so-called influencers.[61] Clearly there is a need for further discussions, exchange, and research to better understand the relationship between spiritual abuse and the abuse of conscience.

Conclusion

Spiritual abuse in accompaniment and community life is an issue that needs to be faced urgently on an interdisciplinary and intercultural level, as Christians, be they Roman Catholics or Protestants, are present in almost all countries around the globe. It has been shown so far that spiritual abuse is not easy to grasp, to describe, and to define. This is also why its definition differs according to the context, experience, and discipline of the author or researcher and can often be understood as a working definition that helps people to understand this complex issue and to operationalize it in a more accessible and comprehensible way. This can be of great importance when it comes to observing or detecting spiritually abusive behavior. As research continues, as awareness and sensitivity grow, and as (hopefully) more victims come forward and disclose, definitions may develop, but also the differences and similarities with other related forms of abuse that may occur in an ecclesial, religious, or spiritual environments will become clearer.

2

The Dynamics of Spiritual Abuse

TO UNDERSTAND THE complexities of spiritual abuse and its effects on the lives and faith of those touched by it requires an understanding of the characteristics and dynamics that underlie a spiritually abusive experience. Like other forms of abuse, spiritual abuse exhibits a systematic pattern of behavior with particular structures, rules, values, and standards that attract potential abusers and put potential victims at risk. A primary aim of abusers, spiritual and otherwise, is to gain the trust of victims while reducing their self-esteem and their trust in others. This gradually leads those affected into an often-exclusive relationship of exaggerated dependency. As Nicola Madge describes, abusers use tactics such as "humiliation, intimidation, and constant criticism of the victims in order to have full mental control over them."[1] More than a simple transgression of boundaries, abuse, including spiritual abuse, usually involves trust and an imbalance of power.

The Role of Power and Power Imbalance

Power, power imbalance, and the abuse of power play an essential role when talking about spiritual abuse in ecclesial or religious contexts.[2]

But what kind of power are we talking about? Scientifically, power is understood as the sum of all possibilities of influence in social, political, economic, and religious respects. It includes the possibility of asserting one's own will in social relationships, even in the face of resistance. Positions of power determine all our interpersonal relationships and contacts, whether in partnership, family, and work or political, cultural, and ecclesiastical life.[3] In the ecclesiastical context, there are two types of power and authority: the power of governance and moral authority. The power of governance, according to its context and the people involved, is defined by canon law,[4] rules, and statues, and refers to an ecclesiastical power or office (for example, bishop or major superior). Moral authority refers to a person or institution having the quality or characteristics of being respected for good character or knowledge, especially as a source of guidance or as an exemplar of proper conduct. Moral authority affects all kinds of institutions and with them all kinds of interpersonal relationships that take place in those institutions, be it the Church, health facilities, politics, or others.

In all these cases, a power imbalance can be observed between those who offer help, care, or cure and those who need it and therefore depend on them. Once a power imbalance exists, there is a risk that power will be misused or abused. But power need not be considered negatively. Power exercised responsibly and in a reflective manner helps to support people and gives them the opportunity to trust and to believe in something. However, it is particularly important to pay attention to the point at which the exercise of power tilts and turns negative. This happens in many areas subtly and unconsciously—for example, behaving, talking, or dressing in order to be recognized as a member of a specific group.[5] How one deals with a power imbalance in asymmetric relationships depends on the individual, but raising as much awareness as possible of the responsibility associated with certain positions (for example, priests, spiritual companions, or superiors) is important.

To ensure that the balance of power does not tip into abuse needs a steady and honest reflection on where potential spiritual abuse begins. Any helping profession and even any helping relationship bear the seeds of potential abuse. Those "in need" who are offered help, care, cure, or accompaniment are automatically those who are at risk of abuse. People need to recognize if they live in a system that is vulnerable or not "at peace" with itself or with its past (such as due to the vulnerability of its leadership or due to abuse cases or other types of scandals in its history) and that therefore uses power in order to stabilize itself or even favors vulnerance, which can be defined as the willingness or power to hurt or attack others in order to protect oneself or own's one reputation.[6] Within such a system, people must take appropriate countermeasures to prevent the abuse of power, which in the worst cases may leave the door open for other forms of abuse, as happened within the Catholic Church.

The Role of Trust

While power is almost automatically linked to abuse as a key element, trust is often ignored, overlooked, or forgotten. At the most, one thinks about trust in cases of sexual abuse of minors and their confidence in adults who are close to them. However, trust plays an important role in other forms of abuse as well because, as in sexual abuse cases in which the abuser is mostly a person known and trusted by the victim, this is also often the case in accompaniment or confession or in medically therapeutic relationships. People who seek advice, help, or cure usually trust in the professional competence and behavior as well as in the duty to confidentiality of their medical doctors, psychologists, or psychotherapists. In cases of spiritual abuse, trust in the spiritual companion, the superior, or the founder of a community or movement is usually a prerequisite for a good and fruitful accompaniment and companionship.[7] As with a doctor-patient relationship or a therapist-client relationship, many personal and intimate details might be shared.

In cases of spiritual accompaniment, catechism, confession, or membership in a religious community or movement, the faith of persons receiving assistance and their trust in God must be seen as fundamental to the relationship. This complicates the issue of trust in cases of spiritual abuse, or generally in cases of abuse in an ecclesial or religious context. Often people who ask for spiritual accompaniment or who decide to join a specific community or movement are convinced that this person, community, or movement might be the right one to help them to grow in their faith and spiritual freedom, to create a stable relationship with God or to intensify the existing one, to find their place in the world, or to overcome a difficult moment or crisis; therefore, trust in the spiritual companion is concomitant with their trust in the person's professional competences, human capacities, and spiritual gifts.

The accompanied person trusts in the companion's confidentiality and judgment and believes that he or she wants their ultimate good. Consequently, the trust of many victims in other people, but often also in God, is shattered or destroyed when victims realize that they have been "betrayed" by a trusted person. A second moment of abuse of trust may happen when a person affected by abuse discloses the abuse and is not believed.[8]

The Violation of Spiritual Boundaries

Both spiritual abuse and sexual abuse are based on the abuse of power and trust and on the violation of boundaries. The asymmetrical relationship between the abusing person and the abused person, which is typical of abusive relationships, is facilitated by structures such as patriarchy, hierarchies, and closed systems. But where does spiritual boundary violation or spiritually abusive behavior begin? Lisa Oakley and Justin Humphreys suggest "spectrums of behavior from abusive behavior at one end to healthy and safe at the other and many shades of these in between."[9] How does one determine the threshold where nonoptimal or incorrect behavior becomes abuse? Unsuccessful interactions, injuries, and attempts to persuade others to do or to leave something are part of our everyday life. The easiest way to find that boundary is to define concrete examples of behavior that is not (yet) abusive as well as examples of clearly abusive behavior, thus establishing standards that must be respected.[10] However, one must remain aware that meeting or violating certain standards does not necessarily mean that a violation of a person's spiritual and psychological integrity has or has not occurred in an individual case.

A violation of spiritual self-determination occurs also if the free choice of the confessor or spiritual companion is restricted. Such restrictions not only can lead to spiritual abuse or be defined as such but also contradict important canonical regulations.[11] Some examples of boundary violations are given below.

In particular, the appropriation of divine power as a central power-related element of spiritual abuse harbors a great danger, since the accompanied person sees the spiritual companion as being chosen by God and consequently the mouthpiece of God.[12]

Various forms of manipulation and control are used to suppress independent thinking and questioning and to provoke feelings of fear and guilt, which in turn lead to blind obedience and loyalty. For example, women who report in spiritual accompaniment the physical or sexual abuse that they experience are encouraged to forgive their partners, to pray continually for change, and not to give up the relationship. Performance-based acceptance in which one's own value is measured solely on the basis of success is also a classic characteristic of spiritual abuse. Many people who experience this type of abuse will be submissive and try to do their best to be accepted. In addition, one's worth is measured only in terms of productivity as the following statement of a victim shows. "I genuinely feared that my children were going to pay the price and die if I couldn't live up to God's expectations."[13]

Spiritual abuse can also happen in the sacrament of confession when certain confessional practices or timeframes are demanded or when the confessing person experiences pressure or affliction during confession.[14] Rather than experiencing a feeling of relief and freedom after the absolution, a feeling of guilt is created. Another example of an abusive use of confession is when the faithful were allowed to receive holy communion only if they had confessed beforehand.[15]

A breach of the confessional occurs when the confessor breaks the seal of confession with third parties[16] or if he invites a third person (for example, a novice or a seminarian) to be present during confession ("to gain experience").[17] It is also a violation as well as a canonical criminal offense when the confessor breaks the seal of the confessional or pastoral secrecy by harassing, embarrassing, or threatening the penitent with the content of the confession.[18]

Who Is at Risk and Why?

Theoretically all individuals who are accompanied in some way spiritually or in an ecclesial or religious context can become victims of spiritual abuse; nevertheless, some persons are more at risk than others. Spiritual accompaniment can include classical spiritual accompaniment or confession, catechism, marriage preparation, individual retreats, spiritual exercises of a community, prayer groups, and religious communities, movements, and orders. One crucial aspect that may put people more at risk is their personal development, the way they have learned to behave, to take care of themselves, and to deal with difficult situations or problems with more or less flexibility and stability. Closely linked to personal development is their life history, including the presence or absence of traumas and adverse childhood experiences.[19] Other parameters that need to be taken into consideration that may increase the risk for spiritual abuse are low self-esteem, an appropriately learned social behavior (for example, not to complain, not to contradict), a high tolerance level (such as for unacceptable behavior, pain, intrusive behavior by others), the tendency to resolve problems quickly, and the tendency to take over responsibilities even without being accountable.[20]

Similar to risk factors for so-called mental abuse, the relationship with authority figures, the conflict-resolving behavior of a person, and the current situation may offer further information in estimating the risk potential for spiritual abuse.[21] Often persons who are more at risk already work or live in codependent relationships, can be easily influenced by others, and may easily feel anxious, ashamed, or guilty. Those characteristics and parameters play an important role when talking about the risk of being abused spiritually.

INDIVIDUALS

At the individual level, young, sometimes inexperienced or immature people are particularly at risk for spiritual abuse, including people who are new to a faith or have converted, who have had no chance to get rooted in faith, and have not yet had sufficient experience in dealing with their faith in everyday life. Today, the dissatisfaction with traditional Churches and religions and the resulting avoidance of them is a decisive factor in spiritual abuse as individuals, especially young people, continue to search for something that offers them a feeling of belonging and sense in their lives. Another risk is that many parents today are not rooted in their faith; therefore, their children have no chance of becoming deeply rooted within a religion or faith. This religious homelessness and inexperience make them receptive to spiritual or religious offers that rely on emotional faith experiences, strongly charismatic leaders, deep devotion, and unconditional obedience.[22]

In addition, "broken or fragmented" people without stable personality structures have a higher risk of becoming a victim of spiritual abuse. Individuals who find themselves in difficult life situations or in a crisis and who ask for accompaniment in this situation are also at risk as they lack personal strength and stability at that time.[23] Persons who have already been victims of spiritual abuse or any other kind of abuse (physical, sexual, mental, psychological) in the past are thus accustomed to abusive structures as a "central emotional position" and are more at risk for being abused again. This is especially true if the affected person never has recognized or psychologically and spiritually integrated the abuse. These people usually try to escape these structures, but often unconsciously end up in them again because they are familiar to them. Further risk factors include overload and stress, isolation, and experiences of foreignness, especially abroad.[24]

Many cases of spiritual abuse affect lay and religious women due to a double power asymmetry, but spiritual abuse can affect male adults as well as children and adolescents. Spiritual abuse can affect laypeople or consecrated people as well as seminarians, novices, female religious, and even male religious and priests.

COMMUNITIES

Spiritual abuse can affect not only individuals but also groups of people as well as whole communities. At a community level, groups of people who have recently been called or converted are at greater risk of becoming victims of spiritual abuse. This is mostly due to their strong idealism and high motivation.[25] A well-known example from the past few years are the Travailleuses Missionaires.[26] Recently founded lay and religious communities or movements around the globe are repeatedly affected by spiritual abuse, as in the case of the secular association Totus Tuus in Germany.[27] This is linked to the lack of traditions dating back decades or even centuries that have not yet gone through a proper development process; furthermore, members are not (yet) questioning their spiritual orientation, and the existing (formal and informal) norms and rules do not allow questions. Spiritual abuse can therefore affect people from all groups of believers.

GROUPS AND FAMILIES

In addition to affecting individuals or large religious communities or movements, spiritual abuse can also affect small groups of people, families, or couples. This may be the case if a married couple, a whole family, or a group of friends decide to look for spiritual accompaniment together with the desire to grow and mature in their faith. Spiritual abuse may also happen within a family as a consequence of the abuse that (at least) one family member has experienced outside the family, for example in spiritual accompaniment. The spiritually accompanied family member behaves at home in a way similar to the spiritually accompanying person, trying to control or dominate and to manipulate other family members either because of imitating the spiritual companion unconsciously or because the spiritual companion asks for that (for example, how often a couple should have sexual intercourse, how many children they should have).[28]

SECONDARY VICTIMS

Spiritual abuse—as with other forms of abuse—may ripple outward to affect family or community members, friends, or other persons close to its primary victims. This type of victimization has been neglected for a long time.[29] People from the social environment of the primarily affected person become secondary victims through witnessing, knowing about, or experiencing the consequences of the abuse on the primary victim. If spiritual abuse occurs in a religious community or movement, the number of secondary victims could be all the members of the community or movement. In some cases, entire groups of society can experience secondary victimization, for example by learning about abuse cases or scandals via third parties or the media. This applies, for example, to cases in which no one could have imagined that one or more individuals would ever be spiritually abused or that a certain person or group of people, due to their good reputations, their influence and charisma, and the values and behaviors they presented to the outside world, could ever be abusers. A high level of identification exists with the community, institution, movement, or person. Frequently in the past, revelations of abuse have shaken the worldview and the faith of many people, and the trust in such communities, institutions, movements, and people is broken.[30]

Another group of secondary victims are individuals who are close to the abuser and have problems accepting and understanding what the abuser has done. They may have to withstand potential attacks or assaults due to this closeness.

Theoretically at least, spiritual abuse can affect all members of the Roman Catholic Church primarily or secondarily, be it on an individual level—laypeople, novices, religious sisters and friars, seminarians and priests—or on a group level as religious communities as well as members of spiritual or religious movements.[31] Nevertheless, some people are at higher risk as they may be (temporarily or generally) more vulnerable.[32]

Abusers and the Dynamics That Permit Abuse

Why certain individuals abuse spiritually is difficult to understand. Even if all people theoretically have the potential to be abusers, certain groups of people are more at risk than others of losing control, abusing power, or violating boundaries. Not all of them notice their wrongdoing but rather violate boundaries unconsciously and judge their behavior as acceptable. Injured people are more at risk of hurting others, and these people are called "helpless helpers."[33] They are often tempted to abuse power, but the reasons may range from seeking to resolve problems in a familiar way to attempting to improve their self-esteem. At higher risk of becoming abusers are people with adverse or traumatizing childhood experiences—such as abuse or violence—who have never processed their wounds and given them a chance to heal. Also at risk are people who grew up in difficult and burdensome power structures and learned from poor role models, who are uncertain about the perception of their own emotions, who have difficulties with closeness and distance, who show narcissistic personality traits, and who feel inferior and worthless.[34]

Similar to other forms of abuse, like sexual or physical abuse, spiritually abusive persons look consciously or unconsciously for "weak victims" who are fragile in the moment, who are unable or only poorly able to defend themselves, and who thus can more easily be led into a relationship of dependency. This can also be interpreted as a sign of many abusers' own inner weakness and insecurity, which is covered up by the victims' dependence on them. In many cases of spiritual abuse, the potential abusers are individuals with an elitist religious or spiritual claim or are part of groups with such an elitist claim within the religious community and society.

The definition of *spiritual abuse* proposed by Lisa Oakley and Justin Humphrey[35] (see chapter 1) helps to explain the motivation of the abuser and the dynamics of the abusive relationship with the accompanied person or community. As in psychological abuse, a spiritually abusive person aims to reduce the confidence and self-esteem of the victim in order to make the victim increasingly reliant on the abuser. For abuse to occur, a framework of conditions within an institution or organization coalesces with the personal characteristics and peculiarities of the potentially abusive person. First, the person must be recognized by the institution or organization by being equipped with certain insignia of power or, at least, may use them.[36] Second, the person has certain personal problems. Finally, potentially abusive people need three types of institutional/systemic support: (1) a hierarchy, (2) a history of the system, and (3) contractually valid regulations.[37] Hierarchy refers to the asymmetrical power imbalance between the potential abuser and the potential victim. Every purpose of the institution or organization can be linked to the hierarchy. In this manner, actions and tasks to achieve the purpose can be subordinated. The history of the system generates expectations and shapes behavior in advance because the institution has publicly enforced its rules during conflicts many times in history. Contractually valid regulations mean that a superior may formulate clear rules for those who wish to withdraw or are disloyal.[38] Lastly, the concept of vulnerance is briefly considered. In summary it can be said that vulnerance is the active capacity, specific to certain contexts, to hurt or to generate wounds. It means that people, institutions, or organizations who feel their vulnerability may think that attack is the best defense. Because of feeling powerless, they may rely on "weapons" for unmistakable strength, and their vulnerability develops into unspeakable power. In recent decades, several Church leaders have also repeatedly resorted to this defense strategy, tolerating and covering up sexual abuse and silencing the victims.[39] This cover-up of sexual abuse by clergy and religious in the Roman Catholic Church over the last decades is a good example of systematic patterns of behavioral abuse. It forms part of a bigger pattern of enforced accountability and pressure to conform, of threats, of requirements for secrecy and silence, of isolation from others external to the abuse context, and of censorship of decision-making.

Often abusers are addicted to the power rush afforded by their ability to control the victims who seem to rank "below" them in class, power, ability, or strength of body, mind, or character. The damage and harm of abuse occurs when spiritual companions claim to themselves power and authority "dominating…and controlling; pressurizing another into an action or course of action using 'God,' scripture or spiritual principles as a tool of coercion."[40] For example, blessing and providence will be only for those who fully submit without disagreement, even when the spiritual companion is wrong. In spiritual abuse involving confession, Eucharist, or preaching, an abusive priest will often satisfy a need for power, control, clerical self-affirmation, and intellectual superiority at the expense of his victims.

Thinking about ideals and idols in this context, spiritual companions, superiors, or founders, susceptible to the lure of power and admiration, like to woo and win followers with big promises. According to Hannah Schulz, this is particularly typical for people with narcissistic personality styles as they usually swarm and ensnare their potential victims (for example, through compliments or promises). At first, everything looks radiant and exciting, and only later do most victims become aware of the high cost they have had to pay.[41]

Most people who accompany spiritually come from and are shaped by a particular tradition, for example, from a spiritual community, a religious order, or a system—with its own structures, life orders, and common convictions. Sexual abuse always leads to queries about the background and circumstances that enable or promoted the abuse. From research on and experience with sexual abuse and abuse of power in institutions, it is known that perpetrators feel attracted to vulnerable systems, which is why the connection between people with responsibility and authority and the respective prevailing rules, structures, and hierarchies must be examined.[42] If there is sexual abuse, the abuser usually dresses it up and justifies it in religious and spiritual terms.

According to the German Jesuit Klaus Mertes, the issue becomes even more difficult when "seduced seducers" themselves occupy certain positions in Church hierarchies. When dealing with spiritual abuse, self-reflection on the teaching of the Roman Catholic Church is necessary in order to avoid its instrumentalization.[43] Generally, exposing the moral failings of many spiritual companions, superiors, or founders of religious communities or movements is difficult because there is still the attempt to make the victims responsible for what happens or has happened when the abuse is uncovered.

Indicators of Spiritual Abuse

Based on what has been said so far, caution is advised if the following "alarm signals" can be identified in individuals, groups of people, or communities:

- loss of personal identity (in communities the group identity comes to the fore)
- violation of boundaries in spiritual accompaniment
- isolation of a person, a group, or a community
- personal and/or emotional dependency of the accompanied person on the accompanying person
- strong emotional ties in communities and close companionship relationships with high loyalty
- elitist thinking
- excessive ("blind") obedience
- ambitious (usually unachievable) missionary goals
- high demands for personal spiritual growth and performance
- spiritualization of decisions and/or actions
- closed systems
- excessive (unattainable and often unrealistic) values and ideals
- lack of differentiation between internal forums and external forums
- strong charismatic leadership figures[44] or communities[45]

A few examples will illustrate what "alarm signals" mean in concrete terms. Personal identity is lost, for example, if subjective feelings and independent thinking must be subordinated to a special doctrine of faith. If the spiritual companion has an influence on the choice of lifestyle, partner, education, studies, or career of the accompanied person, then boundaries are being violated. Isolation often results in neglecting family, friends, colleagues, or other kinds of relationships and is mostly associated with a simultaneous dependency on the spiritual companion, as the latter arranges the accompaniment in such a way that it leads to a relationship of dependency. This dependency may continue up to the point at which the accompanied person, group, or community can no longer do without the companion. Dependency and isolation are reinforced by elitist thinking and/or excessive obedience. Elitism means, for example, the creation of a special way of speaking in which words or certain expressions are assigned meanings that outsiders cannot understand. This creates an "insider-outsider mentality."

High (unreachable) ideals also contribute to elitist thinking. An excessive concept of obedience leads in a targeted way to the decisions, interpretations, and rules of the spiritual companion being accepted without question. Furthermore, elitist thinking and excessive obedience result in feelings of powerlessness, shame, and guilt in the accompanied persons as they may feel weak and inadequate due to the unattainable ideals.[46] With ambitious missionary goals and high demands for personal spiritual growth comes increasing pressure on individuals to achieve these goals and to perform well, whereas spiritualizing many (or even all) decisions and actions in the accompaniment or within a community as "God's will" leads to an even higher pressure to perform and to obey. Closed systems make it difficult for members to confide in people outside and to talk about possible problems, as external communication may be blocked or forbidden.[47] In addition, it becomes more difficult to perceive abuse. In addition, excessive, usually unattainable and unrealistic values and ideals may increase pressure on individuals and make them feel ashamed, guilty, uncapable, and unworthy. In the field of priesthood formation, spiritual abuse may begin when the internal forum and the external forum are mixed up or if information about one's personal and/or spiritual journey given to the spiritual father (internal forum) is not kept there but shared with the rector (external forum) or if the person is the same.

Charisma makes for effective leadership or communities.[48] Attributes such as emotional expressiveness, enthusiasm, visionary leadership, and responsiveness to others "allow a person to be influential and persuasive and therefore able to make others buy their vision for the group and sacrifice personal goals for collective goals."[49] Visionary leaders are able to heighten followers' sense of shared identity; "this shared identity produces a collective 'heroic motive' that puts group goals ahead of personal goals."[50] This explains why and how people may lose their personal identity in abusive relationships.

What Does This Mean in Times of Worldwide Crises?

Spiritual abuse and living through various global crises such as pandemics, financial and climate crises as well as armed conflicts or wars have some intersections. All of them are characterized by restrictions, misinformation, distrust, or even loss of trust in leaders; all of them are accompanied by often complicated and changing instructions. Fear also plays an important role in these situations. In the case of the COVID-19 pandemic, it was the concrete fear of contracting the virus and its possible consequences (illness, sequelae, and so forth). In the case of spiritual abuse, there is the fear of contracting the sinfulness of others and/or of the world. In the case of various crises, fears arise of not having enough to eat and to drink or of spending the winter in a cold home without the possibility of heat. The fear of death can also be observed in all these cases. Unquestionably, the pandemic or the various world crises themselves have been used to manipulate, enforce obedience, dominate, and isolate people in their faith and relationship with God.

3

Consequences of Spiritual Abuse

INDIVIDUALS WHO WERE affected by any form of abuse, be they children or adolescents or adults, were assumed to "just get over it" with time. But the wounds and pain of abuse are deep, the consequences might endure for life, and the effects on physical and mental health are grave. If an abuse occurs in a religious or ecclesial context, it may often take the form of spiritual trauma, affecting the faith of those abused and their relationship with God, causing many victims to harbor doubts about their faith and their personal image of God, up to and including the complete destruction of their relationship with God. Faith and prayer are no longer supportive or a source of hope for them, and victims are left alone with the feelings of shame and guilt induced by the abuser and with the conviction that they have committed an unforgivable sin. These feelings and beliefs, along with the fear of not being believed and the power that the abuser has over them and their lives (whether in an obvious or a more latent way), are serious obstacles and barriers for disclosure. For this reason, prevention work must give everyone affected a voice and create awareness and sensitivity of the devastating consequences that spiritual abuse may have on both primary and secondary victims.

Levels of Consequences

Like any form of abuse, spiritual abuse can have serious consequences for those affected by it directly (primary victims) as well as for their social environment (secondary victims). The consequences of abuse generally and of spiritual abuse specifically vary from person to person and from community to community; the impact of the abuse depends on the personality, sex, and age of the person affected, the culture, the duration and severity of the abuse, and the relationship with the abusing person. The social environment and possible support from it also play a decisive role.[1] This means that some victims, despite their horrible experience, are able to adapt and do not exhibit severe consequences to their physical or mental health. This psychological resilience[2]—the ability to adapt positively during or after significantly adverse life events or risks for adversity—allows the individual to rise above the situation or "bounce back," demonstrating adaptation rather than impairment.[3] Hope, positive emotions, and self-compassion can increase resilience.[4] Interpersonal relationships as well as spiritual/religious systems of belief have also been associated with greater resilience as they may help to give meaning to adverse life events. Strengths such as hope, acceptance, and optimism are "meaningful" resources.[5]

Just because some victims of spiritual abuse may show less severe consequences than others does not mean that the abuse did not happen or that those who suffer more or experience very severe consequences are exaggerating. In cases of spiritual abuse, people usually lose interpersonal relationships and their spiritual/religious belief systems. Without these two powerful resources and protective factors, many victims of spiritual abuse suffer significantly and for long periods of time.

Spiritual abuse can have short-, medium- and long-term consequences. Some of these consequences may occur immediately, while the abuse is ongoing, whereas others may occur only later, when the affected person realizes what has happened. Furthermore, all of the consequences listed below rarely occur together; however, even a few of them may sometimes be too much to carry. The following statements do not claim to be exhaustive, but rather they illustrate the extent to which spiritual abuse can affect or even destroy the life of one or more individuals.[6]

Spiritual abuse can have consequences on seven different levels, which may also influence each other or be the consequences of one another. These seven levels include:

1. Spiritual
2. Emotional
3. Cognitive
4. Psychological
5. Physical
6. (Psycho-) Social
7. Financial

SPIRITUAL CONSEQUENCES

Spiritual abuse can have devastating effects on victims' relationships with God, their image of God, their prayer, and ultimately their faith. In very severe cases, victims may suffer from spiritual trauma[7] and their spiritual integrity may be infringed upon. These consequences can be immediate or long-term. While the abuse is occurring, many victims fear making mistakes or committing unforgiveable sins that may lead to eternal damnation. In short, they fear for the salvation of their souls. This gives rise to uncertainties in faith as well as in their spiritual lives.[8] The supposed "divine position" of the spiritual companion, founder, or superior reinforces these fears because those affected are regularly told that they are not worthy to enter the kingdom of God and that they must try harder to please the Lord. Furthermore, they might lose their spiritual self-determination and freedom and will not be able to grow and mature spiritually.

In the long run, many people affected by spiritual abuse lose their faith or continue to live with a deeply shattered faith; others are not able to pray to God anymore because they have lost their trust in this God who, in their opinion, allowed the abuse to happen and failed to protect them; therefore, they conclude that God does not care about them. Consequently, their image of God may change from a positive one of a loving and caring God into a negative one of a punishing and insensitive God. In some cases, the relationship with God might even be destroyed. Many victims also lose a sense of meaning in their lives and therefore spend the rest of their lives searching for meaning, which in turn leaves them vulnerable to other abusive relationships.[9]

EMOTIONAL CONSEQUENCES

On the emotional level, a feeling of powerlessness and inadequacy as well as feelings of shame and guilt can often be observed in victims. Numerous studies[10] on other forms of abuse show that feelings of shame and guilt are barriers to disclosure; thus, many people affected by abuse in general, but especially by spiritual abuse, may either not open up and share about their experiences or will do so only after many decades, continuing to blame themselves.

Emotions such as fear and anger can also result from spiritual abuse.[11] Fear of going crazy, fear of not meeting the demands of the spiritual companion or the community, fear of being a failure in front of their companion, founder, or community and in front of God are common, but so is the fear of the consequences if they do not adapt or if they try to defend themselves. It is not uncommon for this fear to give rise to anger at the other(s) but also at themselves. Furthermore, people affected by spiritual abuse often have feelings of sadness or resentment.[12] If victims were "caught" by an idol, be it a person, a concept, or a context, fear of losing or breaking away from what has been lived and glorified for so long can be observed. This fear of loss increases the willingness to make sacrifices and can lead to self-abandonment. Afterward, when a manipulated and abused person, group of people, or community realize what has happened and how exaggerated and unrealistic the various promises have been, many former victims may experience a bitter sense of disappointment and the feeling of having been deceived and betrayed.[13]

COGNITIVE CONSEQUENCES

At the cognitive level, confusion in general and confusion particularly about one's identity, perception, and interpretation of what one feels or perceives can be observed. Often within a community or movement, the group identity is more important than the personal identity; therefore, leaders, founders, or superiors of such communities or movements strive toward the group identity they wish to achieve, making members feel "lost and inadequate" as individuals.

Difficulties in decision-making and critical thinking are common consequences of exaggerated obedience, manipulation, and restrictions in decision-making processes. Victims of spiritual abuse are often forced to abandon their own perspective and conform to the mindset and logic of the spiritual companion, community, or movement. This may lead to an inability to make decisions or plans for one's own life because independent thinking is not welcome or allowed.[14] Even after a victim has left an abusive community or accompaniment, his or her thoughts continue to be dominated by the abusive environment and the abuser. This may also happen when the last contact with the abuser or the abusive environment occurred a long time ago, but the victim still feels "persecuted and influenced." This leads to difficulties in "breaking or concluding" with the abuser and an inability to focus on other things and to enjoy the good moments in life.[15] In addition, it consumes much of the victim's time and energy.

PSYCHOLOGICAL CONSEQUENCES

Psychological consequences include a negative self-image, low self-esteem, and uncertain behavior as well as difficulty in enjoying the pleasant aspects of life. An increased risk for various mental disorders such as depressive disorders, anxiety disorders, eating disorders, sleep disorders, or addictions (alcohol, drugs, or medication) can be identified.[16] Spiritual abuse can also have traumatizing effects and lead to post-traumatic stress disorder (PTSD) or even to complex post-traumatic stress disorder (CPTSD). Usually, stressful life events; witnessing events such as serious accidents, illnesses, and natural disasters; experiencing substantial psychological, physical, and sexual violence; and experiencing severe loss or neglect can cause PTSD. Put simply, PTSD is triggered by experiencing or witnessing a traumatic event and leads to reliving it again and again (emotionally, cognitively, and physiologically), for example, through distressing dreams or recurring memories (flashbacks). Other typical symptoms are avoidance, arousal and reactivity, or changes in mood and cognition.[17] CPTSD was first defined as a new diagnosis in 2018 and is mostly associated with a prolonged, chronic exposure to traumatic events, such as long-term abuse or violence, and includes the symptoms of PTSD as well as difficulties in affect regulation, interpersonal relationships, and negative self-beliefs.[18]

Traumatic events and experiences can leave deep (usually invisible) wounds in the soul that will affect a person's life. Just as a physical injury takes time to heal, so do trauma and injury to the soul.[19] Some people also show signs of burnout or self-harming behavior. Others may have suicidal thoughts or attempt suicide when they do not see a way out of the situation or can no longer live with the terrible consequences and the knowledge that they have been abused spiritually. The likelihood of suicidal thoughts or suicide attempts may increase due to the presence of mental disorders such as PTSD or major depressive disorder.[20]

Responses to Stress and Trauma

The complex issue of psychological trauma differs from stressful life events or experiences. Frequently, individuals seem to be paralyzed and are not able to react after an assault or an abusive event. Research has identified two common ways of processing abuse or assault: fight or flight.[21] To fight means to react offensively; to take flight means to withdraw from the situation. Both ways enable the affected person to (re-)act in a self-determined manner. A traumatic situation makes this impossible. Victims are neither able to fight nor to flee, especially when realizing that the person they have trusted—often for a long time—has bad intentions.

To survive and deal with this situation, a victim may resort to freezing. The person may withdraw inwardly, become passive, or feel paralyzed. A freeze reaction usually occurs when people feel overwhelmed and feel that they have no control over the situation.[22] The external situation is defused because the retreat takes place internally as the affected person may dissociate. Trauma-related dissociation aims to enable a traumatized person to act again.

The price paid for freezing is an experience of alienation in which the spatial-temporal classification of events is no longer possible.[23] This means, concretely, that the concerned person no longer acts or feels in a "normal" situation, not showing any feelings and giving the impression of being uninvolved. This avoidant and introvertive behavior usually applies to everything that is related to the abuse. Imaging procedures show that speech processing is blocked in moments of extreme stress and reveal how individuals avoid reality (depersonalization and/or derealization)[24] in order to protect themselves.[25] All these are psychotraumatic backgrounds, operating unconsciously in a person's mind, which is why people with a traumatic experience cannot (re)act, fight, flee, or say no. This also explains why individuals who have experienced one or more forms of abuse in the past are more vulnerable to being abused again.[26] If an abused or exploited person never had the possibility to process the traumatic experience and never received any (professional) support, there is a high probability that affected persons will not be able to defend themselves from abusive experiences and exploitation in the future but will instead become frozen, speechless, and dissociative.[27]

Part of the psychodynamics of trauma is that the victim adopts feelings that should belong to the abuser. For example, victims may feel ashamed or guilty for something they did not cause. The reasons for that are various (see chapter I). First, the person affected trusts the abuser fully and has high expectations. Second, the perception of the victim has been manipulated. Third, the victim becomes more and more dependent on the abuser and is frequently isolated and treated like an object. This leads to a reinterpretation of the reality ("It's actually not so bad!"), as the victim is not able to recognize and name what is happening. Such reinterpretation happens often if a person is repeatedly harmed or abused over a longer period of time,[28] and it may result in some kind of "identification with the aggressor"[29] ("They only want what's best for me!"; "It's my own fault!").

Some victims are so emotionally intertwined with the abuser that they feel pity or responsibility for the abuser. Others are worried or preoccupied and would be willing to support their abuser, who is often their only close emotional contact, by making themselves available with their body, mind, and soul.[30] This may lead to a so-called fawn response, which is characterized by over-adjustment to the needs of others. People in this mode try to avoid conflict by engaging in "people pleasing." Psychologically, this is expressed through over-adaptation and approval and excessive friendliness and submissiveness as well as the neglect of one's own needs. This response is a form of social survival mechanism and often occurs in people who have grown up in environments where they were regularly exposed to threats, neglect, or abuse, and have learned to survive by adapting and accommodating.[31]

PHYSICAL CONSEQUENCES

On a physical level, spiritual abuse often manifests as a result of or in conjunction with the aforementioned emotional and psychological consequences. Physical consequences are often expressed as physiological reactions that are associated with anxiety or anxiety disorders, unhealthy diets, and ways of living, but also with a traumatic reaction, for example, with tremors and sweating, an increased heart rate and muscle tension. [32] Also, PTSD may a have long-term impact on physical health and is associated with increased hypertension, increased blood cholesterol levels, and an increased risk for cardiac problems or vascular diseases.[33] In addition, diffuse physical pain and discomfort to the point of severe physical health problems can be manifested as psychosomatic syndromes,[34] including medically unexplained symptoms, or as a result of a psychosomatic disorder (such as bronchial asthma, headache, psychosomatic gastritis, psychosomatic dermatitis). Physical consequences can also be the result of physical violence experienced in the accompaniment or the community as a way of punishment or pressure, or due to nonhealthy ways of living, such as being obliged to sleep on the floor or on the hard ground, being forced to kneel for hours and pray, or being obliged to follow a specific diet without consulting a physician or nutritionist. These "lifestyles" may lead to severe health consequences as they may have negative impacts, especially in the long-term, on the physical health of a person and the correct functioning of the body.[35]

PSYCHOSOCIAL CONSEQUENCES

Another area of life that the consequences of spiritual abuse can affect is the psychosocial area, mainly due to manipulation by, obedience to, and dependence on the spiritual companion, founder, leader, or superior of the community or movement. The above-mentioned emotional and psychological consequences may also determine the impact of spiritual abuse on the psychosocial level. Affected people lose trust in others. Often, they increasingly isolate themselves from their social environments or are isolated by their spiritual companion or by their community. From this isolation, problems gradually develop in social relationships that manifest themselves in education, work, intimate relationships, everyday cohabitation, and sexuality, as well as in the family life and in the friendships of those affected.[36]

FINANCIAL CONSEQUENCES

Financial consequences are quite common in spiritual abuse, especially for those abused in a religious community or movement. Frequently, new members are asked to leave their "old life" behind and to start a "new life" in the community or movement. This means not only leaving behind family members or friends, studies or work, but also all material possessions (apartments, houses, cars, or other personal belongings) that a person may have. Often members are asked to sell their properties and belongings and to bring all their money to "share" with the community that will be their new family and take care of them.[37] There are many examples of former members of new religious movements and communities who found themselves with nothing after having left the movement or community. At the level of spiritual accompaniment there can be financial or economic consequences, too, if the companion charges excessively for the accompaniment or asks the accompanied person to completely detach from material goods and money in order to be free to grow as the only way to ensure one's salvation in the kingdom of God.

Effects on Secondary Victims

Those persons who are secondarily affected by someone else's spiritual abuse—family members, friends, or other members of a religious community or movement—can develop symptoms that are similar to those of the primarily affected people due to their emotional and/or physical closeness with them. Very often they feel ashamed or guilty for not having realized immediately what was happening to the other person. They may feel frustrated, powerless, and hopeless if they are not able to help a primarily affected person to end an abusive accompaniment or to leave an abusive community or movement. It becomes even more difficult and complex if those secondarily affected are part of the same community and movement. Because spiritual abuse is strongly linked to faith, prayer, and the image of God, secondary victims may also experience difficulties in trusting God, praying, and continuing their spiritual life as if nothing had happened; in extreme cases, they may also be spiritually traumatized. Others may be angry with the Church in general, the leadership of the Church, or the specific community or movement for what has happened to the other person "in the name of God." These feelings lead frequently to psychological problems or mental disorders[38] such as anxiety, depression, sleep disorders, and the possibility for PTSD. People who are part of the close social environment of the primary victim are often involved actively—emotionally, mentally, cognitively and spiritually—in their "fight" against the abuser or the abusive system. Therefore, they also risk that the abuse experienced by the primary victim becomes a central part of their daily life and effort.

Much research has been conducted on how the social environment may help and support primary victims of abuse, but only a little research has been done on the impact that primarily affected persons may have on their social environment. Further research in this area is necessary to better understand the relation between primary and secondary victimization as well as the mutual influence on the healing process and ultimately the necessary professional help that needs to be provided (such as counseling, psychotherapy, group therapy) for those affected secondarily.

Further Reflections

People who have experienced spiritual abuse wonder often whether there is a way out of their personal misery and suffering. Most of those affected say that the silence about the issue of spiritual abuse allows it to continue. This results in a lack of knowledge about the phenomenon of spiritual abuse itself, its dynamics, and the often terrible suffering of those who experience spiritual abuse directly as primary victims or indirectly as secondary victims. Therefore, the Roman Catholic Church and Protestant Churches—as well as other Churches, religions, and society at large—have to accept this problem and maintain or strive to create a "healthy Christian culture," especially in today's world when the Roman Catholic Church and various Protestant Churches are under pressure and criticism due to the many scandals of sexual abuse. For that reason, further reflections and evaluations are needed. Clinicians such as psychologists, psychiatrists, psychotherapists, or physicians must be more informed and aware about the consequences that spiritual abuse may have in general and especially with regard to mental health.

4

Spiritual Abuse and the Life of Faith

AS WE HAVE SEEN in the previous chapters, the phenomenon of spiritual abuse is extremely complex. It will probably take years or even decades to reach a tipping point that will bring a deeper understanding of the challenge. Spiritual abuse is like a scary, muddy swamp that takes courage to cross, but that has wonderful places to explore beyond it. In fact, it is good to remember that the counterpart of spiritual abuse is the desire for a journey of faith. That is why theology is asked to engage in a concrete dialogical exercise with the issue of spiritual abuse, which is not only a challenge to be answered but also a challenge from which to restart the missionary impulse, recognizing, first of all, the core of the Christian faith from which our identity descends. In our view, this is based on two important dialectical tensions: believer-God and believer-community. Therefore, to provide an adequate theological assessment of spiritual abuse, it is necessary to examine these two impulses.

Breaking the Believer-God Dialectic

The fundamental dialectical tension between humanity and God is much more than a slogan—incomprehensible to most. It is a vital relationship that characterizes every authentic experience of faith lived by the believer. At the same time, it constitutes the *conditio sine qua non* of theology itself which, without faith and without an explicit horizon of lived grace, would simply produce further theories about humanity and God. Indeed, it is precisely the explication of this horizon that brings out what vital tensions of the Christian faith are disregarded and shattered in the practice of spiritual abuse.

From Christian testimonies, we know that faith is synonymous with trust and, therefore, is not a teaching but a living relationship with the God of life and the Lord of history.[1] For this reason, when entering into a theological evaluation of spiritual abuse, attention must be paid to the two protagonists in this relationship: the human being and God. Looking at these two entities makes an exhaustive reflection on spiritual abuse even more complicated; indeed, both philosophical and theological anthropology have always emphasized the irreducibility of humanity and God. To maintain a balance that avoids the various forms of escapism and denial that have often been seen throughout history requires a great effort. At the same time, we should avoid attempts at quick and easy solutions that do not recognize either the complexity of the abusive phenomenon or the beauty of humanity, however fragile and constantly growing it may be. Indeed, the wisdom of this balance is precisely the style of Jesus. When he touches and heals the hemorrhaging woman (Mark 5:25–34) or the bent woman (Luke 13:10–13), he recognizes their dignity and integrity without getting lost in theories and abstract discussions. As he expressly states, he does not act as judge or arbitrator (Luke 12:14).

Aware of the limits and the need for a firm theological stance, we believe that the violation of boundaries in spiritual abuse breaks not only the boundaries of a relationship between companion and accompanied but also those relating to a necessary vertical relationship, which companion and accompanied should both maintain in the spiritual life.[2] Christian tradition teaches us that the journey in the Spirit passes through a triangular relationship: companion, accompanied, and Holy Spirit. The listening presence of the Spirit, both in the accompanied and in the companion, paradoxically remains the only guarantee of a walk bearing fruit in faith. In spiritual abuse, the triangular dimension is progressively annihilated, reduced first to a bilateral dimension and finally to a unilateral dimension. Whoever carries out an abusive practice in the area of the Spirit makes use of those instruments previously described (for example, manipulation of Christian teachings, distortion in the interpretation of the Bible) and, in the end, obscures the presence of the Spirit in the accompaniment and, finally, attempts to annihilate the accompanied person who is the protagonist of his or her own spiritual journey.[3]

By expelling God from the relationship of faith, predators indulge in a form of personal self-exaltation and idolatry. Replacing God, predators raise themselves to the level of a deity and go in search of victims to immolate at their altars. They become a "canon" unto themselves, the center of the spiritual relationship, and a one-sided parameter for judging the correctness and validity of their own and others' inner journeys.[4]

That form of idolatry runs through salvation history and is pointed out as harmful by scripture itself and subsequent theological reflection. In contemporary experience, it intertwines with that "throw-away" culture that Pope Francis speaks of in his magisterial teaching:

> Human beings are themselves considered consumer goods to be used and then discarded. We have created a "throw away" culture which is now spreading. It is no longer simply about exploitation and oppression, but something new. Exclusion ultimately has to do with what it means to be a part of the society in which we live; those excluded are no longer society's underside or its fringes or its disenfranchised—they are no longer even a part of it. The excluded are not the "exploited" but the outcast, the "leftovers." (*EG* 53)

In praxis, whether spiritual or pastoral, the person accompanied is not simply expelled from the path of faith but is reduced to a nonperson, that is, to an object and instrument to be used for purposes that are not explicitly declared. This "culture of discarding," which grips contemporary society especially in terms of economics and food, influences all forms of human relationality. Pope Francis states: "This 'culture of waste' tends to become a common mentality that infects everyone. Human life, the person, are [*sic*] no longer seen as a primary value to be respected and safeguarded, especially if they are poor or disabled, if they are not yet useful—like the unborn child—or are no longer of any use—like the elderly person."[5] Pope Francis explains that this culture manifests itself in particular attitudes condensed into the pride of dominating, possessing, manipulating, and exploiting. In fact, this denies that identity and mission of humanity placed at the center of the Garden of Eden to protect and cultivate it. Although the text of Genesis 2 is well known to be an etiological tale, the result of a linguistic and communicative plot interwoven with fantastic and symbolic images, it is also the guardian and spokesperson of a certain anthropological vision that sees humans placed at the center of a garden that God made habitable for them. Human beings, who hold within themselves the divine breath of life, have the task of cultivating and protecting the habitability of this place. So, when an accompaniment becomes abusive, the accompaniment itself no longer exists. The predator fails to recognize that this spiritual relationship is sacred space that God has made habitable and given as a gift to human beings. This is associated with the deterioration of the care of the other but also of that living space that is essentially inhabited by God.[6]

In the end, we can affirm that the very expression "abusive spiritual journey" should not have the right of citizenship in the Christian faith tradition; it is the result of a dissolution of all relationships, horizontal and vertical, because the presence of God and the accompanied one are ingested by the selfish voracity of the predator, who is no longer able to recognize the other and to see in the other the face of God (see Matt 25:31–46). We may, therefore, conclude that on the part of the abuser, spiritual abuse is the denial of the exercise of freedom and of the grace that works and demands cooperation. Cooperative force is annihilated by a coercion that, paradoxically, the abusers first impose on themselves and then extend to their victims.

Shattering the Believer-Church Dialectic

The baptismal vocation grafts the believer onto Christ, making the believer not only capable of relating to Christ the Lord of the world but also of bearing fruit in faith for the growth and progress of the Christian and social communities. In this case, the natural horizontal intersubjectivity that has allowed peoples to grow and progress in history is intertwined with the vertical intersubjectivity that allows the good news of the gospel to continually "incarnate itself" in this human history of ours, to take it on and redeem it.

In spiritually abusive relationships and contexts, abusers dissolve that necessary dialectic between creature and Creator, and doing so automatically shatters another natural dialectic, that between the individual and the believing community. Predators, incapable of any horizontal or vertical freedom, expel themselves from the Church, essentially showing their own "inability" to *sentire cum Ecclesia* and their inability to live the ecclesial mission *ad intra* and *ad extra*. The mission *ad extra* of the Church constitutes the dialogue with the contemporary world, the valorization of secular disciplines, and the dialogue with other religions. The mission *ad intra* of the Church deals with the mission among all Christians and is articulated in two waves that we could define as "archaeological" and "teleological"—rediscovering the foundations of Christian identity and collaborating with the grace of God to achieve the *telos* (the goal) of each Christian and of the entire faith community.[7] We can therefore conclude that, for reasons that are sometimes not deeply understood even by the predator himself, the predator misses the center of his human and Christian identity and dignity and, to use a soccer analogy, he scores in his own goal.[8]

Ignatius of Loyola employs the expression *sentire cum Ecclesia*, "to think with the Church," in his *Spiritual Exercises* as the fruit of a long and troubled inner experience.[9] Historians who have extensively studied the conversion of the Basque saint and the genesis of his booklet recognize that this expression and the eighteen rules on ecclesiastical feeling were focused on and added to *The Spiritual Exercises* when he experienced the Inquisition. Persecuted by the Church itself for a period of about twelve years, Ignatius did not shy away from the confrontation and remained in the Church. In this climate of tension, Ignatius confirms his own identity and fundamental vocation: to follow Christ, to help souls, and to serve the Church.[10] "Thinking with the Church" expresses Ignatius's ecclesiological vision: the Church in its hierarchical structure is that mystical body that assumes the commitment to proclaim the kingdom of God among people:

> Ignatius also viewed the Church as the Spouse of Christ and our Mother. Moreover, in Christ as the Bridegroom and in the Church as his Spouse the one same holy Spirit holds sway, who governs for the salvation of souls. This concept of the Church as the Spouse of Christ and our Mother is the one on which he focuses most in these eighteen rules.

> In them, too, he is thinking, not of the glorified Church as perfected after the Parousia, nor of the abstract, idealized Church of some theologian's dream, but of the Church militant in the concrete, with all the human defects found in many of her popes, bishops, priests, and members—defects which Ignatius knew very very well at first hand.[11]

Ignatius recognizes that the baptismal vocation of every believer takes place in a human and ecclesial reality, at times marked by limitation, error, and sin. Here, the task of every baptized person is to participate in that mission of the Church that seeks to transform reality, including ecclesial reality, from what it is to what it should be, according to a model descended from the light of the gospel. Therefore, abusive practices could represent an escape from reality and from *sentire cum Ecclesia*, a distorted view of human and ecclesial reality, the denial of that principle of historical awareness that allows the Church a sincere dialogue with the world and the proclamation of the kingdom of God in earthly affairs. Thus, when the two fundamental dialectics of humanity are dissolved within spiritual abuse, predators who had proposed themselves as guides and companions effectively renounce their baptismal identity and divert the path of that mission *ad intra* and *ad extra* of the Church. In our humble opinion, this perspective may help us to develop and maintain, even toward abusers, an attitude of mercy and compassion. However, this does not reduce their guilt or civil, criminal, and ecclesial responsibilities.[12]

For this reason, spiritual abuse is not a private affair between the abuser and the abused. Every conversion represents a personal stance and cannot be delegated to others. It is, at the same time, a community affair because the purpose of that individual conversion is community building. Similarly, when in spiritual abuse predators deny their baptismal identity, they renounce their conversion, and this renunciation has repercussions on the community, which, deprived of one of its members, is shattered. This shattering process occurs on a large scale, showing its perverse effects beyond the space and time in which the abuse itself is committed. Paying attention to abuse is in the interest of the entire Church community, which must ultimately recognize that if the expulsion of grace in spiritual accompaniment leads back to a Pelagianism of ancient memories, similarly, a theological reflection on abuse prepares one for "healthy" practices in collaboration with grace.

Abusing the Three Theological Virtues

Up to this point, we have theologically evaluated the spiritual abuser. Here we will briefly consider abuse from the perspective of the victim. The lesser space given to the abused is not synonymous with a lack of attention to the abused person but is an attempt to reconstruct the framework that best enables us to understand abuse and imagine practices to prevent abuse and care for the abused.

Spiritual abuse seen through the eyes of its victims is an abuse of faith, hope, and charity, those three theological virtues that determine the bond between humans, God, and Christian moral action. As revealed by Jesus Christ, God is a God of love and mercy. God always allows humans to experience God's enduring mercy, even amid all of humanity's inadequacy and guilt. God values human freedom unconditionally and constantly offers humans a new choice. That is why nobody can be "forced" to believe, to hope, or to love. Rather, the experiences of trust, love, and confidence can promote and deepen these divine virtues.[13] In contrast, the abuser unknowingly works inside a Pelagian perspective, emphasizing the importance and sanctity of one's own actions, the achievement of higher goals through extreme personal performance and renunciation. Faith, hope, and charity lived out in an abusive praxis is a dull ape of true faith, hope, and charity.

FAITH

Vulnerability and dependency in those seeking accompaniment can also be seen as gifts through which God enables or leads people to trust; according to Matthew 5:3, "Blessed are the poor in spirit; for theirs is the kingdom of heaven." Human need and poverty before God turn people into petitioners and lead them to trust and believe in God. In spiritual abuse, this gift of God serves the abuser as a means of increasing power. If faith is reduced to performance, and trust is replaced by mere outward obedience, faith is "emptied" and remains just as an outward form of law.[14] Trust in God is abused.

HOPE

If the person being accompanied, rather than being encouraged to listen to God, is told to listen to the ideas, teachings, wishes, and demands of the spiritual guide, then the accompanying person replaces God's position.[15] Instead of the hope for eternal salvation and redemption through Christ, trust in one's own achievements and power of redemption takes place. As a result, self-redemption replaces hope in the unconditional faithfulness of God.[16] The hope for salvation is replaced by ethical and moral demands that are used to judge the person in accompaniment or the members of a community.[17]

LOVE

Love is the core of the spiritual path. In the abusive path, love is replaced with ethical and moral judgments that allow abusers to exercise and deepen power over those who depend on them. Consequently, the love of God is replaced by an emotional dependency on the abuser. Thus, love is gradually degraded to a requirement, and in the end, an empty lovelessness takes its place.[18] As with the example of the pharisees and scribes in the Gospels, the external insistence on law and order only serves as security to guarantee the power of the abuser because it leads away from the ministry to which Jesus invites us. A service that oppresses others and is exercised "in the name of authority or responsibility," thereby undermining human freedom and fulfillment, is not service but a pure exercise of power.[19] Jesus wants to set us free and to lead us to the full development of freedom as stated in John 8:31: "you will know the truth, and the truth will make you free." Furthermore, as Anton Witwer explains, the needy person longs for the love of God and the love of humans. However, abuse prevents this experience of God's love, generating instead an affective dependence through which the perpetrator exerts further and increased pressure ("I just want your best!"), repeatedly demanding something of the abused person but without being ready for real devotion (see John 15:13). Thus, love remains absent, and the kind of tangible love Jesus lived for us and of which we should be witnesses remains unattainable.[20]

Spiritual abuse results in a big lie about God, the Church, and its baptismal and missionary identity. Intervening on these aspects is the task of the Church, which is called to live God's plan.

An Argument for a Category of Spiritual Abuse

The concept of spiritual abuse requires a better understanding of its psychodynamic and psychopathological aspects. A focus on (potential) victims and the possible consequences that spiritual abuse may have for them as well as a better understanding of who are spiritual abusers and why they abuse is needed. More investigation of their personalities, behavior, and possible psychological problems needs to be done. Such investigation also includes the question of whether people who have been victims of spiritual abuse might have a higher risk of spiritually abusing others if they do not get help or find a way to leave the abusive relationship or environment.

Let us make clear once again that focusing on those who abuse spiritually does not change the suffering of the victims, whose interests must always be in the foreground. Nonetheless, we should not forget what we already know from other types of abuse (such as sexual abuse or physical abuse), namely, that some of those who abuse in the present have experienced sexual or physical abuse in the past. So far, no studies or data are available to explain the correlation between victims of spiritual abuse and spiritually abusive behavior later when they themselves might be in leadership positions or accompanying someone spiritually.

Because the main psychological element of spiritual abuse is power, spiritual abuse is sometimes called "the spiritual abuse of power" or "the abuse of spiritual power." Such a point of view is too limited and could never do justice to the phenomenon itself or to those affected by spiritual abuse. Power is a central element of all forms of abuse and violence (sexual abuse, spiritual abuse, psychological abuse, abuse of conscience, and so on) even if the types of power (such as organizational, situational, interpersonal, social, or personal) and the sources (such as legitimate, reward, coercive, expert, informational, or referent) can be different.[21]

A closer look at power-related concepts such as authority, authoritarianism, and authoritativeness is needed. In the field of spiritual accompaniment and consequently in spiritual abuse, the power of the abuser could be obtained illegitimately—not necessarily authorized and accepted by others or linked to a leadership position—and without concern about moral aspects. But it could also be obtained in a legitimate way, as is mostly the case, with the authorization of and acceptance of others. It may include the position and the right to rule or to command as well as oral evaluations (authority) or be due to personal aspects and characteristics (authoritativeness). In contrast, authoritarianism legitimizes itself, including an improper use of its authority.[22] Authoritativeness is a term that is widely used in the Italian context (*autorevolezza*) strongly linked to authority and wisdom. Authoritativeness is optional as it depends upon the free recognition of it.[23]

Too often in discussions about the role of power in abuse, such differences and nuances of forms, sources, and origins of power have been neglected. A difficulty is also linked to various theories about and approaches on power that may differ between disciplines and single authors who deal with these issues. Another challenge consists in the fact that certain terminologies come up against semantic difficulties, not least because of the need to translate them into different languages and to make them match completely. Therefore, there is the urgent need to reflect more about the differences and similarities of *power*, *authority*, *authoritativeness*, and *authoritarianism*, especially in the ecclesial context and within the field of spiritual abuse. The reflection becomes more complicated if one also considers the concepts of divine power and spiritual power and their differences and similarities.

Attributing every kind of abuse to the same big category called abuse of power leaves aside other elements central to spiritual abuse such as the abuse of trust (see chapter 2). Trust is a necessary element in accompanying relationships and often goes along with authority and authoritativeness but not necessarily with other forms of power, especially if its illegitimate. In spiritual accompaniment this trust is not only present in the horizontal direction of this relationship (person in accompaniment and accompanying person) but also in the vertical direction of it (person in accompaniment and God). This is why more attention and significance should be paid to trust.

Regarding the question of whether spiritual abuse could simply be seen as a form of psychological abuse in a religious or spiritual context, we clearly have to say no. Even if the dynamics and techniques used in cases of psychological abuse are similar to or even the same as those in cases of spiritual abuse, one important element makes a huge difference: God. God's name, power, and will are abused by the spiritually abusive person, and as a result, God's image and relationship with the affected person can be shattered or destroyed. Of course, one may note that spirituality and faith are part of the human person and ask whether the interrelationship between psychological and spiritual processes[24] should qualify spiritual abuse to be classified as psychological abuse. Does this argument lead to the consequence that psychological, mental, emotional, and spiritual processes, as they are all part of the human being, should cause psychological, mental, emotional, and spiritual abuse to be put within the same category without differentiating the various aspects of the human person?

The spiritual dimension cannot simply be reduced to psychological processes, which makes it necessary and also justifiable to emphasize the specifically religious and spiritual moments of spiritual abuse, such as a dramatic distortion of the actual intention of the gospel and the Christian faith. Against the background of a holistic anthropology, however, it is equally clear that any spiritual event is always at the same time a psychological one, and spiritual salvation and calamity always have a social and emotional quality and dynamic.[25] Therefore, it is important to describe and analyze the psychological dimension of spiritual abuse and its consequences, but to also work hand in hand with theology and spirituality.

How to classify spiritual abuse and how to distinguish it from other related forms of abuse, especially psychological abuse, is certainly not easy to clarify. In addition, the Roman Catholic Church is represented in almost every country around the globe, and spiritual abuse is a phenomenon that affects not only the Catholic Church but also many Protestant Churches as well as other religions and Churches. This creates further difficulties with the conceptual definition and classification, since not all terms can be easily translated into other languages and cultures. Consequently, the question arises whether a general understanding and definition for spiritual abuse is necessary and helpful or whether each religion would need its own, linked to its own faith, to find adequate and effective ways to prevent it and to offer help and support for those affected by it.

Having a proper category for spiritual abuse within the field of abuse and maltreatment would underline its importance and give more attention to this widespread form of abuse that affects so many people in multiple Churches, religions, communities, and movements. If spiritual abuse had its own category, victims would be taken more seriously, as would the severe consequences that spiritual abuse can have on the life, faith, and health of those who experience it. As with psychological or medical diagnoses, the more detailed the distinctions of abuse are, the better the symptoms can be described and the more effective the prevention and intervention work can be.

The need exists for a better understanding of ecclesial leadership and spiritual-religious leadership—including the contexts of spiritual accompaniment, spiritual exercises, religious communities, movements, and formation—which are oriented not only to images of power but also to the experience of Jesus's powerlessness on the cross. In addition, a proper understanding of grace in its relation to human nature is needed to counteract the temptation to achieve spiritual growth against and at the expense of nature. Humans grow spiritually in personal freedom and in their capacity for love. Knowledge, attentiveness, and sensitivity toward psychological processes as well as the interdisciplinary exchange and collaboration between psychology and theology are necessary for the evaluation of spiritual abuse.

5

Toward a Theological Evaluation of Spiritual Abuse

IN REFLECTING ON spiritual abuse, psychology is of immense value. Indeed, spiritual companions and other religious leaders need to become ever more aware of the psychological dimension of the human person. However, the spiritual quest of the human person is not completely explained by the tools of psychology. The spiritual journey involves an openness to God and an openness to the action of God within consciousness.

Interdisciplinary collaboration between psychology and theology stems from an awareness of the content, boundaries, and similarities between the two disciplines, which both deal with human subjectivity; however, the two are not interchangeable. A theological reflection on spiritual abuse becomes, first and foremost, an evaluation of the identity and mission of theology in the world and in the Church. Theology has a prophetic function, capable of bringing God to humanity and humanity to God, and of maintaining, in dialectical tension, creature and creator, humanity's finitude and God's infinitude. Theology makes it possible to understand which elements of the Christian faith are challenged by the perpetration of spiritual abuse and what damage spiritual abuse does to the Church in its efforts to carry out its mission in history.

The recovery of this perspective approaches the heart of the believing life, animated by the dynamics of grace and faith and a deep dialogue between humans and God. In this chapter we will deal with the theological reflection on grace and the cross, exploring from a theoretical point of view how it has developed throughout the Christian tradition, and in chapter 6, the reflection will move to a more practical level. We will consider the role of grace in discipleship and especially in spiritual accompaniment.

The purpose of theology is not to make simple matters complicated, but to bring out the complexity of seemingly simple and trivial issues that seem to have no impact whatsoever on Christian faith and life. The Congregation for the Doctrine of the Faith describes the vocation of the theologian thus:

> The service of doctrine, implying as it does the believer's search for an understanding of the faith, i.e., theology, is therefore something indispensable for the Church. Theology has importance for the Church in every age so that it can respond to the plan of God "who desires all men to be saved and to come to the knowledge of the truth" (1 Tim 2:4). In times of great spiritual and cultural change, theology is all the more important. Yet it also is exposed to risks since it must strive to "abide" in the truth (cf. John 8:31), while at the same time taking into account the new problems which confront the human spirit.[1]

The task of the theologian is to dialogue with the world. This is represented both by the constant challenges to faith and humankind and by the secular disciplines, which are valuable in their own contribution and tools of investigation. For example, one issue to explore through interdisciplinary collaboration is the crossing of boundaries. Where are the boundaries between influence and suggestion, between persuasion and indoctrination, between spiritual accompaniment and the creation of dependencies, between religious doctrine and idealized ideas or teachings, between "good" and "bad" charismatic leaders, and between obedience and a lack of freedom?

The spiritual dimension of some abusive practices directly involves the relationship of faith and the reciprocity between nature and supranature, freedom, and grace. This chapter offers a historical overview, not particularly exhaustive, of how theology has understood the relationship between grace and freedom, the foundation of every authentic Christian life. The aim is to show how much the experience of faith, lived in the balance between freedom and grace, also needs critical scrutiny, to give rise to pastoral praxis and forms of spiritual growth that never lose sight of the core and purpose of believing identity.

Grace and Human Freedom: Insights from Theological Tradition

Every spiritual experience is intertwined in theory and practice with two poles: divine grace and human freedom. In the theology of Eastern Christianity, we find no obvious difference between nature and grace, creation and redemption. Influenced by scriptural experience, the Eastern fathers qualify grace as God's way of acting with humanity. The basis of their reflection is the idea that the human being is made in the image and likeness of God (Gen 1:26). Despite sin, this image is preserved, although it needs to be liberated through a long process of education, which has its culmination in Jesus which is also manifested in history, in the world, and in human nature, with all its predispositions and capacities. In this educational process, God respects human freedom: "If God, therefore, approaches man's [*sic*] freedom pedagogically, man will only follow his own force of gravity when he entrusts himself to divine pedagogy. By educating him, God frees the man to be himself."[2] This way of seeing Christian salvation is deeply influenced by Plato and his way of understanding education. According to Plato, humans can achieve their true humanity and freedom if they follow a *parádeigma* (model) that allows them to participate in its prototype. Greek patristics, following Plato's suggestion, believe that the true paradigm is Jesus of Nazareth through whom God educates humans about Godself. In this process, the initiative belongs to God, although humans are called to collaborate freely. "This educational activity is envisioned as a cosmic process of universal proportions, which embraces both creation and redemption, both nature and history, all of humanity and the single individual."[3]

The doctrine of grace formulated by the fathers of the Western Church is completely detached from this Eastern conception because of a vastly different sociocultural context. The Greeks saw the cosmos as a unitary harmonious whole; they were interested in the spiritual figure and risked forgetting the single in the whole. The Latins, on the other hand, posed more practical problems, linked to ethics and a juridical-positive form of community.

The Latins sought to implement the ideal; therefore, they paid much attention to the dispositions of the will, to the problem of responsibility, guilt, and reward. In this context, Christianity presented itself as the religion of divine right, as the implementation of a new relationship between humans and God. Greater attention was paid to individuals and their needs, and theologians pondered how the individual, endowed with freedom and autonomy, could realize the history of salvation. In the West, the answer to this question was completely different from that of the Eastern fathers; Western theologians believed that the individual can be saved with the help of grace, communicated to humans through Christ. Thus, reflection on freedom also has a dual connotation: freedom from and freedom to. The two are complementary because humans are freed from sin to be free to be realized.

The theological connotation of grace intertwines with an anthropological question: how can humans reach freedom? This question is central to the controversy involving Augustine and Pelagius.

AUGUSTINE: THE PRIMACY OF WILL AND FREEDOM

One of the most significant examples of this attention to the concrete human subject is represented by Augustine (354–430), who, in his *Confessions*, expresses his intense experience of individuality, freedom, and responsibility, but also of misery. Here a new way of envisioning humans emerges, marked by the primacy of will and freedom and by the experience of being placed directly in a relationship with God that is to be lived and built. In this unique experience, face-to-face with God, humans also discover their absence of freedom, their slavery to themselves, and their inability to collaborate with God. Here, then, the grace of God becomes necessary to break into the subjectivity of humanity and renew it. For Augustine, then, the grace humans need is not an external force but an inner strength that gives them true freedom, true love, and salvation. Unlike the Eastern fathers, Augustine affirms that humanity, with only its will, is not able to conform to Jesus, *parádeigma* for the

Christian. An element emerges that will be better developed throughout Western theology: the grace of God and the freedom of humanity are closely linked. The greater the divine grace, the less the freedom of humans and vice versa.

PELAGIANISM: A FLIGHT FROM GRACE

Against this Augustinian position arose a British theologian, Pelagius (ca. 354–418), and his followers, influenced by Platonism and the Eastern Church. Commenting on the passage from Romans 5:12, Pelagius believed that humanity was prone to sin through imitation of Adam and that this tendency could be interrupted, thanks to the human will to live a sinless life. The Pelagian claim that the will must be free to choose either good or evil was founded on a simple syllogism: if human beings are responsible for their actions (as all Christians believe), to hold individuals responsible for deeds for which they are not totally in control would be unjust. Since God is clearly just, human beings must therefore have the ability to choose.[4]

According to Pelagius, humans are not completely abandoned to themselves and to their will; the saving events of the Old Testament, the words of the prophets, the teachings of the New Testament, and, above all, the person of Jesus of Nazareth are instruments that God uses to lead humans to definitive salvation. Pelagius accuses Augustine of an anthropological pessimism, similar to that of Manichaeism, a spiritual movement that states that humans, a priori, are inclined to evil. Instead, Pelagius believes that even in sinful humanity and in its will to be saved, the grace of God exists. Given once and for all, this grace allows the individual to do good. For Pelagius, grace is communicated in a concrete way, especially through Jesus, and immediately produces beneficial effects on humanity and the Church. For Augustine, the grace is interior. In the words of Saint Paul, it is the love of God poured into the hearts of humans (see Rom 5:5).[5]

The tension between Pelagius and Augustine—the need for grace on the part of humanity—was resolved with the Council of Carthage (418), which declared Pelagianism to be a heresy. Beyond the theological implications, Pelagius was not able to confront the new demands of the Western world and proposed a model in which the subjectivity of faith was completely absent. Understanding why Pelagius's position was considered a heresy allows us to unmask those modern positions that, while not explicitly labeled as heretical, represent a deviation from that Christian anthropological vision that sees the collaboration between grace and freedom as the realization of humanity's true self-transcendence.

THOMAS AQUINAS: "UNCREATED GRACE"

New and unsolved questions of grace and nature would be addressed by medieval theology: What is the relationship between nature and grace? What can humans do with and without grace? These questions spoke of *uncreated grace* (that is, the love of God in the hearts of humans capable of transforming them inwardly) and *created grace* (the effect of this transforming power). But how does uncreated grace become reality in the life of humans? Influenced by Aristotelian philosophy, medieval theology speaks of *habitus* (habit)—a stable condition of human action. *Created grace* is *habitus,* the root of human action, which allows human beings to love God and neighbor. It is also called *sanctifying grace*, to suggest that God sanctifies the whole person with his love. It does not repress human freedom but promotes it, allowing humans to collaborate with God.

Aristotelian philosophy will also influence medieval theological thought on the "nature and grace" debate. For Aristotle, "nature" is the aprioristic frame within which being is realized. This nature and its realization are determined by an immemorial past. These presuppositions generate new theological questions that concern both the relationship between nature and grace and the relationship between the nature of humanity and the supernatural. Thomas Aquinas addresses these questions and faces the Aristotelian challenge in action. For Aquinas, the human being is characterized by an unlimited openness and transcendence to God. Therefore, an intimate communion with God belongs to the very nature of humanity, and this can be fully realized if by grace this nature is elevated beyond itself. "Grace is not only the ultimate satisfaction of our desires but also the ability to walk the path that leads to this end. Human nature thus finds itself involved in the process of supernatural grace, which will have the most intimate communion with God and with Christ."[6] Therefore, in the perspective of Aquinas, the supernatural is the end to which humanity is led through grace. Aquinas invites us to look up to the merciful God who neither erases nor crushes human nature but presupposes it.[7] Humans' natural desire for grace is a presupposition of grace itself; we find ourselves before a God unconditionally open to humanity's deepest desires. In fact, for Aquinas, there is only one end: the communion of God with humanity, possible only if God gives Godself to humanity in grace. And thus, God addresses humanity's natural faculties, which are brought to fulfillment.

The Thomistic position comes into crisis in the modern age, when in the secular sphere, thanks to the spread of humanism and the Renaissance, there is a greater focus on human beings and their capacities. A new concept of nature develops, an autonomous datum, held by humanity, that enjoys possibilities and purposes. With such premises, grace is likely to be understood as an added element falling on humanity from above.[8]

In the face of this anthropological exaltation, Christian theologians tried to bargain their way through, bringing Augustine's perspective back into vogue. The return to this tradition was not painless because Augustine's thought was misunderstood. Exaggerating the appearance of a corrupt and powerless nature, they appealed to grace as an ontological necessity for humanity. Of the earlier reflection on grace, the dimension of gratuitousness and gift was lost. These views were advanced by the Reformers, by a group of theologians in Louvain during the 1500s, and by Jansenism in the 1600s. They led to a new theological conviction in which people began to speak of two natures. On the one hand, "pure," concrete nature is the human being who, possessing certain abilities, can address the challenges of the world and live an ordinary life. In this case, humans find purpose and fulfillment in themselves. On the other hand, above the order of nature is the order of grace, freely given by God so that humanity can come to communion with God. This abstract grace can be accepted or rejected by humans, precisely because it is experienced as an added and not indispensable fact. To speak of grace as an a posteriori addition to humanity's nature implies that grace is no longer able to enter into dialogue with the concretely existing human.

Thus far in this brief history of the theology of grace, we have encountered two extremes. By reducing grace to an "indispensable" element for humanity, we lose sight of that biblical connotation that considered grace as the concrete manifestation of God's love for humanity. By moving away from this relational dimension, both God and humans are automatically deprived of their freedom. The other extreme clearly separates nature and grace. While the total freedom of God and human beings is guaranteed, it is also true that grace is reduced to a superstructure that humans can do without because they are already fulfilled in themselves. Again, faith as relationship disappears completely.

MARTIN LUTHER: A THEOLOGY OF THE CROSS

Within Christianity, these different theological approaches toward grace produced much disagreement, which would become amplified when the Augustinian monk Martin Luther initiated the Protestant Reformation.[9] Luther drew on the monastic tradition of medieval theology and expressed an aversion to the metaphysical terminology of the scholastics, making instead an appeal to the direct experience of God's love as described in St. Paul's accounts of faith. He believed that the confidence in reason displayed by the scholastics represented nothing less than a parallel with the confidence in good works shown by Jewish Christians in the time of St. Paul or the Pelagian heretics in the time of Augustine. Luther espoused three characteristics of the kind of Christianity he proposed: "faith alone, Scripture alone, the cross alone." In some respect, this can appear like a traditionalist step back to the way theology was in the time before Aquinas and the other scholastics; however, Luther represented another step forward: the stress on personal experience anticipates the "turn to the subject" of modern philosophy and even the existentialism of philosophers such as Søren Kierkegaard.

According to some scholars, the "theology of the cross" belongs, above all, to the young Luther, who was influenced, as was Ignatius of Loyola, by *devotio moderna* and its mysticism.[10] In his writings, Luther bears witness to the numerous medieval practices of piety, born of contemplation of the suffering Christ. In his *Commentary on the Epistle to the Hebrews*, he criticizes the practice of meditation on the cross with the sole goal of identifying in compassion with Christ's sufferings. To Luther, the only worthwhile goal of a meditation on the cross is to enliven one's faith in Jesus Christ who forgave human sins through the cross itself. The themes of his reflection are set out in his programmatic *Heidelberg Disputation* (1518). Summarizing his thought, we can say that for Luther, humans can only understand God in the visible tokens of the cross and suffering, which are the only means through which God has chosen to be made manifest.[11]

Luther placed his attention on the word of God, the way through which God acts in humankind and which Luther himself called the word of the cross. Indeed, in the confrontation with the word, the old person is destroyed and crucified in order to give birth to a new person whose vocation is the service of God and other people. Put in these terms, it almost seems as if God imposes the cross so that grace will flourish. Drawing on Galatians 3:13 and 1 Corinthians 5:21, Luther affirms the identity between the word of the cross and the word of grace. Beginning with the death and resurrection of Jesus, Luther wants to recast what humans are. Awareness of themselves as sinners causes individuals to experience absolute passivity, in which they strip themselves of their own righteousness, truth, and wisdom in order to find themselves before God. For this reason, many scholars recognize in Luther's theology of the cross a deep anthropological element; at the center of the Christian faith, there is the fragility of human life. And the passion of Christ is experienced as a model of life. Thus, Albert Brandenburg, one of the most prominent Catholic experts on Martin Luther, considers his theology of the cross as one of the most important contributions to the *koinonia* of the Christian Churches.[12]

Luther himself criticizes a certain scholastic theology that fails to deeply understand the cross on an affective level. That affective understanding is the element that differentiates between a theology of the cross and a theology based on the idea of a God who hides and suffers.

> It begins from the cross upon which Jesus of Nazareth died outside Jerusalem in (approximately) AD 30. This is not simply an exemplar of the hiddenness of God or of divine revelation in humiliation but the historical event in which God is definitively revealed, the event that illumines all other phenomena and makes it possible for them to speak to us of God. The demand that faith be able to rely on general truths, accessible to people of all times and places through their intelligent observation of the world, is precisely what Luther rejected as false theology of glory.[13]

IGNATIUS, LONERGAN, AND DORAN: A NEW PERSPECTIVE

Ignatius of Loyola, who lived at the same time as Martin Luther, believed that concretely existing humans, fully and freely involved at the level of intellect and choices, can stand before their past, accept it in its stratification of grace events and sinful choices, and transform it into a new story of salvation for themselves and others. The theology of his *Spiritual Exercises* might seem to limit the freedom of the individual, who is designated firmly as a creature serving the Creator, but it is through embracing this identity as mediated by the practices and disciplines Ignatius prescribes that genuine freedom can be found.[14] We will explore the anthropology and spiritual practices of Ignatius more fully in our discussion of spiritual accompaniment in chapter 6.

Living four hundred years after Ignatius, Bernard Lonergan also places humans at the center of their own processes of reflection and discernment, trusting in the human capacity to transcend themselves, to open themselves to God and to religious experience. As he expresses in his masterpiece *Method in Theology*, Lonergan returns to the experience of grace; he resumes the language of Thomas Aquinas, speaks again of *gratia operans* and *gratia cooperans,* and sees in the return to the subject and its interiority the keystone that can allow theology not to present itself as an abstract science but to be a force that drives redemption.

> All love is self-surrender, but being in love with God is being in love without limits or qualifications or conditions or reservations. Just as unrestricted questioning is our capacity for self-transcendence, so being in love in an unrestricted fashion is the proper fulfilment of that capacity.[15]

Lonergan recognizes in every human a common and innate cognitive structure that makes us able to continuously move our horizons, raising more and more questions. Indeed, the journey toward God, which translates into unconditional love for the Almighty and other people, is not the fruit of a simple intellectual exercise, nor of a human being's sole choice; it is the fruit of a love that makes humans able to overcome the limits of their selfish values, to open themselves to the highest Good. This total openness to God asks humans not only to welcome the grace given freely but also to collaborate with it. As Lonergan himself points out, grace, received in the hearts of humans (see Rom 5:5), has the power to transform humanity itself: "Though not the product of our knowing and choosing, it is a conscious dynamic state of love, joy, peace, that manifest itself in acts of kindness, goodness, fidelity, gentleness, and self-control (Galatians 5:22–23)."[16] With this statement Lonergan did not want to consider humans as puppets exposed to the grace of God which automatically transforms us. On the contrary, this reflection on *grace operans* allows Lonergan to develop a reflection on the inevitable collaboration that humans offer to God and to God's grace for the redemption of the world.

In this context, Lonergan can speak of a triple conversion, religious, moral, and intellectual, to which all can aspire, at which some arrive, and that never represents a perennial conquest. In the Lonerganian perspective, it is desirable that the theologian struggles to move according to this triple conversion that concerns the relationship with God, the values with which to make ethical choices, and the way of knowing.[17] The effectiveness of these three conversions allows theology itself to rise to the challenge of the times and to escape those ideologies that, after all, constitute an escape from the cognitive structure of humanity and that produce destruction and divisions in the human community. A theology understood in this way, capable of mediating the witness of faith of the past in a world in continuous evolution, also succeeds in recognizing and defusing the risks of neo-Pelagian claims.

Robert Doran, a systematic American theologian, is considered one of the greatest interpreters of Lonergan's thought. Probably the most innovative element of Doran's proposal is his insistence on transcendental anthropology that makes humans, and therefore, theologians themselves, grow in authenticity and enter into dialogue with grace so as to create a new civil community in which theology itself can make its own significant contribution. As Doran states in the introduction to his *Theology and Dialectics of History*, the kingdom of God is still humanity's business because it is realized by humans among themselves, in this time and in this world. Here the themes of grace and freedom and the theology of the cross return again, but this time they are proposed as a "glue" for interdisciplinary collaboration between theology and other disciplines, especially the social sciences.

CONTEMPORARY THOUGHTS ON GRACE

The debate about grace continues to the present day, seen especially in the process of secularization. Pope Francis states:

> The process of secularization tends to reduce the faith and the Church to the sphere of the private and personal. Furthermore, by completely rejecting the transcendent, it has produced a growing deterioration of ethics, a weakening of the sense of personal and collective sin, and a steady increase in relativism.... We are living in an information-driven society which bombards us indiscriminately with data—all treated as being of equal importance—and which leads to remarkable superficiality in the area of moral discernment. In response, we need to provide an education which teaches critical thinking and encourages the development of mature moral values. (*EG* 64)

Anthropologically speaking, this secularization has produced fragmented human beings incapable of reconciling and integrating the sphere of the natural and the supernatural and unable to open up to themselves as a transcendent mystery. This anthropological bias, which presents an inevitable existential crisis, has reverberations on Christian identity and ethics; it represents for the believer a de facto denial of baptism and incorporation into Christ, which enables us to live as the Risen Ones (see Rom 6:1–14). This image is expressed strongly by the Apostle Paul through the verb *sumphuó* (v. 5), which already in classical Greek meant "implanted by nature, united with, growing together." The significant symbolism of the verb, together with the expression "walk in newness of life" in the same verse, authorize us to think that Paul did not mean to direct the community of believers to experience resurrection confined just to Church dynamics or within the walls of sacristies.[18]

Evangelii Gaudium (2013), which echoes *Gaudium et Spes* (1965), is an invitation to return to humanity as a sacred space capable of opening up to God and dialoguing with God in order to grasp and face the small and great challenges of life, both at an individual and collective level. Both documents, in fact, are based on a healthy anthropological vision that recognizes in individuals a continuous ability for conversion, an ability to grasp those resources and potentialities that recognize in individualistic culture "a vacuum left by secularist rationalism" (*EG* 63). This healthy realism calls for a radical process of reform in the Church, which is reduced neither to the mere way of doing and thinking about pastoral care nor to a general renewal of the Church's internal organization and structures of authority. "They relate directly to the sacramentality and sign-value of what the Church is *before* God *for* the world; and directly, therefore, to the Church's witness and mission."[19]

In this desire for reform and renewal, theology plays an important role. Rooted in a profound spirituality and a balanced way of living the relationship between faith and grace, nature and the supernatural, theology can foster that aggiornamento of the Church already called for by Pope John XXIII in his opening address to the Second Vatican Council.

Thus, the *historical excursus*, dealing with the issue of grace and freedom, alerts us not only to the drama of the separation between life and spirituality but also to the serious loss that society and the Christian suffer when theological reflection ceases to concern itself with the world, human beings, and their decline.

In Search of an Anthropological Balance

From these pages comes an anthropological proposal for both theology and psychology. During the early centuries of the Christian community, numerous heresies arose that were in danger of disfiguring the face of God and of the Church. We may think that these heretical drifts are only a faded memory of the past, but in reality, certain heresies such as Pelagianism continue to survive in disguise. The language may have adapted to new times, but the attempt to exclude grace from the life of the believer and to ascend to salvation by human strength alone persists. In this way, the cross itself loses its redemptive meaning and becomes an amulet emptied of the resurrection that reunites the scattered fragments of humanity and the Christian community.

The risk of Pelagianism, which has affected some spiritual traditions in the past and which today continues to affect some psychological currents,[20] calls for a greater and sincere dialogue between psychology and theology. Both disciplines need to leave their comfort zones and create common ground for work and discussion. To answer the questions "Who is a human being?" and "Who or what makes humans truly free?" implies the construction of a common workspace and an unveiling of the identity of the theologian and psychologist concretely in action. This interaction is not a simple theoretical game but helps to verify or rethink, if necessary, the various forms of accompaniment and spiritual formation, both individual and collective.

The questions raised reveal the reality in which we live; humans are not abstract beings, "predictable" and "knowable" or judged as "right" or "wrong" according to the indications written in the pages of a manual. The human we can investigate and accompany in a process of growth and integral development is the one who exists and who has concrete actions and determinations. In fact, overcoming a "gap" between textbook humans (as they should be) and real humans (as they actually behave and relate), we realize that humans are capable of choosing, struggling internally, pondering their own choices, transcending themselves, and "seeking and finding God in all things." Humans can overcome personal interests and act according to common values.

The choices can be made within an ethical and moral horizon or can push human beings beyond the natural boundary, aiming their gaze toward the supernatural horizon. In this case, the human capacity for self-transcendence acquires a theocentric value: humans show the desire to go beyond themselves and enter a relationship with God. In the following chapters, we will offer an explicitly Christian understanding of this conversion event; nevertheless, we believe that an experience of religious conversion is universally available, although it will be understood differently by different people. Christians undergo religious conversion by centering themselves in Christ. In this openness and in the encounter with Jesus, the elements of religious experience and profound dialogue with God are transformed into actions, behaviors, and rituals "observable" from a psychological and sociological point of view but not reducible to them.[21]

Here the fruitfulness of a thoughtful balance between psychology and theology is evident, helping the spiritual companion to envision human beings as dynamic units who are capable of explaining the mystery that is in them. In this way in the journey of faith, persons who are accompanied are progressively helped to experience themselves, overcoming for themselves any form of emotional dependence and stasis in the search for their own Christian identity and vocation.

This perspective also helps the companion to keep in balance, both from a theoretical and a practical point of view, the tension between tending toward the Infinite and having to deal with one's own finitude. In this way, it is possible in spiritual accompaniment to recognize with the help of psychology which forms are attributable to the sphere of sin and which, instead, pertain to the area of the unconscious and psychopathology. In this path of knowledge, it is useful for the companion and for those on a spiritual journey to have a deep contact with themselves to discover and accept the unconscious motivations that govern human beings.[22]

This anthropological vision brings out how freedom is the distinctive trait of humanity who sets out in search of God and who freely responds to God's call. Clarifying the meaning and depth of this freedom allows us to understand the value of every spiritual journey and, conversely, the gravity of an abusive spiritual accompaniment. Freedom characterizes all life in the Spirit. For this reason, an abusive spiritual relationship violates not only the boundaries of human freedom but also shatters and obscures the free action of God, whose role is supplanted by the abusive companion posing as the creator. This perverted role shows a cognitive and experiential flaw, linked to an inadequate understanding and a shallow experience of freedom, both in an anthropological and a theological sense. Freedom is transformed into indiscriminate action, which loses all relational traits with oneself, with others, and with God.

Authentic freedom reflects the theology of grace concretely experienced in the daily spiritual journey.[23] The two poles, freedom and grace, in fact, account for the internal dynamism of the human person and allow us to give value to the "spiritual struggle" and to recognize in the "healthy" anthropological vulnerability the true spring of inner growth. So, to escape the concrete and impending risks of Pelagianism, psychology needs to learn from an authentic theology of grace. Thanks to theology, grace itself can be phenomenologically described, although only attentive eyes can recognize it.

PART 2

WHAT IS HEALTHY SPIRITUAL ACCOMPANIMENT?

6

Healthy Spiritual Accompaniment

A Theological Perspective

THE CHRISTIAN TRADITION of spiritual accompaniment has a very ancient history.[1] With its roots in biblical literature,[2] it is modeled on Jesus's accompaniment of his apostles as narrated in the Gospels, and is widely attested in the early monastic communities and in the experience of the desert fathers and mothers.[3] In the early Middle Ages and the early modern period, spiritual accompaniment experienced fervent growth, aimed at Christians committed to following Christ whatever their state in life.[4] Today, in the era of postmodernity and because of increasing secularization,[5] a certain ambiguity surrounds the concept of spirituality and the experience of spiritual accompaniment.[6] Indeed, whereas not so long ago the term *spirituality* was almost automatically associated with the idea of the Christian God, today it is not. There is a growing desire for spirituality, but it is often associated, even in Christian communities, only with psychophysical well-being and with mental and emotional health, which can be achieved without an explicit encounter with God and without recourse to religion.

Even in contemporary life, new "spiritual" tendencies emerge, but often they are not related to the real identity of humankind. In fact, we can witness a desire of "transcendental forces" and a lack of "self-involvement," as if we were not the main characters of our inner life and must wait for quick miracles to see changes in our lives. Many adults do not take care of their spiritual health. Indeed, they do not know that an inner life and the possibility to choose how to act and to live in a responsible and free mode exists, even in the realm of Christianity.

And so, spiritual accompaniment is sometimes misunderstood and emptied of meaning by those who seek only personal well-being, without God and without Christian community. Moreover, the idea prevails that the spiritual journey is an elitist proposal, addressed only to those who have chosen a priestly or religious vocation. Another common perception is that laypeople who seek or follow spiritual accompaniment show signs of dissatisfaction and behavioral uncertainty, leading them to seek an "omniscient" guide who tells them "what to do" in matters of faith and morals.

In truth, the Christian tradition, especially that which developed until the Middle Ages, testifies to something quite different, and rediscovering it is useful both to clear the field of misunderstandings and misinterpretations and to orient and nourish that contemporary desire for spirituality which, even in its shadows, represents good news. Let us begin by describing spiritual accompaniment.

What Does It Mean to Accompany Someone Spiritually?

In the Christian tradition, spiritual accompaniment is an ecclesial ministry undertaken by a person, lay or religious, with a deep maturity of faith and a strong and constant spiritual experience. As an ecclesial ministry, it is free of charge, reflecting the gratuitousness of God's self-revelation to and love of the world. Notes Sandra Schneiders,

> Spirituality in the Christian context is vested in the triune God as revealed in Jesus and his Holy Spirit as being the ultimate value to whom Christians aspire in their spiritual quest. Christians share in the life of the Holy Spirit and find life integration and transformation in Christ.[7]

This ministry is directed toward the person who wishes to be accompanied. At the same time, it witnesses to the love of God, which the accompanying person has already known and experienced. Spiritual accompaniment is a ministry of thanksgiving, an individual and an ecclesial act of gratitude for the divine love that is received freely. Furthermore, it is a tangible experience of being an individual within the Christian community, which cares for individuals and guides them toward the fullest realization of their creaturehood in God.

A THREE-CORNERED RELATIONSHIP: GOD, THE SUBJECT, THE COMPANION

Spiritual accompaniment is a journey together toward God, the Creator and Lord of life who, manifested in human history, continues to appear in the life of the individual believer and in the Church for the salvation of humanity. Therefore, spiritual accompaniment is a path of trust between a human being and God. In this relationship, God continues to love and trust human beings, despite being aware of their finiteness. On the other side, believers, aware of their own limitations, embark on a path of trust, sometimes feeling the ground shake beneath their feet and sometimes walking securely, hand in hand with God. In this way, those who are accompanied grow in their sense of belonging to the Church and mature in their commitment to the Church's mission in the world.

As the term *spiritual accompaniment* suggests, the Spirit is the true "companion" of the journey, enlightening the minds and hearts of both the accompanied and the companion. In fact, the companion is not a "guru who knows exactly where the 'directees' should go and guides them to that end."[8] Spiritual fathers and mothers are mature and integrated persons, profound connoisseurs of Scripture and of their own spiritual lives, who can help others in the art of discerning and listening to God's will amid the noise of the world, without ever replacing the person or God. For this reason, companions remain disciples of the Spirit, not dispensers of religious advice to people who need to be "guided" in a moment of crisis or existential weakness, unable to make decisions. Nor are the companions "perfect" people who, having completed the cycle of formation, have nothing more to learn. Companions themselves seek and listen to the voice of the Spirit; they venture on a path that is not standardized and predictable, knows no age limits, and welcomes and supports their creatureliness and their constitutive and necessary vulnerability. This allows them to take off the "superhero" costume, to avoid playing a leading role in the journey, and to be at the side of the accompanied person who in the search for God remains free to be open to grace and to dialogue with it or to reject it.

In all this work of the Spirit, the companions have a complex and delicate task. Their own inner freedom is a precious condition; without it, they interfere in the work of the One who never uses human beings, who proposes the true good to them without imposing it, respecting their freedom of choice, their fears, and their uncertainties, since he came not to be served but to serve (see Mark 10:45).[9] Companions themselves are "converts" who have not ceased to be converted and who place their lives in the merciful hands of God. In this unique journey toward God, the person accompanied is recognized as a space "made holy" by the silent presence of the Creator and Redeemer. "In spiritual accompaniment, we honor a person's outward ways of engaging with life, but from a stance nourished by inner reality. This frees the one accompanying to offer the whole of their supportive attention to the other, in whatever situation they are."[10]

This interior attitude, based on faith and freedom, capable of accepting one's own finiteness and of opening oneself to the infinite love of God is the same attitude that allows the companion to recognize, accept, and refrain from judging the yearning of the persons being accompanied, who, still awkward and trembling, want to strengthen their own humanity, which is made up of fragility and virtue, their love, and their ability to follow God. Thus, the accompanying person

> does have an agenda, namely, to help the directees to recognize the presence of God or Jesus in their lives and to foster an intimacy with Him. However, the directors are not as directive about the outcome of the accompaniment as they are of the process. The directors cannot determine the nature and timing of the directee's relationship with God.[11]

Although the practice of spiritual accompaniment resembles other practices that can be experienced in both ecclesial and extra-ecclesial contexts (the sacrament of reconciliation in the Catholic tradition, spiritual conversation, nondirective counseling, psychotherapy),[12] it aims to integrate the story of the person accompanied into

God's will. A journey under the banner of wonder, spiritual accompaniment can experience progress but also stagnation and deep spiritual conflicts, which then suddenly open up to unexpected vistas of faith and love. This is where the Lord God appears. Accompanying someone spiritually means, for the accompanied and the accompanying person, opening themselves to the adventure of gratuitous love that can do all, hope all, and endure all (see 1 Cor 13:1–8).

RECOGNIZING THE NOTES ON WHICH TO DANCE

What are the key elements that shape the experience of spiritual accompaniment? While discernment is often associated with this process, spiritual accompaniment is not simply a matter of choosing a specific path in life but a continuous journey that allows one to navigate the complexities of life's choices. Not being a finite process, it does not end with a single decision. Instead, this ongoing process shapes one's understanding of life's possibilities and challenges.

Spiritual accompaniment takes different forms depending on the seasons of the accompanied person's life and his or her inner growth. It is a path that leads to a growing and consolidated sense of belonging to the Church as well as to a maturing commitment to the Church's mission in the world, based on the model of love.[13] This path does not lead accompanied persons away from the world nor create an enchanted place where they can live with themselves and God without hindrance. They are accompanied on the road they must take to learn how to be in the world, dancing to the notes God plays for them. Accompaniment does not teach how to perform dance steps to perfection. It sharpens the ear to recognize the musical score played by God for each individual.

The companion must first identify where and how to stand in order to hear and recognize the melody of love. That place is the reality of the person being accompanied. Each person is a creature inhabiting space and time shared with other people. In this space, which the accompanied person sometimes perceives as cramped and at other times as excessively deserted, the accompanying person has unwavering faith in the creative power of God, who silently inhabits the story. Accompanying persons must continue to discover God within themselves and discover themselves in God. Without the continuous discovery and confirmation of this identity, there is no substance to being a companion. It becomes merely a role to be played or a trophy to be flaunted.

Spirituality in the Christian context is vested in the triune God as revealed in Jesus and the Holy Spirit as being the ultimate value to whom Christians aspire in their spiritual quest. Christians share in the life of the Holy Spirit and find life integration and transformation in Christ.[14] For this reason, spiritual accompaniment is far from being a profession or a theological information service with pneumatological and trinitarian content. Above all, the awareness of the free love received from God makes spiritual accompaniment not something to be done but an orientation along the path of love. God's free love is the treasure that accompanying people have experienced personally in their own lives and that they cherish to keep themselves humbly "competent" to recognize God's action in the life of the accompanied person and to remain a step behind in order to facilitate the encounter between that person and grace.

TOGETHER ON THE WAY

Together the companion and the accompanied person seek out God, One and Triune. The relationship is not static but presents a horizontal and a vertical dynamic. The two see together but are not to be fused or confused; each is unique with an individual history. "Together" becomes a call to mutual trust, to the recognition of human dignity and creatureliness, to the mirroring of the loving God. Moreover, the two are on a journey with God, who is the goal of the journey, with Christ, who is the way to be traveled, and with the Spirit, who is the guide. Together, the accompanied person and the companion are protagonists in a necessarily asymmetrical relationship in the companionship of the Spirit, who is the true companion of the journey and who effectively enlightens the minds and hearts of both the accompanied and the companion.

In addition to the asymmetry of accompanied person and companion, similar to that of master and disciple,[15] there is another, more radical asymmetry: that of the master/disciple pair in relation to the Master, who is the Spirit. This means that the companion remains a disciple of the Spirit, involved in a continuous "apprenticeship" in which he or she will "learn," experience, and perceive more and more deeply God and God's grace. Indeed, some mysteries of faith may be revealed to the companion by the very person being accompanied, who becomes an epiphany of the Lord.

So, spiritual accompaniment exalts and enhances the qualities of humanity, which are themselves a divine gift, opens a person to the gratuitousness of the encounter with God, and suggests that human beings can realize their true selves in the encounter with God and with the Spirit. When the true self unites with God, the basis for discipleship and discernment is created.

Ignatian Spiritual Accompaniment

In the long tradition of the Christian Church, spiritual accompaniment has known various forms, enriched by the example of the saints and of fathers and mothers who founded new religious orders and animated new spiritualities. In the following pages, we will focus on the figure of Ignatius of Loyola who gave a strong impetus to the experience of spiritual accompaniment and discernment. The personal experience of Ignatius of Loyola and the witness of his *Spiritual Exercises* teach us that the spiritual path has no fixed rules nor a right or wrong time to become aware of our spiritual gifts and of the special call that God addresses to us.

THE BIRTH OF IGNATIAN SPIRITUALITY

Ignatius lived in the sixteenth century, an era marked by spiritual renewals promoted by Franciscans, Dominicans, *devotio moderna*, and the Lutheran crisis.[16] During this epoch, the first *recolectorios* (retreat houses) were built to help Christians deepen their relationship with God. The authors of the time encouraged recourse to a spiritual father and a daily review of everyday life through the lens of the gospel. The first exercises for the spiritual life, *Ejercitatorio de la vida espiritual*, were written by García Jiménez de Cisneros.[17] In the Catholic Church, a need for moral reform and for changes in the exercise of authority emerged. This led Martin Luther to a spiritual reformation, which in turn called for radical innovation in the guidance of the Church itself. Rejected by Rome, Luther and his followers were excommunicated. While these renewals happened, the Basque soldier Iñigo (whose name was later latinized to Ignatius)[18] was concerned with beautiful ladies and life at court.

In 1521, during a battle in defense of the castle of Pamplona, a French cannonball wounded Ignatius, and he was compelled to recover in his family castle in Loyola. For a while, he fought for his life; later he fought with boredom. Asking for books to pass the time, he received the only two books available in the castle: *The Life of Christ* and *The Lives of Saints*.

> By frequent reading of these books he grew somewhat fond of what he found written therein. Setting his reading aside, he sometimes paused to think about the things he had read, and at other times he thought of the worldly things that had formerly occupied his mind....There was this difference, however. When he thought of worldly matters, he found much delight; but after growing weary and dismissing them, he found that he was dry and unhappy. But when he thought of going barefoot to Jerusalem and eating nothing but herbs and of imitating the saints in all the austerities they practiced, he not only found consolation in these thoughts, but even after they had left him he remained happy and joyful.[19]

As Ignatius gave attention to his varied inner movements, he found that they fought each other and produced different effects, which he later called *desolation* and *consolation* (Exx. 314–37).[20] He decided to follow the second movement as it gave him happiness, peace, and joy. Ignatius understood this movement as the way through which God was showing him his personal path. Ignatius left his service to the Spanish king and began to serve Jesus Christ, seeking the greater glory of God. Ignatius became a pilgrim journeying toward Jerusalem.

During his journey, Ignatius stopped at Montserrat Abbey in Catalonia, where he developed a more intimate and methodical prayer. Here, he read the *Ejercitatorio de la vida espiritual*, which pointed out that the pivot of Christian life is an experiential knowing of God through love. Later, Ignatius rested for eleven months in Manresa, near the Cardoner River, where he lived a life of prayer and penitence and received spiritual visions related to the Trinity, the humanity of Christ, Christ's presence in the Eucharist, and the divine presence in the created world. He came to recognize that the Lord's mercy was always with him in the shape of a force that could heal him from his weakness.[21] During this time, Ignatius jotted down the rudiments of his *Spiritual Exercises*. This work was not intellectual but strictly connected to his new understanding of himself, thanks to his personal trauma and conversion. Ignatius now began the second wave of his spiritual journey: his apostolic vocation and spiritual accompaniment offered to other people.

Even though Ignatius of Loyola had no direct contact with Martin Luther, the two arrived, in the end, at the same image of God-Love.[22] Indeed, they both considered that discernment and the spiritual life were not to be an escape from the world but a way to live in service to Christ and the world. "Despite their different methods in theological discernment, both ultimately locate their hope in a God Who wants nothing more than to love His children."[23]

Ignatius eventually reached Jerusalem, but the Franciscans, custodians of the Holy Land, refused to allow any additional pilgrims to stay. So, back in Spain, Ignatius began to study Latin in Barcelona and philosophy in Alcalá. In 1528, he moved to Paris to study Latin grammar and philosophy. Here, he met his first companions, Peter Favre and Francis Xavier. With them and four others, Ignatius shared his apostolic project, guided them in *The Spiritual Exercises*, and, on August 15, 1534, seven men vowed poverty and chastity and decided to present themselves to the pope so that he could send them to the most needy. In 1540, Pope Paul III approved the new religious order, called *Societas Jesu* or the *Society of Jesus*.[24]

THE SPIRITUAL EXERCISES

In 1548, Pope Paul III approved Ignatius's booklet, *The Spiritual Exercises*; since that moment, it has been an important part of the spiritual patrimony of the whole Church and beyond.[25] This booklet and the spiritual path proposed were not written to be read and studied in an abstract manner, but to be lived. Listening to Ignatius in his autobiography *Pilgrim's Journey*, we can recognize that *The Spiritual Exercises* reflects his personal experiences of the discernment of spirits that led Ignatius to his religious conversion and the awareness of his apostolate.[26] Starting from his time in Manresa, he noticed how spiritual experience worked, so he kept a journal in which he recorded his spiritual journey, his personal insights, notes, prayers, meditations, reflections, and directions. The notes were revised over the next twenty years. The result was a book, different from any other up to the time; it was a practical tool to help individuals to keep in touch with themselves and the divine actions in their own lives (Exx. 15).

Listening to the Spirit as his guide, Ignatius created a "retreat," an interior journey organized into four weeks, a spiritual path whose goal was to help people gain their inner freedom in order to serve God, consonant with their personal gifts and personality. During the retreat, people are helped "to discern the way God wants the retreatant to follow Jesus Christ."[27] Thus, spiritual discernment is central to the process of *The Exercises*, strictly connected to an intimate mystical union with God. Here, the grace of God, prayer, freedom, and discipleship are threads woven together into the spiritual journey. Thus, *The Spiritual Exercises* is a handbook useful for the companion of spiritual exercises and flowing from Ignatius's concrete inner experiences. Any accompanier of these *Spiritual Exercises* must have already experienced this particular inner journey.

When Ignatius wrote his booklet, he was a layman, and *The Spiritual Exercises* was intended as a useful tool for all people to manage their own spiritual life. Initially, it played a decisive role in the formation of the Jesuits. "At the time, no other religious order had a program for its novices that was anything like it."[28] However, despite Pope Paul III's approbation, over the sixteenth century *The Spiritual Exercises* was accused of being a dangerous mysticism that pointed out God's personal communication with the individual. The Spanish Dominican Melchor Cano (1509–1560) argued against this practice that offered everybody spirituality. Indeed, he was right that the Jesuits believed that people could assure their own salvation through the experience of "spiritual exercises." According to Melchor Cano, this assumption could endanger clerical supervision and lead believers to Pelagianism and vainglory.[29] Despite this opposition, the practice of spiritual exercises continue to this day.

IGNATIUS ON NONINTERFERENCE IN THE GOD-SUBJECT RELATIONSHIP

The introductory annotations of Ignatius's booklet explain what "spiritual exercises" mean: they are "every way of examining one's conscience, of meditating, of contemplating, of praying vocally and mentally, and of performing other spiritual actions....to seek and find the Divine Will as to the management of one's life for the salvation of the soul" (Exx. 1). In the light of this statement, the second annotation becomes an important guideline: "the director should give 'only a brief or summary explanation' of the text for meditation or contemplation, because 'what fills and satisfies the soul' of the retreatant 'consists, not in knowing much, but in our understanding the realities profoundly and in savouring them interiorly'" (Exx. 2). *The Spiritual Exercises* is not to be considered a treatise of spirituality because the booklet presents exercises to do—a month-long retreat during which the participants spend five hours a day praying.[30] During this journey, retreatants are not alone; they proceed accompanied by an experienced spiritual companion who helps them shape the retreat and understand what they are experiencing. But the true actors of *The Spiritual Exercises* are the retreatant and the grace of God, experienced in thoughts, emotions, and insights.

The Spiritual Exercises has two main features: it is a notebook of the spiritual companion, and it is a path toward making a decision. In some ways, we can consider *The Exercises* a humble witness of the spiritual journey of Ignatius. They are a method of prayer and discernment and even a guarantee that it is possible to follow Jesus Christ even when we feel tired and disheartened. Ignatius realized that every person is unique and, consequently, that each human being reacts to the same exercises in different ways and needs an individualized kind of help. So, the task of the spiritual companion is to adapt the text to the various requirements of the retreatant. Adaptation does not mean to betray Ignatius's intentions nor to manipulate *The Exercises*. The booklet cannot be reduced to a handbook filled with rules and laws to be followed blindly. It is more like a road map that the spiritual guide has learned to read and live in order to grasp the spiritual status of the retreatant. Thus, the guide can lead retreatants on their own spiritual journeys, giving advice to let retreatants be aware of dangerous curves and dark roads.

The core experience is one of trusting God and the human guide, electing this spiritual journey instead of others.[31] The task of the one who guides in *The Exercises* is not to get ahead of the action of the Holy Spirit but to be a facilitator who does not interpose between the exercitant and the Other who is sought.[32] *The Exercises* itself states:

> The director of the Exercises ought not to urge the exercitant more to poverty or any promise than to the contrary, nor to one state of life or way of living more than to another. Outside the Exercises, it is true, we may lawfully and meritoriously urge

> all who probably have the required fitness to choose continence, virginity, the religious life, and every form of religious perfection. But while one is engaged in the Spiritual Exercises, it is more suitable and much better that the Creator and Lord in person communicate Himself to the devout soul in quest of the divine will, that He inflame it with His love and praise, and dispose it for the way in which it could better serve God in the future. Therefore, the director of the Exercises, as a balance at equilibrium, without leaning to one side or the other, should permit the Creator to deal directly with the creature, and the creature directly with his Creator and Lord. (Exx. 15)

The companion is like a flashlight, able to brighten the path without replacing the retreatant's freedom. This stance comes from faith and trust—faith in God's work in God's creatures and trust in the human ability to recognize and answer freely to the Creator. In this way, Ignatian spiritual exercises are an invitation to reach a special experience of faith in which the retreatant remains in touch with him- or herself and God. Thanks to three special tools—meditation, contemplation, and discernment of spirits—retreatants develop a sense of collaboration with God's action in the world and gain spiritual discernment in decision-making. Spiritual integration of contemplation and action, prayer and service, emotions and reason is a prominent goal of *The Exercises*.[33]

SANCTIFIED BY GRACE...FAITHFUL FOR VOCATION

The companion offers retreatants exercises through which they can trust the value of their own personal experience for a purpose that is intimately connected with the exercises. The retreatant gains experience in how to proceed, step by step, in order to be transformed by the call of Jesus Christ. Retreatants recognize and welcome the signs through which God manifests Godself in their lives, even in unpleasant and unexpected situations. We need to point out that, according to the pedagogy of *The Spiritual Exercises*, inner growth must not be rushed; we can learn this lesson from the life of Ignatius himself. After his mystical experience in Manresa, he went to Jerusalem to follow in the footsteps of Jesus, but his wish was only partially fulfilled. Without his dashed hopes, he might never have written *The Spiritual Exercises*, a treasure for generations of Christians. So, when retreatants begin their journeys, they should prepare themselves for a great adventure and bring along a sack of patience and an attitude of expectation; they will learn to wait as they acquire the tools needed for the next leg of their journey. Thus, *The Spiritual Exercises* helps the retreatant to develop a spirituality of the "present moment"; Ignatius "invites us to think and pray about the where we've seen God presently, for example in our daily path."[34]

At the core of *The Spiritual Exercises* is the personal effort to be guided by the desire to know and make a decision according to faith in Christ. The aim of the spiritual journey is to find out incrementally the divine desire for our lives, so that God's desire becomes our own desire. Grace is experienced as a slow, transformational power; the retreatant needs just to trust it and wait. "One of the struggles of the walk of faith…is the pace. For those who long to go forward in the love of Jesus, it can be dismaying to know that a s-l-o-o-o-o-w road stretches before us."[35]

Each of the four weeks has a particular goal to reach. The decision-making process begins from a total availability to God and God's grace, declared in the *First Principle and Foundation*: "Man [*sic*] is created to praise, reverence, and serve God our Lord, and by this means to save his soul" (Exx. 23). The spiritual journey develops from there. The retreatants recognize that God fills their lives with gifts. They become aware of how some of their concrete choices are not always suggested by an evangelical style. Step by step, the director helps exercitants to shine light on themselves and to recognize when their inner freedom has been conditioned by external elements, leading them far from God.

Within the *First Principle and Foundation*, Ignatius expounds his anthropology most clearly. Human beings are created by God, and their existence only makes sense in relationship with the Creator. This foundational relationship gives the individual meaning and purpose and provides humans a healthy way of navigating the relationships with others and with things. This is one of the greatest achievements of Ignatius of Loyola, especially if we consider that, in the historical moment in which he lived, the individual, taken in singularity, had value only in relation to society. Ignatius brings out the importance of the individual while not isolating people from the rest of the universe. At the end of *The Exercises* individuals recognize that they do not exist without the whole: "It is God who is the centre and the one for whose praise and loving service human beings were created."[36]

According to the anthropology and the theology underlying *The Spiritual Exercises*, humans are able to undertake a "practice of authenticity" through which they reach their own spiritual freedom. "Conversely, the theology of the Spiritual Exercises might seem to limit the freedom of the individual, designated firmly as a creature serving the Creator, but it is through embracing this identity, as mediated by the practices and disciplines Ignatius prescribes, that genuine freedom can be found."[37]

Starting from the first week of the spiritual journey, Ignatius points out the importance of the personal relationship with God, through memory, understanding, and will. The goal of spiritual autonomy does not mean the complete independence of human beings; they should always be understood within relationships. When people experience themselves as creatures in the hands of their Creator, then they can grasp the purpose of their existence according to divine will. So, crossing the map of their life, the exercitants can recognize the presence of God and God's mercy from moment to moment. As such, their identity will not be grounded in the self, but in relationship with God.

The issue of a person's identity before God allows a fundamental question: how to live in the world according to the divine will. Here, the central point, personally experienced by Ignatius himself, is choice, also called *election*. Election could be approached through the divine work undertaken on our desires, and it fulfills our personal union with God. Thanks to this lens, we can better grasp the meaning of freedom and choices according to Ignatius. Freedom is not related to self-determination, reduced to the personal ability to make choices and fulfill one's own life. In *The Spiritual Exercises*, all choices have one and the same goal: the service of God (Exx. 169). Ignatius points out that indifference to created things and states of life is the secret of true freedom. "The process of election…is a dialogue between our freedom as human beings and God's freedom. When our choice is for God, our freedom is affirmed and expanded rather than diminished. We receive the gift of a freedom from attachment to any created thing, which is the expansiveness of God's freedom."[38] So, the *election* is the fruit of this special encounter, and it gives new freedom in which individuals agree to shape their will by God's transforming gift; this acceptance is the image of the personal union with God. Some authors recognize Ignatius's ways of doing election to be a kind of "anticipation" of the "see-judge-act" pastoral method.[39]

The spiritual journey ends in the final meditation, the *Contemplatio to Reach Love* (Exx. 230–237). All these threads—identity, freedom and choice, desire and possession—are drawn together in the prayer of offering, the *Suscipe*. The individual, aware of the spiritual gifts received from God, offers to God memory, liberty, understanding, and will. After the contemplation of the mysteries of Christ connected to his life, the cross, and the resurrection, human beings can imitate Christ's own *kenosis*. Individuals completely submitted to the divine voice do not disappear but choose and align their personal will to the divine will. This *kenosis* concretely shapes their life, fulfilling the personal *election* and giving God's love and grace in return. So, the fourth week of *The Spiritual Exercises* and the prayer of *Suscipe* are not a flight from the world but a concrete way to live one's personal mission.

In Ignatius's personal conversion, imagination and self-discipline played an important role; he imagined himself to be like the saints whose witnesses kept him company during his convalescence, and through his self-discipline he created a school of prayer that emphasizes the affections, stirred up by the will, more than intellectual experience (Exx. 3), and prayer that values the depth and richness of the resources a person brings, which is ignored by the more "traditional" instructions on prayer. The attention to the present moment, required by Ignatius himself, does not allow retreatants to separate prayer from life. Retreatants do not deal with the chronological rhythm of nature and the cosmos, but they attend to the moments of their interiority, so crucial in a human being's moral and personal history.

The Spiritual Exercises helps the retreatant to develop a spirituality of the "present moment." Ignatius "invites us to think and pray about where we've seen God presently, for example in our daily path."[40] *The Exercises* presupposes that retreatants enter fully the reality of their lives, with deep trust in the given moment that is being lived out. "St. Ignatius is concerned to integrate and deploy our human energies for the particular moment in time in which it is our task to live."[41] *The Exercises* gives the moment of time a shape, an expression, through an act or decision that, once and for all, releases any sort of dream and roots us in the present that is at once ours and God's. The attention paid to the moment lets retreatants be attentive to what is distinctive of each moment. So, in *The Spiritual Exercises*, retreatants discover the precise moment in which everything falls into place and the heart can gain what it was seeking all along. "There are three key features of this 'hour,' this *kairos*. Things come together; mere 'circumstances' take on a new significance; decisions are taken."[42] The *kairos* lets the human existence gather all its energies. Our affective capacities, our concrete experience, our sources, our desires, our obstacles, and our doubts represent a school of life where we can measure and balance our fidelity to God. "And our judgment is then either confirmed by how it works out in daily life, or else, by contrast, it is shown to be illusory—because it lacks foundation in the truth of what we are."[43]

Election is the core of both *The Exercises* and daily life. With *election*, human beings stop being ambivalent and move toward integration, freeing all their energies for action. When the decision comes, it ends the time of waiting, typical of a seeker of God. The yes of the conscience is the precise reply, today's reply, to God's grace. The energy employed during the process of election continues to bring forth its fruit. The *kairos* opens to the future, which demands us to take care of it, because the future is not just something that will happen in some way. We need to be able to live the present, but in such a way that, from within it, the future gradually reveals itself in a new encounter with God. The booklet *The Spiritual Exercises* aims to be endless! The inner exercises do not end on the last day of the retreat but on the last second of our earthly life. So, the Ignatian method of prayer helps the believer to manage uncertainty, to discern occasions, and to live within God's time. In a word, this method is lifelong.

Thus, the exerciser learns how to dance in this time to the melody played by God and does so through contemplation, which is not a pure intellectual act:

> Though ignatian contemplation is primarily a companionship in love, because it is such a profound companionship, it does also have a definite secondary side-effect. The intimate experience of the awesome mystery of a loving God in all the details of Jesus gives special vision to the eyes of the soul and a vigorous touch to the hands and fingers of an active presence in the world.[44]

In the tangled activity of daily life, by seriously valuing all the details of this time and this place, and precisely by not escaping the circumstances and options of the here and now, we can touch a God mysteriously laboring and loving continuously. Contemplation lets us appreciate the interpenetration of mystery and history and allows us to act according to the same dynamic fusion of detailed earthly history and divine mystery. The continuing rhythm of contemplation and action transforms people into apostles. "Through contemplation we truly become whom we contemplate and whom we are all meant to be. For, whether we realize it or not, it is in God's love, and in our loving response in prayer and service, that we live and move and have ourselves."[45]

Through the Ignatian *Spiritual Exercises*, we have discovered that the life of prayer and discernment is not a gift for a few, but a precious objective for anyone who wants to live their baptismal identity.

Conclusion

The history of Christian spirituality and spiritual accompaniment is long and colorful. At its core, it reveals a strong human desire to draw closer to a God who first and freely loved us. In fact, this history tells a special story of love between the Creator and creature in which each person experiences him- or herself as unique and unrepeatable in the eyes of God. It is on this element that Ignatian spirituality is based, which, by valuing humans' experience and feelings, helps them to look at themselves with God's merciful eyes and to find in God the fullness of life and happiness. Even though Ignatius's experiences may seem distant in the eyes of a cybernetic, hypertechnologized, and fragmented world, they remain valid and extremely creative. *The Exercises* facilitate a process of anthropological and spiritual integration into the whole of salvation history. They are respectful of each person's time for growth, valuing each person's strengths. They strengthen inner freedom and awareness.

These anthropological and theological premises, previously and personally experienced by a spiritual companion, enable that person to welcome and respect the human frailty of the accompanied, which is itself the site of divine manifestation and *kairos*. In this way, the spiritual companion testifies, on the one hand, to the motherhood of the Church and its power to produce happy and spiritually fulfilled sons and daughters. It also helps the individual to get rid of false or negative ideas about God, religion, and faith that are generated by modern and contemporary culture. For this reason, Ignatian spirituality offers important insights on which to build a solid and healthy spiritual accompaniment.

7

Psychological Principles for Spiritual Accompaniment

SOME VICTIMS WHO have identified spiritually abusive elements in their own history have at the same time experienced spiritual accompaniment as helpful and healing. Above all, the decisive factor for success seems to be that the accompaniment is understood and offered as a professional relationship, which, like psychotherapy, includes a continuous reflection of the structural and professional personnel power asymmetry and a corresponding code of ethics. What has been said so far makes it clear that every person who holds a spiritual office has a special responsibility for those being accompanied spiritually as well as in pastoral relationships. For the sake of clarity, we need to point out that the professionalism of spiritual accompaniment is not subject to an employment contract and a pay slip. Nor can it conform to someone's goodwill alone. It is a charism and ecclesial ministry that calls for compassion and competence in collaboration with and for the benefit of the entire Christian community. This is the perspective derived from 1 Corinthians 12:1–14, where Paul deals with fractures and tensions within the community because of a variety of "services and workings" and *karismata* there.[1] He can "solve" this trouble through the lens of the expression *pros to sympheron*, literally translated as "according to what is advantageous" (v. 7). It creates a link between the individual and the community.[2] Spiritual accompaniment is a Christian service, even a *karisma*, freely given by God for the sake of the whole community.

With a total of more than 1.3 billion Roman Catholics living or working in about 190 countries, a great deal of sensitivity toward cultural issues is required, and common standards of good behavior are not easy to realize. This is due to the influence of culture on the way in which faith and one's personal relationship with God are lived, but also due to its impact on values, norms, and traditions. In addition, all those who accompany spiritually—whether they be priests, religious, or laypeople—must be made aware of the great responsibility they bear and the high level of confidence that goes along with it on the part of the people they accompany.[3] Therefore, general ethical principles and standards of good behavior are needed—similar to those already developed and implemented for various other helping and accompanying professions such as psychologists or psychotherapists. Such general principles serve as a common foundation and understanding and should be communicated openly and transparently.

Various dioceses and Catholic and Protestant religious communities and institutions that train those who will accompany others spiritually or that offer spiritual exercises and retreats have developed guidelines or quality standards and have included the issue of spiritual abuse in their formation programs.[4] By referring to the concrete example of ethical principles and codes of conduct of the American Psychological Association, concrete suggestions for signs of quality in accompanying relationships and especially in spiritual accompaniment are made in this chapter. Furthermore, these suggestions should help to ensure standards for healthy accompaniment. Quality standards specify the basic attitudes of the accompaniment for particular situations as well as the role of the accompanying person, their basic training, and further education. This helps to raise awareness of possible boundary violations. The Catholic Church has recently been questioning the different forms of accompaniment offered to young people and families, both in an individual and a collective context.[5] Moreover, by imagining new paths of faith, it has insisted on the identity, role, and qualities of the accompanying person.

Understanding Closeness and Distance

In everyday life, closeness and distance are usually associated with social or physical distances; however, in the context of accompanying relationships, these terms contain much more than pure descriptions of distance, as accompanying relationships challenge spiritual companions, counselors, or psychotherapists not only in their professional role but also as human beings. In spiritual accompaniment as well as in counseling or psychotherapy, the question arises regarding how much closeness is necessary (at this moment/in this specific situation) and how much distance should be maintained. Because every accompanying relationship is characterized by an asymmetry between the accompanying person and the person being accompanied, the appropriate closeness and distance can be decisive to the success of the accompanying process. Therefore, closeness and distance can be consciously designed in order to control and change the interaction.[6] Closeness and distance are related to well-being and malaise, sympathy and antipathy, trust and alienation. For the person being accompanied, many of their relationships take place unconsciously, meaning that the effects of the closeness-distance configuration can be perceived positively as well-being and trust or negatively as defensiveness and resistance, or even as boundary crossing. To design an accompanying relationship adequately, the experience of closeness and distance of the person being accompanied must be considered.[7]

The difficulty linked to the understanding of closeness and distance is that no uniform and universal definitions of "closeness" and "distance" exist. Depending on location, culture, and language, different definitions and descriptions can be found. Regarding closeness, some definitions accentuate individual characteristics such as security, reliability, and freedom in a specifically good relationship quality;[8] other definitions emphasize an empathetic understanding of the other person.[9] Distance is positively connoted in many respects, since it contains the potential to create "distance from what is close, as a free space that opens up opportunities for expanding closeness and thus for the stubbornness of coping with life."[10] Nevertheless, a negative form of distance is also described, for example, as a lack of sympathy, being inflexible, and relying on routines or roles.[11]

These short examples highlight the complexity of the two constructs closeness and distance and their different understandings. Closeness is often associated with trust, understanding, justice, empathy, and reliability, but also with restriction or plight. Distance has positive connotations such as freedom, unfolding, delimitation, extension, tolerance, and professionalism, but negative connotations such as instability and lack of empathy. As a consequence, the idea of closeness and distance as an essential element in accompanying relationships is shaped by different theoretical approaches and heterogeneous terminology. Some theoretical and professional frameworks, such as pastoral theology, pastoral psychology, (social) pedagogy, and psychotherapy, pursue dedicated concepts of closeness and distance, whereas others do not. Specific (professional) roles associated with specific tasks and role expectations can also be expressed in a specific closeness and distance.

Closeness and distance are not objectively calculable categories but are based on the subjective perception of interpersonal relationships. Consequently, the perception of closeness and distance is not a purely intellectual question but is strongly related to physical perception.[12] Therefore, often a complex interplay between the basic need for closeness and the simultaneous need for differentiation can be observed. Due to the subjective dimensions, the relationship between closeness and distance cannot be understood as a static measure but as a fluctuating and changing one. Different perceptions of closeness and distance are reflected in interpersonal relationship patterns and can lead to tension and misunderstandings in spiritual, pastoral, or therapeutic contexts.[13] This is a challenge in the creation of a common and mutual understanding of closeness and distance. The lack of clear and objectifiable boundaries entails the risk of boundary violations, assaults, or abuse.[14] Thus, in accompanying relationships, closeness and distance cannot be seen as opposite poles but as two poles that are related to each other, that are fluid and modifiable according to the situation, the process, the relationship, or within the accompanying relationship. For example, it might happen that the accompanied person needs lots of distance at the beginning and, as time goes by and stability and trust are created, is able to accept more closeness. The opposite can also be true; a person may need more closeness at the beginning of the accompaniment but less as more freedom, autonomy, and independence are gained. Finding the right balance between closeness and distance is crucial.

Reflections on boundaries and on the necessary closeness and distance help better to ensure the effectiveness of any journey of accompaniment, be it individual or communal. Every inner journey aims to develop the three cardinal virtues—faith, hope, and charity[15]—and implies constant growth toward freedom and in inner dialogue with oneself and God. In this process, the main protagonist is the Holy Spirit, who, as a creative force, speaks and transforms the person's values and choices. The process is not automatic but calls for the active collaboration of those accompanied. The transformation takes place over time in a movement from one's interior to the exterior with concrete actions that reflect the interior life. It is, in any case, a process that can never be taken for granted, with impulses and setbacks that are not always easily foreseeable. Here, an individual's unpredictability linked to one's internal mystery comes into play. For this reason, the spiritual companion must develop an adequate sensitivity to put into practice concrete choices regarding closeness and distance that facilitate and do not hinder the dialogue with the Spirit by the person accompanied.

THE PHYSICAL DIMENSION

While culture is an important factor to consider when dealing with closeness and distance in accompanying relationships, the multidimensionality of the two constructs is also significant.[16] The physical dimension is the most obvious but at the same time the most complex and ambiguous dimension. As a means for spatial demarcation, localization, and networking, the body is of particular importance. It can be understood as a kind of censor that provides information about perceived distances and perceived emotions. The physical dimension may vary from situation to situation and person to person; in particular, cultural characteristics, age, gender, and personal experiences play important roles.[17] Strongly linked to the physical dimension are touching behavior and physical contact. An important difference between touching behavior and distance behavior is that touching happens primarily consciously. Routines that involve physical contact (such as greeting the client or person in accompaniment) can be described as conscious touching behavior only to a limited extent, so they require a lot of reflection on the part of the accompanying person in order to work out the right amount of closeness and distance. This is particularly true if the accompanied person belongs to another culture in which people could physically be closer or more distanced from one another.

THE TEMPORAL DIMENSION

The temporal dimension refers to the duration or frequency of conversations, meetings, and sessions (consistency or frequent changes), but can also mean the speed or timeframe of answering or reacting to phone calls, messages, or requests.[18] Also, during the COVID-19 pandemic and various forms of online accompaniment linked to it, another aspect of the temporal dimension of closeness and distance became obvious: time differences due to different time zones. Accompanying or being accompanied by a person in a different time zone requires finding a time frame that suits both individuals without requesting one party to get up in the middle of the night or to stay awake until late in the evening. Neither option is favorable for a healthful and effective accompaniment as they go against the human biorhythm.

DISTANCE FROM ONE'S OWN EMOTIONS AND BIOGRAPHY

To be able to deal appropriately with closeness and distance in accompanying relationships, the accompanying person must be aware of his or her own feelings and biography but be able to professionally set them aside. Distance from one's own emotions includes the ability to switch between one's own emotions and the emotions of the person being accompanied.[19] One example could be grief counseling or accompanying a mourning person spiritually or therapeutically. Offering this kind of support and accompaniment requires an empathic understanding of the feelings that accompany the loss of a beloved person. Without empathy, the support remains a formality that does not help the bereaved. Therefore, the accompanying person needs to be emotionally close to the other person while at the same time distanced from his or her own emotions or memories of similar experiences in his or her personal life. Furthermore, the accompanying person needs to be able to combine emotional closeness with a professional distance without falling into routine or indifference. This is particularly important because allowing oneself to be guided solely by emotions or intuition can impede the view of solutions and increase the level of stress of the accompanying person.

THE SOCIAL DIMENSION

Closely related to the physical and emotional dimension is the social dimension of closeness and distance. Since the beginning of the COVID-19 pandemic, almost everyone has become aware of this dimension. The social dimension relates strongly to the spatial behavior of the accompanied person (for example, how the person moves, sits, and behaves in the room). However, spatial behavior is determined not only individually but also culturally and can express confidentiality (closeness) or distance, status and dominance, as well as the professional role. Over the past years, this dimension has expanded to include more of the digital world (for example, online accompaniment, computer-based psychotherapy, and so on).[20]

DISTANCE TO INSTITUTIONAL/ ORGANIZATIONAL AFFILIATION

Professionals in spiritual accompaniment, counseling, or therapeutic contexts should be able to relate their understanding of closeness and distance to the realities of their affiliation with a particular professional society or institution.[21] This requires having a sufficiently distant perspective to recognize institutional or organizational processes that are dysfunctional in nature or that could allow for, favor, or cover up boundary crossing or abuse.

MEETING CHALLENGES

In accompaniment, dealing with closeness and distance has various challenges. One is cultural issues, which are subject to change due to globalization, migration, and the pandemic (the experience of social distancing, face masks, and so on). Knowledge of cultural differences in the perception of and response to closeness and distance is fundamental as it enables the accompanying person to react according to the situation and reduce or even avoid culturally based misunderstandings (such as misinterpretation of behavior).

The distance requirement in accompaniment can also change depending on the situation and the people involved.[22] Too much closeness in accompaniment risks having the person being accompanied become dependent on the accompanying person and lose independence during the accompanying process. Too much distance risks that the person being accompanied will feel alone and neglected.[23] These dangers can be countered by consciously designing the accompanying relationship and the accompanying process.

The following factors may assist in finding the necessary level of closeness and the appropriate distance, thus making accompanying relationships wholesome.[24]

A professional approach. Clear rules for shaping professional relationships can be of help here.[25] Regarding the outer framework of the interaction, the choice of place, space, time, and the presence or absence of other people are crucial. Also, the role of the accompanying person's attitude should not be underestimated, as empathy, acceptance, and congruence (genuineness) have been identified as basic variables conducive to a positive relationship.

Self-reflection and self-competence. Empathy includes self-reflection and thus self-competence. Self-reflection builds the ability to recognize one's own fallibility and one's vulnerability to abuse professional power for the fulfillment of personal needs and desires. Self-competence means a reflexive, self-critical attitude combined with the ability to continuously perceive and analyze one's own emotional reactions, patterns of thought, and behavior. A self-competent accompanier does not trivialize uncertainties or technical gaps and seeks support if needed. Involving another expert if one has reached one's professional limits demonstrates self-competence.[26]

Attention to voice and body signals. A large part of interpersonal communication is nonverbal or paraverbal. Apart from what a person says, essential aspects of nonverbal behavior, such as posture, gestures, gaze, and eye contact as well as facial expressions need to be considered seriously as these often reveal more about the real state of a person than spoken words. Also, paraverbal communication cues including, for example, tone, volume, and speed of a person's voice, add extra meaning and information to a message.

Guidelines or codes of conduct. Clear rules cannot be made for every single situation, but basic attitudes or a valid code of conduct can be established. For example, the professional group or institution a person is linked to can make its own guidelines, as have many professional associations around the globe.[27]

Self-care. Due to its high demands, responsible accompaniment requires continuous training, supervision, or intervision (a form of collegial consultation), self-care, and regular self-reflection.[28] Periodically, a supervisory specialist agency should provide qualified feedback, as is already practiced in various other supporting professions (such as psychology, psychotherapy, counseling, some contexts of spiritual accompaniment). Further self-care strategies include: being clear about one's role, protecting one's privacy, seeking out collegial and professional support, paying attention to one's own level of stress, ensuring an appropriate work-life balance (that is, eating properly, getting enough sleep, exercising, paying attention to one's social life).[29]

The inclusion of these practical pointers does not solve the challenge of accompaniment because every spiritual journey is unique. On the one hand, the person accompanied is unique, a mystery, known to God and loved in an unreserved manner. On the other hand, that divine creator and transformer Spirit who flattens mountains, generates life in barrenness and old age, and makes deserts bloom is actively at work. Before these two mysteries in creative dialogue with each other, the companion must be open to "believing" listening—listening based on trust and faith both in God and in the accompanied person. For this reason, continuous training accompanied by the care and growth of one's own inner life is important. Formation can be reduced to sterile formalisms and perceptualist practices if these are not integrated into the interiority of the companion, who, like all people, is always on a journey. Signs of a fully integrated life are inner freedom, the desire to meet people without imposing one's own point of view and opinions, the ability to unconditionally welcome all the people one accompanies without judging them, the disposition to inner space to make room for others and one's own stories, to involve oneself without becoming overwhelmed. The quality of formation should be tested at the level of the quality of relationships with oneself, God, and others. Formation should shift from an external requirement to an interior need so that companions are fortified for the mission that, through the Church, God entrusts to them. In this way, competence is shaped by biblical compassion, enabling life to flourish.

This compassionate attitude is related also to the loving gaze (see Mark 10:21), docility to the Spirit, and discernment of spirits. These inner aptitudes and personal knowledge of God are not acquired in the schoolroom but in the ongoing experience of being a creature in the hands of the Creator, living in a secular world and its challenges.[30]

Ethical Principles from Psychology

The ethical principles of psychologists and code of conduct that follow are those of the American Psychological Association (APA) in 2017, the current version when we wrote this book. These principles are widely known in the field of psychology and used by other psychological associations as examples. Deontological ethical principles and codes of conduct are similar in many countries around the globe; however, while these principles and codes are relevant for psychologists and psychotherapists enrolled in professional associations, not all professional associations for psychologists or psychotherapists have published them.

The ethics code of the APA "is intended to provide specific standards to cover most situations encountered by psychologists" and aims to safeguard and protect "individuals and groups with whom psychologists work and the education of members, students, and the public regarding ethical standards of the discipline."[31] The standards are divided into ten sections: resolving ethical issues, competence, human relations, privacy and confidentiality, advertising and other public statements, recordkeeping, education and training, research and publication, assessment, and therapy.[32]

In addition to the ethical principles, the APA proposes five general principles that "are aspirational in nature" and try "to guide and inspire psychologists toward the very highest ethical ideals of the profession....[I]n contrast to Ethical Standards, [these principles] do not represent obligations and should not form the basis for imposing sanctions."[33]

PRINCIPLE A: BENEFICENCE AND NONMALEFICENCE

Beneficence means that psychologists strive to benefit those with whom they work and take care to do no harm. They "seek to safeguard the welfare and rights of those with whom they interact professionally and other affected persons and the welfare of animal subjects of research."[34] Beneficence requires providing a context of safety; it means acting on behalf of the person's or group's welfare and promoting growth and development. It also includes respect for the autonomy and freedom of the person and care for the dignity of others.[35]

Nonmaleficence means to avoid harm or damage to the person. Professionals need to be attentive as harm can also be caused unintentionally through unthoughtful behavior (such as losing a recording that contains confidential information, forgetting notes on a desk in a shared office).[36] Furthermore, nonmaleficence includes avoiding the harm or damage a client may cause to other people. Sometimes these two principles may lead to an ethical dilemma, and one needs to decide which of the two to follow in a specific situation. When conflicts occur among psychologists' obligations or concerns, they attempt to resolve conflicts in a responsible fashion that avoids or minimizes harm.[37] In addition, they must be alert to and "guard against personal, financial, social, organizational, or political factors that might lead to misuse of their influence,"[38] as their scientific and professional judgments and actions may affect the lives of others. Finally, they "strive to be aware of the possible effect of their own physical and mental health on their ability to help those with whom they work."[39]

PRINCIPLE B: FIDELITY AND RESPONSIBILITY

Principle B asserts that psychologists establish relationships of trust with those with whom they work. Awareness of their professional and scientific responsibilities to society and to the specific communities in which they work is important, as is upholding professional standards of conduct, clarifying their professional roles and obligations, accepting appropriate responsibility for their behavior, and seeking "to manage conflicts of interest that could lead to exploitation or harm."[40] "To the extent needed to serve the best interests of those with whom they work," psychologists "consult with, refer to, or cooperate with other professionals and institutions"[41] and "are concerned about the ethical compliance of their colleagues' scientific and professional conduct."[42] In addition, they "strive to contribute a portion of their professional time for little or no compensation or personal advantage."[43]

PRINCIPLE C: INTEGRITY

"Psychologists seek to promote accuracy, honesty, and truthfulness in the science, teaching, and practice of psychology."[44] They "do not steal, cheat, or engage in fraud, subterfuge, or intentional misrepresentation of fact."[45] They avoid unwise or unclear commitments in an effort to keep their promises. "In situations in which deception may be ethically justifiable to maximize benefits and minimize harm, psychologists have a serious obligation to consider the need for, the possible consequences of, and their responsibility to correct any resulting mistrust or other harmful effects that arise from the use of such techniques."[46]

PRINCIPLE D: JUSTICE

Fairness and justice entitle all persons "to access to and benefit from the contributions of psychology and to equal quality in the processes, procedures, and services being conducted by psychologists."[47] Psychologists must exercise "reasonable judgment and take precautions to ensure that their potential biases, the boundaries of their competence, and the limitations of their expertise do not lead to or condone unjust practices."[48]

PRINCIPLE E: RESPECT FOR PEOPLE'S RIGHTS AND DIGNITY

All people have dignity and worth and rights to privacy, confidentiality, and self-determination. Special safeguards may be necessary "to protect the rights and welfare of persons or communities whose vulnerabilities impair autonomous decision making."[49] Psychologists must be aware of and respect "cultural, individual, and role differences, including those based on age, gender, gender identity, race, ethnicity, culture, national origin, religion, sexual orientation, disability, language, and socioeconomic status."[50] They should consider these factors when working with members of such groups and try "to eliminate the effect on their work of biases based on those factors. They must not knowingly participate in or condone activities of others based upon such prejudices."[51]

This short outline of the general principles of the ethics code of the APA could offer orientation and food for thought not only for the training of those who accompany spiritually or who lead religious communities or movements but also to formulate standards of good behavior as well as the consequences that may follow if people do not respect the rules, codes of conduct, or principles.

The Importance of Trust, Confidentiality, and Freedom

The relationship between psychologists or psychotherapists and their clients plays an essential role in the accompanying process itself and in its success. Thus, if the accompanied person is to be helped to grow and to mature, he or she must have the freedom to choose the accompanying person and be able to trust that person. The same is true for spiritual accompaniment.

Privacy, privilege, and confidentiality are important aspects in psychotherapeutic or psychological accompaniment in creating and maintaining a trusting relationship. Privacy means the fundamental right of persons to decide how much of their personal properties, thoughts, feelings, and data will be shared with or known by third parties. It ensures the dignity of every person and the freedom of self-determination. Confidentiality, professional secrecy, and privileged communication derive from this essential right.[52]

> The concept of privilege (or privileged communication) refers to specific relationships that enjoy protection from disclosure in legal proceedings..., in which the communications that have taken place cannot be disclosed without the explicit permission of the interested party....Traditionally such privilege extends to relationships such as lawyer-client, husband-wife, doctor-patient, mental health expert-client and certain types of religious relationships.[53]

The two concepts of confidentiality and privileged communication are often confused, but their distinction is vital. Confidentiality in clinical practice is often seen from a rule-based ethics perspective that includes the duties to protect or to warn, with mandatory reporting in specific cases and contexts (for example, safeguarding issues, therapeutic privilege), with the overall goal of avoiding legal liability and professional censure. From a more integrative perspective that includes the professional and the personal dimension of the psychologist, psychotherapist, or counselor, confidentiality is a cornerstone of effective counseling or therapeutic relationships. Positive therapeutic relationships make corrective secure attachments, and therefore positive therapeutic outcomes are more likely when they are based on beneficence, nonmaleficence, and respect for privacy. In brief, confidentiality today is seen as an ethic of care that goes beyond duties and rules.[54] Maureen Duffy describes confidentiality as "a relational, multicultural, contextual activity designed to promote and enhance client welfare."[55] It is a "sacred trust between the healer or helper and the patient or client that has been recognized as a value."[56]

Together with autonomy and the fidelity toward clients, the principles of beneficence and nonmalificence are part of the so-called ethic of care. An ethic of care includes the obligation to protect clients and, if necessary, the duty to warn. Three concrete cases requiring warning are the risk for suicide, threat of harm to others, and the abuse (physical and/or sexual) of minors or vulnerable persons. In such cases, reporting can be mandatory in many countries around the globe, and therefore, they are exemptions to confidentiality.[57] The ethic of care principle gives priority to the maintenance of the relationship and the needs of the other for acknowledgment, attention, and responsiveness to physical, emotional, and social needs. An ethic of care requires a commitment to the balance between ethical obligations and the safeguarding of the confidential nature of the relationship in order to develop an optimal level of trust. A trusting relationship favors the process of self-reflection, self-disclosure, and self-censorship.[58] Therefore, a relationship that is built upon trust and openness is the cornerstone of a solid alliance.

The reality is quite different in spiritual accompaniment in ecclesial environments, as there are usually no official ethical codes or principles available. Nevertheless, the basis for a trustful relationship between the accompanied person or group and the accompanying person as well as for successful accompaniment are similar. This is why in some countries reflections on and discussions about whether and how these principles could be adapted for spiritual accompaniment have started.

Signs of Healthy Accompaniment

Ignatius describes in his annotations to *The Spiritual Exercises* the relationship between the accompanying person and the person in accompaniment. He also names essential attitudes and forms of intervention that today can still be considered valid guidance. From the Ignatian tradition we can derive various signs of healthy spiritual accompaniment based on attitudes in the accompaniment, the promotion of the personal preferences of the accompanied person, which means, for example, his or her own ways of praying, and the capacity of making independent and responsible decisions.[59] We divide these signs into signs of the accompanied person, signs of the companion, and signs of quality.

SIGNS OF THE ACCOMPANIED PERSON

Growing freedom. An increase of freedom (Exx. 23) is the decisive criterion for assessing the quality of spiritual accompaniment of individuals and groups.[60] This includes the freedom to

1. assess one's own possibilities as they are given and limited by God
2. use one's own gifts, not in order to realize oneself, but to let God work through one and, understood in this way, to live sacramentally
3. recognize failure as such and to interpret it as something that has been committed consciously (sin and guilt) or as something that happened unconsciously (human error) and thus to entrust oneself to the Lord in hope
4. remain calm even under personal or social, private or ecclesiastical dramatic circumstances, to trust in the one who is always greater than human beings and also more powerful than any form of church and religiously based community[61]

As those accompanied let go of false images of themselves and others, they are freed to believe in God, to hope in God, and to love God.[62] But how can spiritual companions guard spiritual freedom? A first important step is to respect the personal freedom and dignity of each person that is accompanied. This includes respecting not only the person's individuality but also individual choices, decisions, and actions as well as individual approaches to issues such as sin, guilt, salvation, grace, forgiveness, and reconciliation. Self-determination should be encouraged. Furthermore, accompanying individuals should regularly question their own claims, ideals, or patterns of thinking, accept and appreciate diversity with regard to personal biographies and the personal development of faith, and recognize that every person makes use of spiritual accompaniment in different life situations (such as after illness or separation) and for various reasons (for example, to find a way out of difficult life situations, to make important decisions, or to strengthen one's personal relationship with God). Some spiritual companions testify to the pedagogical usefulness of pausing in prayer at the end of each spiritual meeting and asking oneself what one has experienced while listening to the accompanied person. It forces one to look inside oneself to discover dynamics of consolation and desolation and to understand whether one's attitude at that moment was more rooted in legalism, which stiffens, or in love, which sets free.

Self-determination. Closely linked to growing freedom is self-determination. The persons accompanied take responsibility for making decisions about meaningful dimensions of their lives, including sexuality. Nobody is urged to make promises to the accompanying person (such as about the duration of the accompaniment), and the accompanying person refrains from any form of discrimination based on sexual orientation or identity. Attention to sexual self-determination requires a careful interpretation of biblical statements about sexuality by the accompanying person in relation to the context and time. Spiritual companions should not actively address topics related to sexuality; in any case, they should communicate cautiously about sexuality and refrain from offensive questions about intimate life and relationship status.

SIGNS OF THE COMPANION

Avoiding spiritual manipulation. Manipulation in accompanying relationships does not always happen consciously. Therefore, it is important to be aware of and to know one's own weaknesses, wounds, and risks. To avoid and resist spiritual manipulation in accompaniment means first to not confuse one's own voice with the voice of God and to actively counteract such a confusion on the part of those who are accompanied.[63] Furthermore, it means not to claim any sovereignty in the interpretation of life situations or strokes of fate as well as to avoid exercising any presumptuous pressure of expectation through elitism (for example, exaggeration of one's own personal experiences, reference to a specific spirituality) and not to demand obedience or submission. Other important steps are to clearly reject any kind of coercion to certain spiritual actions through manipulation or threats of any kind and to convey friendly and empowering images of God and to classify threatening ones theologically.

Additional practices to avoid include stirring up fear or intimidating people with pious arguments; interpreting everyday life as a sign from God in order to achieve hidden or personal goals; exerting influence on private life through paternalism, control, or interventions in personal contacts; and provoking feelings of guilt and shame in the accompanied person(s). Quotations from the Bible or beliefs should never be instrumentalized for discriminatory behavior or manipulative statements.

Avoiding role confusion. Being consistent and clear with one's role and behavior makes it more difficult to conceal power and to spiritually exaggerate one's own function and position. Clear and open communication of roles and tasks can help to prevent misunderstandings or unrealistic expectations. It is also the right and duty of the accompanying person to draw boundaries between work and private life.[64] According to the life state of the accompanying person (layperson, religious, or priest), these boundaries cannot always be easily defined. Nevertheless, it is important to do so, especially to avoid overlapping roles with the person in accompaniment or taking issues linked to the accompaniment home.

Being aware of own's one professional competences and limits. Because spiritual accompaniment often affects the mental well-being of the accompanied person, a basic knowledge of psychological dynamics is essential. As a minimum standard, the accompanying person must be able to recognize psychological stress to be able to react accordingly. If necessary, the spiritual practice must be interrupted, or the intended form changed. During spiritual practice, psychologically stressful situations and experiences such as becoming aware of biographical burdens or trauma, adjustment crises, but also sudden flare-ups of mental illnesses can never be completely ruled out.[65] Therefore, the accompanying person must be able to provide at least immediate first aid and ensure the transition to appropriate medical, psychological, or therapeutic care. Similarly, psychologists, counselors, or psychotherapists who do not have the necessary competences regarding spiritual crises linked to faith or spiritual life should involve or recommend a spiritual companion. In short, individuals without the respective training, competences, and qualifications should not start to "psychologize" or to "spiritualize," as such behavior may create damage and harm the person in accompaniment.

Attention to transference and countertransference. Accompanying persons must pay attention to their own inner movements and feelings. It can happen easily that an experience sounds familiar to the spiritual companion, and they react on the basis of their own experience.[66] However, it is possible that the person being accompanied perceives the situation differently or that there is a different message to be learned in the situation. To avoid transference and countertransference as much as possible, mindfulness and self-reflection are required. If the accompanying person has had traumatizing experiences, those experiences should be worked through first. Awareness about these tendencies, self-reflection, and regular professional supervision or consultation with colleagues (intervision) can also help to reduce this risk.

Paying attention to self-care. Individuals who accompany spiritually—as with other helping professions—should ensure in a variety of ways that their personal needs are met outside of the accompaniment.[67] That means that they need to pay attention to their work-life balance, their spiritual practice, recreation, and personal relationships (for example, family, congregation, movement, friends). They must face the difficulties that multiple roles and relational contexts pose for the clarity and professionalism of spiritual accompaniment and stay away from all situations that could damage their integrity.

Maintaining contacts with other professionals and networking. Persons who accompany spiritually should seek collegial contacts with other pastoral and helping professions. This is especially true if someone is accompanied not only spiritually but also in a psychotherapeutic treatment. It is vital to respect the work of the other practitioner and not to speak badly of the other in public or in front of the accompanied person. A release from the duty of confidentiality should be obtained if necessary for the well-being of the person being accompanied.[68]

Growing with God. Embracing the sacredness of the stories being told, it is good to ask: "Where is God here?" This is not a judgment on a person's life but a recognition that accompanied persons are gifts of God who, unconsciously, can help the accompanying persons in their own continued growth in faith.[69]

SIGNS OF QUALITY

Guidelines, ethical principles, and standards. As working tools, guidelines, general ethical principles, and codes of conduct should be part of the quality standards of spiritual accompaniment. Similar to the guidelines developed by many institutions of the Roman Catholic Church for cases of sexual abuse, guidelines are needed for cases and suspicions of spiritual abuse.[70] Furthermore, general ethical principles and codes of conduct, similar to those proposed by psychological associations, should be prepared by ecclesial institutions and associations with regard to spiritual accompaniment and related forms of counseling and care. Such principles should focus on human rights and dignity, integrity, fidelity, responsibility, benevolence, and nonmaleficence or justice. Special attention should be paid to persons who are minors (think, for example, of catechism classes), particularly vulnerable (such as people who suffer from a severe mental or physical illness), who disclose an abuse in accompaniment, or in cases where the accompanying person suspects that the accompanied person is exposed to an abusive environment, is suicidal, or is a threat to others. If such principles and codes of conduct already exist, they need to be revised—and, if necessary, modified—regularly. These general principles or codes of conduct will build the framework of the accompaniment and provide standards for good behavior that every accompanying person must be aware of. Furthermore, these principles and codes should regulate who can become a member of the professional association or institution and who can offer any form of spiritual accompaniment.

Basic requirements, training, and ongoing formation. Participation in prevention courses and training should be mandatory for all those involved in spiritual ministry and accompaniment, formation, pastoral work, and counseling, whether they be full-time personnel or volunteers.[71] This training should gradually be extended to all Church workers and be open to other interested parties. In this way, communities can be created that can combat manipulative and abusive situations by welcoming exchange, reflection, discussion, and resistance.[72]

To make the training more professional, models and regulations similar to those governing psychotherapists could be required, such as including a selection process, many hours of practical experience, professional supervision, and ongoing formation courses each year. We are aware that this model cannot correspond one-to-one to the training for spiritual accompaniment, but it may still serve as a landmark and provide information for reflection.

Regular evaluations. Regular evaluations of the accompanying person as well as the process of accompaniment would be a helpful tool to assess and ensure the quality of the accompaniment. This could be done with a questionnaire or with some open-ended questions that focus on the preparation and competencies of the accompanying person as well as on the satisfaction of the accompanied person with the process and the way the accompaniment takes place. To have a clear and broad picture of the situation, such evaluations should take place on a regular basis, including various persons that are accompanied by the same person and/or in a longitudinal way, conducting several observations of the same subjects over a longer period of time. Based on the results, the suitability and professionalism of the accompanying person could be evaluated and, if necessary, consequences (adjustments and modifications in the process, special training for the accompanying person, or replacement or exclusion) could occur.

Concluding Reflection

The aforementioned signs for quality accompaniment are not exhaustive or even complete, as they are based on spiritual accompaniment as well as on personal and professional experiences, reflections, and insights in a European Catholic reality characterized by Ignatian spirituality. Moreover, consider that many cases of "anonymous" spiritual accompaniment occur. People who ask for accompaniment in the faith may turn to parish priests, laypeople, and religious who do not belong to any institution, yet they perform their service with great success, in a deep listening to the truth of God and others. They are generally recognized by their wisdom and numerous spiritual gifts: meekness, kindness, and longsuffering.[73] Nevertheless, the present suggestions can be a starting point and give orientation for further reflection and discussion in other contexts and with other Churches, religious denominations, and cultures.

We should do everything we can to reduce the probability of manipulation and abuse in accompaniment and to strive for healthy accompaniment. To date, spiritual accompaniment is rarely regulated or guided by codes of conduct or ethical principles, but perhaps psychology and psychotherapy could offer a helping hand in their development. Guidelines and principles are no guarantee that abuse will never happen, but at least they may help to create more sensitivity and standardize personal and professional requirements for those who accompany.

8

Theology and Psychology Guiding Accompaniment

THE RELATIONSHIP BETWEEN psychology and theology has not been an easy one due to various stereotypes and stigmatizations from both sides. The historical development of the relatively new discipline of psychology did not create trust in the discipline itself, its methods, or its representatives. Furthermore, many people think only about pathologies, mental disorders, and problems when thinking about psychology. Psychology was seen as mainly dealing with the "sick side" of human behavior. On the other hand, faith and the expression of religion were devalued. Just as psychology cannot be reduced to its pathological side, human action does not meet only rational criteria. Human beings are a unified whole; they put everything into play in every relationship, all of themselves, their personal identity, and their complex history. "Real" people cannot be reduced to a dichotomy.[1] The distinctions between psyche and spirit, body and soul, brain and mind, nature and culture, ontogenesis and phylogeny—or, in the words of Thomas Aquinas, nature and supernature—are methodologically useful but substantially reductive. Browning affirms that "until now, modern psychologies have not yet identified a way to avoid faith; and faith is an essential argument of the most comprehensive concept of religion."[2]

In May 2022, Pope Francis highlighted that dialogue and interdisciplinary collaboration are needed between theology and psychology to face the issues and problems of humanity.[3] Today we confront an anthropological crisis, a postpandemic society, various wars and armed conflicts, abuse scandals in the Church and society, and the like. By being equipped and enriched with different approaches and instruments, psychology and theology cannot offer pre-fixed solutions and answers. But they can help in an individual and community process of discernment, to manage such an anthropological crisis. Indeed, the complexity of the phenomenon and its specific characteristics, as well as the resources available to deal with it, should be considered in the decision-making process.

The Importance of Inter- and Transdisciplinary Collaboration

Living in a rapidly changing and hyperconnected world, we face increasingly global, complex, and dynamic issues. All of this cannot be adequately addressed from the sphere of a single discipline because these issues are interconnected and consistent.[4] The need for an inter- and transdisciplinary dialogue between theology and psychology becomes clearer and more urgent, as attested in the Roman Catholic Church's teachings on education and formation.[5]

Interdisciplinarity can be understood as cooperation or interaction between different disciplines, while transdisciplinarity emphasizes criticism of and general reflection on scientific work.[6] Interdisciplinary work focuses on greater knowledge, whereas transdisciplinary work aims at other and new knowledge and opens to transcendence. This means going thematically and methodically beyond the boundaries of one's own discipline while remaining rooted in one's disciplinary position. This requires an attitude of (self-)critical reflection on and awareness of the potential and limits of one's own discipline and other disciplines and takes into account their historical development and their cultural roots. Only by being open to other disciplines can one's personal disciplinary pride and self-centered mentality be overcome and transformed into a self-giving and benevolent one. Metaphorically, one should look beyond one's own world and be ready and prepared to work at the frontiers and to abolish boundaries for the common good and for the benefit of humankind. Inter- or transdisciplinary collaboration will not be easy and conflict-free, but the openness and willingness on individual and disciplinary levels build the foundation for it, together with the awareness of the barriers and aids of one's own discipline and the conviction that an inter- or transdisciplinary collaboration will enrich all the disciplines involved and make a precious contribution to face current challenges.

In the wake of Vatican II and the increased use of the social sciences in theological reflection and pastoral practice (*GS* 62), the latest *Ratio Fundamentalis Institutionis Sacerdotalis* (2016) points out:

> During formation for priesthood, the presence and the contribution of experts in certain disciplines is helpful, owing to their professional abilities and for the support they can give, where particular situations call for it....In the field of psychology, this contribution is valuable both for the formators and for the seminarians principally in two areas: in the assessment of personality, expressing an opinion as to the psychological health of the candidate; and in therapeutic accompaniment, in order to shed light on any problems that may emerge and to assist the growth in human maturity.[7]

This issue emphasizes both the unity of the person and the complementarity of charisms and vocations; different professional figures within the educational community let the young person thrive in a path of deep growth and integration. The presence of professional figures not only performs an instrumental function but is part of that general attention to the person, to promote the goodness of the candidate.[8]

This topic was the focus of a document produced by the Congregation for Catholic Education: *Guidelines for the Use of Psychology in the Admission and Formation of Candidates for the Priesthood* (2008).[9] This document emphasizes how the candidate's well-being affects the well-being of the gospel proclamation and the redemptive mission of the Church itself. Already *Pastores Dabo Vobis* (1992) had emphasized certain inner dispositions related to the intellectual and spiritual spheres that are necessary for the path to the priesthood.[10] The guidelines offer an additional list of qualities and virtues: inner freedom, the ability to cooperate, soundness, integrated sexuality, knowledge of oneself and one's limitations, self-correction, and love for the truth. Candidates for the priesthood need a path of formation in which these predispositions are shaped in the candidate's constant cooperation with grace.[11] The suggestions provided by the various documents of the Catholic Church are not merely practices to be performed or avoided, but they manifest the theological structure that generates them. It is useful to recall Thomas Aquinas's reflection on nature and supernature, *instinctus* and the gifts of the Holy Spirit. In his *Scriptum super Sententiis*,[12] he deepens his teaching on a human mode of action concerning the human virtues, acquired and infused. He shows how the human mode concerns those acts produced by human reason. Later, Thomas explains that the gifts of the Holy Spirit go beyond the human mode, perfecting human virtue. In this way, he recognizes that human virtue is under the rule of human reason and the spiritual gifts are under the rule of God. The Thomistic word *instinctus* refers to God moving the human person through the gifts of the Holy Spirit as *habitus* in conjunction with the infused virtues toward one's supernatural beatitude.[13] Through the lens of Thomas's reflection, we can better consider the relationship between human virtues and operative grace, human reason and the Holy Spirit's action, and recognize that grace does not abolish nature, but the former looks for the latter. So, the recourse to psychology in religious formation and education is not just a guarantee of the issue of vocational discernment. It is a valuable aid in restoring inner freedom, which lets people move to self-transcendence and a free response to the divine call.[14] This process is evident both in the dynamics of the Ignatian *Spiritual Exercises* and in the just quoted *Ratio*.

Regarding formation, the human dimension of young seminarians, as stated by the former secretary of the former Congregation for the Clergy[15] Archbishop Jorge Carlos Patrón Wong, is a priority challenge for the Roman Catholic Church today that does not allow any superficiality, underlining the importance of having fully human pastors.[16] This requires the ability to open up to experience and learn from it in order to grow and mature as a person, always keeping in mind the age, life situation, and training of the person involved. That process of growth and maturation is articulated according to a progressive path of self-knowledge, becoming aware of one's emotions, motivations, expectations, behaviors, and attitudes, but also of one's desires, needs, ideals, strengths, and weaknesses.[17] All these are areas in which a psychologist or psychotherapist can help young people in formation through psychological accompaniment, psychological intervention, counseling, psychotherapy, or psychospiritual accompaniment.

Once again, we want to indicate that the involvement of psychology is not necessarily linked to the presence of mental health problems or mental disorders. It would be a big mistake, in fact, to try to reduce the mental well-being of an individual to two categories such as "mentally healthy versus mentally ill" or "normal versus abnormal." Such a reductive perspective would neglect the individuality of each person and the many nuances that lie between these two poles.[18] Furthermore, the discipline of psychology would be reduced to its clinical and therapeutic aspects with many other important areas remaining unacknowledged, such as social psychology, organizational psychology, work psychology, psychological evaluation and research methods, educational psychology, pedagogical psychology, and neuropsychology, to mention a few.

Two Fields of Collaboration

In an earlier article,[19] the authors of this volume raised questions on the issue of how psychology and theology may collaborate and enrich each other with regard to the complexity and variety of their respective subdisciplines and the differences in their ages and histories. The collaboration between theology and psychology is new but has already been realized and lived for several decades in various Western countries. Two examples will be presented briefly—pastoral psychology and psychology of religion.

PASTORAL PSYCHOLOGY

Pastoral psychology is part of practical theology and has its origins mainly in the English- and German-speaking world. Pastoral theology is a Christian theological discipline that is interdisciplinary in its hermeneutic and methodological approach. It understands itself as a connecting science and aims to bring various subjects and disciplines, as well as people who represent these subjects and disciplines, together to relate with one another in both theory and practice.[20] Concrete examples are university courses[21] or the scientific journal *Pastoral Psychology* founded in 1950.[22] Pastoral psychology combines the perspectives of human science with Christian spirituality; furthermore, it helps to model communicative situations and consultative pastoral care in a responsible way by living the dialogue between theological and psychological visions of reality. Therefore, new perspectives and opportunities for pastoral work can arise.[23]

PSYCHOLOGY OF RELIGION

The psychology of religion is a discipline that arose already in the late nineteenth century as a self-conscious discipline within the field of psychology. However, many tasks and challenges of the discipline—such as the systematic description of religious contents, attitudes, experiences, or expressions; the explanation of the origins of religion; or the illustration of consequences of religious attitudes and behaviors—have a long history going back many centuries before that.[24] The psychology of religion is related to pastoral psychology but is not limited to the Christian theological context, as it takes into consideration different religions. In addition, it starts from the psychological point of view as part of so-called applied psychology. The psychology of religion seeks with its concepts and theories as well as with its methods and tools to understand better the psychological needs and processes in religious consciousness and experience and in religious attitudes and behaviors on an individual and on a group level.[25] Topics that the psychology of religion deals with are: believing, doubting, prayer, penance, confession, and the experience of God, among others. The question of spiritual transcendence as an important factor of personality has also been proposed and discussed.[26] For this reason, the development of spirituality as well as its influence on human well-being and health is a vital part of the psychology of religion.

These two examples show the importance of integrated approaches and how psychology and theology can enrich each other and learn from each other on a theoretical and practical level. This is even more important when it comes to existential questions, health issues, pastoral work, or the accompaniment of individuals or groups of people. For example, Fr. Franco Imoda, SJ, one of the founders of the Institute of Psychology of the Pontifical Gregorian University in Rome, stated in 2000:

> The understanding of the human person in terms of mystery calls for an approach which combines the human sciences, psychology/psychiatry, and theology, in a spirit of open dialogue.

> This dialogue should address three areas of importance in the study of the human person: the cognitive, the conative (action) and the affective.[27]

According to Imoda,

> psychology, psychiatry, and religion must not only talk to each other but, through a dialogue of mutual questioning, be able to integrate. The reciprocal references and connections between the humble events and concomitants of the development of human life and the great themes of life and death...which often tend to persist into adulthood, is perhaps one of the most amazing manifestations of the mystery of the person.
>
> That human dignity, the very image of God, is consigned to and comes to depend on fragile relationships with other human subjects in which the vulnerability of the parties predisposes to illusions, limitations, and abuse, and that, at the same time, it is precisely these fragile human relationships that become the channel and mediation for the constitution, for the obfuscation or often the reconstitution of this dignity, is something marvelous and "tremendous."[28]

As the coronavirus pandemic and the various crises of today's world have revealed, this affects the whole world and has led to serious consequences and questions about life and death as well as respect and human dignity on various levels for individuals and for entire societies and nations.

Spirituality and Religion in Counseling and Psychotherapy

Especially in times of uncertainty, doubt, suffering, and fear, people look for meaning and stability in their lives. Many of them seek this meaning in faith or, more broadly, in spirituality or religion, while they seek support in counseling or psychotherapy. So, it is not surprising that these individuals are looking for a counselor or psychotherapist who is able to incorporate the spiritual dimension in treatment. How such an incorporation can look like is described by Len Sperry.[29] He differentiates four levels of incorporation—none, limited, moderate, and maximum—on the basis of the extent of incorporation of three therapeutic factors: (1) a spiritual history or assessment, (2) some degree of processing patients' religious and spiritual issues and/or utilizing spiritual practices with clients/patients, and (3) the extent of referral and/or collaboration with religious/spiritual personnel (for example, priests, spiritual guides, pastoral counselors).[30] A spiritual assessment helps the counselor or therapist to understand whether religion or spirituality is important to clients/patients, whether they belong to a religious or spiritual community, whether their spiritual or religious beliefs influence their way of looking at problems and thinking about health. Furthermore, a spiritual assessment gives the clients/patients the possibility of addressing spiritual or religious beliefs or practices with the counselor or therapist.

The four levels of incorporation can be summarized as follows.

TABLE 1: SPERRY'S LEVELS OF INCORPORATION OF SPIRITUAL DIMENSION IN COUNSELING PRACTICE		
Level I	None	No spiritual assessment No processing of spiritual issues No spiritual advisor, even if indicated
Level II	Limited	Spiritual assessment No, or brief, single processing of spiritual issues Referral to spiritual advisor if indicated
Level III	Moderate	Spiritual assessment Some processing of spiritual issues Collaboration with a spiritual advisor if indicated
Level IV	Maximum	Spiritual assessment Full processing of spiritual issues Collaboration with a spiritual advisor if indicated

According to Len Sperry, these four levels are related to the types of personal and professional commitment of the counselor or therapist to religious or spiritual sensitivity. That means that both the personal commitment of the respective counselor or therapist can be low (for example, disinterest, agnostic personal stance) or high (for example, faithful, personal spiritual journey) and the professional commitment can be low (for example, "scientific" professional stance, value-free) or high (for example, sensitivity toward clients'/patients' spiritual/religious issues).[31] The professional as well as the personal commitment of the counselor or therapist to spirituality or religion may determine the process and the success of the treatment if spiritual or religious issues play an important role. Thus, the Association for Spiritual, Ethical and Religious Values in Counseling (ASERVIC) in the United States proposed in 2009 a revised version of religious and spiritual competencies for addressing religious and spiritual issues in counseling. These competencies are divided into six main aspects: (1) culture and worldview, (2) counselor self-awareness, (3) human and spiritual development, (4) communication, (5) assessment, and (6) diagnosis and treatment.[32] The revised version underlines that it is no longer about "if" spiritual or religious issues can be incorporated and addressed in counseling but about "how" this can be done in the best way possible.[33]

Spiritually oriented psychotherapy needs to be distinguished from other forms of accompaniment and care, such as spiritual accompaniment (sometimes still called spiritual direction or spiritual guidance), spiritual care, pastoral care, and pastoral counseling. First, spiritually oriented psychotherapy is based on psychological theories, approaches, and research. As with other forms of psychotherapy, it is practiced by competent clinicians who are licensed due to their training and experience.[34] This kind of treatment aims, first, to bring about psychological change and, second, to favor spiritual growth. As Len Sperry notes,

> The goals of this treatment include help with spiritual struggles, spiritual emergencies, spiritual growth, increased psychological well-being, self-fulfillment or individuation, or reduction of symptomatic distress and the restoration of the baseline functioning.[35]

Table 2 summarizes the four other forms of religious and spiritual treatment.

TABLE 2: TYPES OF SPIRITUAL AND RELIGIOUS TREATMENT		
Type of Treatment	**Scope**	**Basic Assumptions**
Spiritual Direction/ Guidance/ (Accompaniment)[36]	Facilitating spiritual growth and fostering psychological change Development of spiritual health and well-being	Moderate to high degree of psychological functioning and well-being The individual is already whole
Spiritual Care[37]	Addressing the relationship of the individual to the transcendent and spiritual needs resulting from that relationship	Involvement of four functions: Taking a spiritual assessment Identifying spiritual needs Ensuring that these needs are addressed Providing mental health care in a spiritual way
Pastoral Care[38]	Bringing about religious or spiritual change Facing personal problems and crisis	Listening and responding to individuals experiencing change, confusion, or distress with health and nonhealth concerns
Pastoral Counseling[39]	Assisting in coping with physical, emotional, or moral stressors and/or a crisis of meaning	Addressing spiritual or religious needs is essential in effectively dealing with personal problems and crisis

Please note that the description of scopes and basic assumptions of the four types of spiritual or religious treatment and the terms used to describe them may vary among authors, cultures, religions, and languages. The training may also differ, which is why it is not described here.

Interdisciplinary Challenges in Spiritual Accompaniment

It has become clear over time that psychological approaches to accompaniment and care can be enriched by spirituality, and spiritual accompaniment needs to have recourse to human sciences, primarily to psychology. From these developments, several challenges have arisen.

First, *the* psychology does not exist, nor does *the* theology. The diversification and fragmentation of psychological science engenders a big theoretical and practical problem because each branch of psychology has a particular view of human persons and their "functioning."[40] This entails a significant epistemological problem where one attempts to use a tool such as psychology while failing to consider that the anthropology underlying the chosen psychological approach might not parallel some crucial instances of theological anthropology. Based on the epidemiology of each individual psychology and each individual theology, an epistemological framework of their interaction needs to be further developed. Otherwise, the risk for inappropriate encroachment and inevitable confusion could result.[41]

This results in a further challenge: the dissemination of literature and advice regarding the "practical side" of spiritual accompaniment and the hesitation toward using specific tools. In some situations, a lack of common/formal and/or concrete theological practices of spiritual accompaniment can still be observed; this easily leads the spiritual accompanier to use his or her own way of conducting the accompaniment based on personal insights, literature, formation courses, and the like. Similarly, psychological issues may come up in spiritual accompaniment that should not be neglected.[42] The possibility that the spiritually accompanying persons may not have a background in psychology does not mean that they will not have recourse to it, either through common sense or, less obviously, by using paradigms that are typically psychological but renaming them with more spiritual language.[43]

Another issue involves the assertion that what is considered "mental" or "psychological" should be kept separate from what is considered "spiritual." This often implies that the former, particularly if pathological, must be dealt with by a psychologist who, of course, will be strictly bound not to deal with spiritual aspects. Such a perspective would understand the human person in too simplistic a way, as if changes in the psychological realm do not have spiritual repercussions, and as if spiritual accompaniment does not have important consequences on a mental/psychological level. In any case, it is not uncommon for the spiritually accompanying person to sense issues intruding into accompaniment that demand a few more interpretative keys and practical tools. Not finding them easily in texts on spiritual accompaniment, the accompanying person tends to "import" these keys and tools from the literature on diagnostic or therapeutic interviewing and on professional helping relationships.[44]

Interaction, dialogue, collaboration, and perhaps integration of spiritual and psychological knowledge could help accompaniers understand that psychology and theology are complementary. In fact, many levels are simultaneously present.[45]

Today, more than ever, in a fragmented and complex world, the encounter between theology and psychology can be a decisive factor in favoring of a new anthropological balance. The founders of the Institute of Psychology of the Collegium Maximum of the Pontifical Gregorian University in Rome (a university run by the Jesuits), and subsequent professors and alumni of the institute have tried to integrate psychological and anthropological aspects in the development of the human perspective. As stated in the first two volumes of the *Anthropology of Christian Vocation*,[46] humans reach authenticity in self-transcendence.[47] The two important realities on this path are the ability to transcend oneself theocentrically and the freedom given to humans by God. Theocentric self-transcendence and freedom are interdependent and convergent; theocentric self-transcendence orients and sustains freedom.[48] In this sense, a spiritual accompanier may face different challenges; like the challenge of educating accompanied persons toward predominantly transcendent values in the presence of a significant freedom or the challenge of dealing with people characterized by fragility that significantly limits authentic freedom, especially in living transcendent values. Other challenges could be the accompaniment of individuals with more or less severe pathological issues. In these cases, consultation with or the involvement of another specialist (e.g., psychotherapist or psychiatrist) might be necessary.

The Christian journey is an ever-evolving process, which that involves the whole person—freedom, intellect, and will. Every authentic Christian life, founded on baptism, implies a cooperation between freedom and grace (see chapter 5), and in this path there is no room for external interference (that is, spiritual companions or religious leaders imposing external ethical or religious rules and rites and dictating the timing of the path). The question is how to foster the integral and harmonious growth of Christian believers concretely engaged in living their vocation. How can they act responsibly as they welcome the divine mystery that is in themselves and in their lives?

A collaboration between psychology and theology is vital. Only together in a mutual and respectful collaboration, learning from each other and being aware of their own competencies, strengths and limitations, can psychology and theology "accompany" individuals, groups, and communities living in and facing the challenges of the twenty-first century.

9

Preventing Spiritual Abuse

DO WE HAVE TO accept that people will suffer from spiritual abuse? Is there a way to prevent it? To avoid complicating the situation or losing time and energy "reinventing the wheel," we must build upon previous knowledge and experiences derived from dealing with other forms of abuse, especially sexual abuse. Mistakes made when dealing with suspicions and cases of sexual abuse should be avoided in cases of spiritual abuse—denying and covering up the abuse, believing it happens only elsewhere, trivializing the suffering as well as the impact that the abuse had (or still has) on the lives of many victims and survivors, or not listening to and believing them. Actions like these have allowed abuse to continue and increased the suffering of those already wounded. These mistakes and what has been learned from the past should help to quickly develop effective prevention measures and to start an immediate process of reappraisal. Because spiritual abuse is an issue that concerns many (if not all) religions, denominations, Churches, and religious or spiritual communities or movements on a global level, prevention work should be done in an international, intercultural, and interdisciplinary way.

Creating Awareness and Sensitivity

Creating awareness and sensitivity for this issue as well as an active approach to prevention, reappraisal, and intervention are essential. The only way to deal with spiritual abuse is to give a voice to those affected and to prevent further victimization. Prevention is a long-term process that needs continuous engagement and commitment. Even if there is not 100 percent protection against spiritual abuse, conditions can be created that make spiritual boundary violations difficult. Many effective preventative measures in religious or ecclesial contexts are already known from the prevention of sexual abuse on three different levels—primary prevention, secondary prevention, and tertiary prevention. Primary prevention refers to measures that are taken to reduce spiritual abuse from the outset. Secondary prevention includes measures used in high-risk situations (such as putting a stop to abuse that is emerging or in progress). Tertiary prevention is different from care and includes reactions to spiritual abuse already committed and aims to mitigate its immediate consequences and to minimize secondary consequences.

One problematic issue is that spiritual abuse is still not considered abuse in many religions, Churches, movements, and cultures; nevertheless, it has similar dynamics to other types of abuse and leads to severe and sometimes life-devastating consequences for those who have experienced it. These consequences are often overlooked because they are rarely apparent or perceived clearly, or they are ignored when they become more obvious. This is why first impressions and feelings that make one think, "There is something wrong!" should always be taken seriously. Victims of spiritual abuse still receive little attention when they try to disclose their abuse. They continue to suffer secretly and silently. For this reason, awareness of and sensitivity to alarm signals of spiritual abuse is crucial to prevent it from happening.

As mentioned in chapter 2, caution is advised if the following signs and indicators can be identified in individuals, groups of people, or communities:[1]

- loss of personal identity (in communities the group identity comes to the fore)
- violation of boundaries in spiritual accompaniment
- isolation of the person, the group, or the community
- dependence of the accompanied person on the accompanying person or
- strong emotional ties in communities and close companionship relationships with high loyalty
- elitist thinking

- excessive (or blind) obedience
- ambitious missionary goals
- high demands for personal spiritual growth
- a closed system
- excessive (unattainable and often unrealistic) values and ideals
- lack of differentiation between internal forum and external forum
- strong charismatic leadership figures or communities.

Awareness of and sensitivity toward these indicators of spiritual abuse can be created through concrete prevention measures aimed at different at-risk groups; research and various types of publications targeted to diverse groups of people in multiple languages; interviews, websites, and documentaries; statements, regulations, and guidelines from Church leaders; prayer days for victims of spiritual abuse; and informative events, conferences, study days, workshops, and public campaigns.

Reflecting on Potentially Abusive Elements

To prevent spiritual abuse in accompaniment or in the daily life of a community or movement requires active reflection on and engagement with the elements that can increase the risk for spiritual abuse.

RESTRICTION AND LACK OF FREEDOM

Freedom is a core issue in *The Spiritual Exercises* of Ignatius[2] and generally in all forms of Ignatian spirituality and accompaniment. In assessing for spiritual abuse, the key question is that of the restriction or the lack of freedom. The Jesuit Anton Witwer has worked out four criteria for the determination as well as the severity of spiritual abuse based upon freedom.[3]

1. *Compulsive attempt to commit others to a particular practice of faith.* People cannot freely choose what kind

of offers or help suit them best and what is helpful for them.

2. *Discreditation of other forms of religious practice.* Other people are judged negatively or even condemned. The inner freedom of those who "follow" is subtly restricted with a certain religious practice. Consequently, they see themselves as the "chosen ones" and "superior" to others; at the same time, they feel bad when they fail to live up to expectations of their companion, superior, or founder.
3. *Increase of demarcation from others.* Contact with others is restricted or banned, isolating those in accompaniment from the members of a community or movement, by making contact with others as difficult as possible or by judging "outsiders" in a negative way.
4. *Attempt to create a special bond between the "chosen ones" and the "abuser."* The companion, founder, or superior makes people feel special but is only concerned with the instrumentalization, manipulation, and control of others for the sake of power.

Freedom is a paradigm of spiritual accompaniment,[4] and this is why spiritual processes need the acknowledgment by both the accompanying person and the accompanied person that one person cannot do this for the other. An essential aspect of accompaniment is the recognition and acknowledgment of the fundamental and irreversible human reality that there are natural conditions to which each person is subject as a human being. This includes the fact that humans have received gifts and opportunities that they can freely dispose of.[5]

POWER AND ITS MISUSE

Failure to address the various aspects of power, to come to a common understanding of power (see chapters 1–4), and to reflect on power in accompanying relationships may foster abuse in general and spiritual abuse in particular. In spiritual accompaniment, a high degree of power asymmetry exists. This stems not only from the official distribution of roles but also from structure. For example, the accompanying person knows a lot of private details about the person in accompaniment, but the self-disclosure is not mutual.[6] Two types of power are particularly relevant to spiritual abuse. Sociological power concerns legitimate power, the power of reward, coercion, identification, or knowledge and is foundational to accompaniment. Psychological power is primarily concerned with the emotional exercise of power, which is at the heart of spiritual abuse. How power is demonstrated and lived, especially by leadership, draws together both sociological and psychological power.

From an ethical point of view, the concept of power is ambivalent, since power is constructive but can also be used destructively.[7] In a constructive sense, power forms the basis for law and order. In a negative sense, power can be seen as a component of evil, which is expressed in sayings such as "craving for power" or "fantasies of omnipotence." Power can be neurotic, compensatory, compulsive, sadistic, and personality based.[8] In addition to egocentricity, complacency, arrogance, envy, and hypersensitivity, power is one of the main symptoms of narcissism, the main social disorder of our time. Narcissistic persons are addicted to recognition and admiration and are convinced of their positive personal characteristics, for example, success. They greedily strive for power and the exercise of power. A malignant form of narcissism in which self-worth derives from devaluation of others is of great importance to our discussion of spiritual abuse.

Power is a diverse and contradictory psychic entity, which remains inscrutable due to its complexity.[9] However, the relationship between power and theology in the Church is even more complex. Despite the claimed equality of all human beings before God, a massive inequality can be observed on several levels based on life status, sex, role, and culture:

- theological level: clerics versus laypeople
- anthropological level: men versus women
- professional level: leaders versus employees
- pastoral level: accompanying person versus accompanied person
- metaphorical level: "shepherds" versus "flock."[10]

These levels can be more or less pronounced according to the respective culture. In addition, one culture could see itself as more important, powerful, or privileged than another culture, which may have consequences in accompanying relationships, communities, or movements too (for example, decision-making, acceptance, responsibilities, privileges, and so on). Apart from communities, movements, or accompaniment, professional ecclesial contexts also bear the risk of abuse of power, resulting, for example, in spiritual abuse or sexual abuse, permeated by a double asymmetrical power relation and thus also by doubly asymmetrical privileges between priests and laywomen. In these cases, the negative attributes of male and clerical power can culminate, and the double asymmetry plays a role not only in the abusive behavior or acts but also in cover-ups and defense mechanisms.[11]

Spiritual abuse concerns not only the victims(s) and the abuser(s) but also the Church as a whole. Prevention includes the further dismantling of unequal power relations that bear a risk for spiritual abuse, such as clericalism and its roots. Consequently, the need to reappropriate the common baptismal identity—through which every member of God's people is "priest, king and prophet" (*LG* 10–14)—emerges clearly, letting Christians bridge any form of fragmentation, imperialism, idealism, and class struggles within the Church.[12]

THEOLOGICAL AMBIVALENCES AND ABUSIVE TEACHINGS

Since spiritual abuse is also a theological question, one cannot help but demand a theology beyond polemics and politicization.[13] All Church service requires a profound theology and spirituality that stand in the middle of Church tradition and are not one-sided. The devaluation of personal, spiritual, and theological considerations is not what leads to a critical reflection, but, rather, taking seriously and honestly the introduction of a deeper perception of the entirety of Catholic teaching.

For some years now, theology has been dealing self-critically with its role in abuse, mainly in sexual abuse of minors and vulnerable adults.[14] Everything can be manipulated, both theology and Sacred Scripture, because the bias is in the manipulator and not in the vulnerability of the contents. To have a watchful eye on the contents proposed is important, not just through a coercive force of control, but through renewed theological practices. And renewal does not only lie in new content or new techniques but in the renewal of the theologian. The principle of "historical awareness," which matured during the Second Vatican Council, helps theology to remain anchored in reality and not give in to idealism and abstractionism.[15] Often, in fact, manipulation is not a lack of intelligence but a witness to the abusers' escape from themselves and the world and an attempt to find plausibility in their own ears. Theology can become toxic when abusers use it as a strategy to justify spiritual, sexual, or other forms of abuse with theological concepts. As examples of religious-theological motifs susceptible to abuse, the following are worth noting:

- understanding and dealing with Christian obedience
- understanding and exercising religious authority and spiritual accompaniment
- understanding the way God speaks to humans
- understanding sin and divine punishment
- interpretation of suffering and the need for human atonement
- understanding evil and how to fight it in people and in the world.[16]

Looking at the narratives of victims of spiritual or sexual abuse in an ecclesial context, we find a quasi-implicit ministerial theology, including an exaggerated image of priests. When theology is abused, it is striking how often abusers move away from the ethical and theological mainstream by characterizing the respective abusive situation as "special" or as an exception[17] or by justifying themselves. Companions need to constantly question the quality of their own conversion and inner life. It is precisely for this reason that companions need to be accompanied on their own journeys of Christian love and perfection. In fact, people capable of loving according to the model of God (see 1 Cor 13:13) do not need to manipulate either others or the teachings of the Church. They simply love God, themselves, and others.

As mentioned in chapter 1, the question arises of how far biblical, religious, or spiritual texts, concepts, ideas, or practices can be described as abusive. A crucial distinction was made between texts and teachings and their interpretations by particular individuals as well as by religious communities or movements. Many key biblical and theological concepts have an amazing plasticity and are repeatedly reinterpreted and reappropriated in the course of tradition.[18] Making explicit the epistemological and ontological horizon from which one interprets remains important. The key question is: "What am I doing when I do it?"

From this point of view, it is primarily about how certain texts and teachings are appropriated and possibly misused by a person or a community. However, texts, teachings, or practices that are repeatedly and regularly used to legitimize abusive behavior should be corrected by the faith community, and abusive hermeneutics should be clearly named and prevented as far as possible. A concrete example is given by Pope John Paul II in 1988 in his apostolic letter *Mulieris Dignitatem*.[19] In article 24, he states that one should not continue to interpret Ephesians 5:24 literally.[20] Another example is offered by the report written to evaluate the case of Jean Vanier. In the section dedicated to the investigation of his theology, scholars noted how the evolution of his thought, as indicated in his writings, went hand in hand with increasingly imprecise references to Holy Scripture. Sometimes, passages were quoted generically, sometimes they were given as subtexts. This favored imaginative and psychologizing biblical interpretations, sometimes based on nonexistent data in the Gospels.[21]

Although the Bible could be misinterpreted abusively, it can also encourage victims to speak out against the imposed silence and cover-up, to lament, and to accept the painful truth. For example, John 8:32 says, "And you will know the truth, and the truth will make you free." Psalms such as Psalm 126:5—"Those who sow in tears reap with shouts of joy"—may be associated with a God that gives hope and comfort. Likewise, figures of the Bible and the history of the Church can be liberating resources (for example, Tamar, Teresa of Ávila, or Edith Stein) or examples of growth after traumatic events or experiences (such as Job or Naomi). The experiences of many victims underline the biographical significance of theology. For some, believing in God is a liberating resource in their life, but for others, the instrumentalization of theology makes trust in God hard.[22]

IDEALIZATION AND IDOLATRY

The idealization or idolatry of one's own community, movement, companion, or superior as well as of the way of life promoted creates a deep gap between one's own world and the world "out there." Frequently, people affected by spiritual abuse are convinced or are made to believe that the members of the community and the spiritual companion are all that they need. They think that they do not have anyone else in their lives, an illusion that makes the gap between their world and the world outside even bigger. This way of thinking is nurtured by the spiritual companion, founder, or superior[23] to make the members or person in accompaniment believe that they are the holy chosen remnant and that the others—the evil world—should be avoided. The mere thought of leaving the community is therefore associated with an existential fear of loss. An abused person may fear loneliness due to social isolation and a communal family consciousness as well as fearing the loss of meaning in life, which consists of the community or the accompaniment and its rules, structures, and ideals without an alternative. Finally, a victim of spiritual abuse may be afraid of losing faith by leaving, having been convinced that the community and its distinctive spirituality is the "only right" way of living their faith.[24]

These frequent existential fears make it extremely difficult for those affected by spiritual abuse to break away from the community or accompaniment, since they would have to start from scratch in many areas of their lives: build new social relationships, reorient themselves, define new values and ideals, regain access to their own wishes and needs, which have often been severely repressed, reengage with personal beliefs, and in some cases start over financially and professionally. Added to this is the challenge of recognizing and acknowledging that what was thought to be the ideal way of life was abusive in nature and caused profound hurt. Affected persons fear not being able to survive and continue to live within the abusive context or community because leaving seems not to be a liberation but is mainly perceived as a free fall without a parachute.[25] This is why it often takes years before an abused person ends an abusive relationship and leaves an unsafe place or an abusive community or movement.

Concrete Actions for Prevention

Apart from the sensitivity toward the signs and indicators of spiritual abuse and a profound reflection on the potentially abusive use of freedom, power, theological teachings, and idealization, the following section offers concrete proposals for actions for the prevention of spiritual abuse.

RESPONSIBILITIES AND COMPETENCIES

In order to prevent spiritual abuse from happening and to intervene in cases where it has already happened, responsibility and competences are needed on various levels, including leadership as well as on the part of people "on the ground" who may offer direct contact and support to those who have been victimized.

As outlined by Pope Francis on various occasions and explicitly asked for in the *motu proprio Vos Estis Lux Mundi*[26] with regard to sexual abuse, the leadership of the Church must act with responsibility, accountability, and transparency in cases of spiritual abuse as well. This includes working on the above-mentioned points and participating actively in them. Supervision and control should also be included. But giving up power and influence does not go far enough. What is needed is the acceptance of responsibility and accountability. Church leadership should not be about power, authority, and influence but about responsibility and accountability, which includes a responsible way of dealing with power and authority as well as an oversight and the need to intervene where abuse, in whatever form, occurs.[27]

CONTACT PERSONS AND PREVENTION CONSULTANTS

An expansion of support for primary and secondary victims of spiritual abuse in the Church as well as in secular contexts is crucial. Victims need help to classify, understand, and process what they have experienced. Therefore, all dioceses should have competent prevention consultants or contact persons who are trained and qualified, similar to safeguarding officers and consultants in cases of sexual abuse. If they do not have them (yet), dioceses, religious orders, and religious movements should move to select and find consultants and experts to train their members or personnel. The involvement of external experts could be of great help, too, especially when those affected (initially) need distance and detachment from everything related to religion, faith, Church, and spirituality.

GUIDELINES AND NETWORKING

As with sexual abuse, spiritual abuse needs clear guidelines, policies, and codes of conduct to be drawn up and procedures laid down. Guidelines should discuss physical, psychological, and spiritual boundary violations and how to prevent them by describing the format and the setting of the accompaniment as well as the role and the tasks of the accompanying person. Furthermore, guidelines should sensitize personnel to possible boundary violations. Risks as well as the quality of the support become tangible. An appropriate information structure is required, based not only on internal but also on external professional expertise. An independent, interdisciplinary training and advisory network is essential for the prevention and processing of spiritual abuse. This includes an unmistakable definition of responsibilities and accountability on the part of those responsible in the Church.

INSTRUMENTS OF EVALUATION

A German diocese made the first attempt to develop a checklist for the assessment of spiritual abuse[28] with the aim to offer orientation about (1) the form and severity of spiritual abuse, (2) strategies used by the abuser, (3) phenomena linked to the abuse, and (4) frame of the abuse. This list is primarily intended for individuals as a form of self-evaluation to determine for themselves whether they have experienced any form of spiritual abuse. A checklist could be developed for the area of prevention as well as intervention, which could offer orientation to people in the leadership of dioceses as well as in religious institutes and associations about whether a group should be awarded status under canon law.[29] Such a checklist would be a first attempt and does not purport to be exhaustive, nor can it in any way guarantee that spiritual abuse has or has not occurred. However, it would indicate whether spiritual accompaniment or a way of living (say, in a religious community or movement) is a matter of a spirituality and way of life that promotes human beings, or whether there are serious problems in some relevant areas or grievances that need to be identified.[30]

Canonical Implications

Canon law can protect against spiritual abuse and regulate its consequences;[31] therefore, it can be a fundamental tool for preventing spiritual abuse. At the end of 2024, the Dicastery for the Doctrine of the Faith in collaboration with the Dicastery for Legislative Texts established a working group whose task is to analyze the possibility of classifying a delict of spiritual abuse, avoiding the overly broad and ambiguous expression of "false mysticism."[32] Article 10.2 of the Regulations of the Dicastery for the Doctrine of the Faith defines "false mysticism" as "problems and behavior connected with the discipline of the faith, such as cases of pseudo-mysticism, alleged apparitions, visions, and messages attributed to supernatural origin." In some cases, the term "false mysticism" is used by canon lawyers in relation to abuse offenses, even though it is not currently an offense or crime under canon law.

While the outcome of the analysis and the kind of proposal the working group will make are not yet clear, the establishment of the working group is a real achievement. The process of reflection will take a long time, but the task of the working group represents an important change of perspective, overcoming the vague notion of "false mysticism" and finding an explicit definition of the crime of spiritual abuse from a doctrinal, theological, and spiritual point of view. A real synergy exists between canon law and theology. The phenomenon of spiritual abuse is being given a status of objectivity and reality, thanks to theological reflection capable of drawing a line between authentic doctrine and spiritual abuse.

Problematically, most Catholics, including many officials, are not familiar with canon law. How to make canonical regulations better known and facilitate their implementation is a big challenge.[33] Canon law states, "a person who abuses an ecclesiastical power or function is to be punished according to the gravity of the act or omission, not excluding privation of office, unless a law or precept has already established the penalty for this abuse."[34] It is also true that "for a person who through culpable negligence illegitimately places or omits an act of ecclesiastical power, ministry, or function with harm to another is to be punished with a just penalty."[35] In order to respect the fundamental rights of the faithful to their own rite, their own form of spiritual life, the free choice of social status, good reputation, and privacy, all members of the Church—lay, religious, and clergy, and especially those in formation—should know their rights. Above all, those who hold responsibility in the Church must know and respect the applicable norms of canon law and not try to suspend them.

As mentioned in the first part of this book, spiritual abuse often happens in the context of confession. This is true for seminarians, religious, and laypeople. Therefore, it is crucial that violating the norms of canon law linked to confession[36] and the seal of confession lead to serious consequences,[37] up to the dismissal from the clerical state or excommunication.[38] Furthermore, there must be a stronger focus on this complex topic of confession and spiritual abuse in training. It should be discussed seriously whether every priest receives the jurisdiction to confess or whether this should be revoked under certain circumstances.[39]

In addition to punishment, ecclesiastical criminal law also offers the possibility of warning[40] and the imposition of a penance.[41] Church officials should not shy away from using canonical tools when it comes to protecting spiritual rights and spiritual self-determination.[42] Of particular importance is the application of the law by those who hold the authority to recognize new religious or spiritual communities or movements. As has happened in many cases in the past, the intercession of powerful sponsors can prevent the examination of the constitutions, which in turn creates conditions for abuse—by the mixing of the internal forum and the external forum through the stages of formation, or from idolatry of the founder (similar to a cult).[43] In the recognition of new religious or spiritual communities or movements, the statutes play an important role; the constitutions are a fundamental legal book from which the charism of the institute should clearly emerge.[44] The constitutions must also contain "fundamental norms regarding governance of the institute, the discipline of members, incorporation and formation of members, and the proper object of the sacred bonds."[45] The examination of statutes and regulations is necessary to ensure that possible abuse is prevented from the beginning. This duty of supervision, which is part of the responsibility of the Church leadership, should find concrete application. In this way, canon law could truly serve as a preventive measure against spiritual abuse.[46]

Education, Training, and Formation

Education, training, and formation (initial and ongoing) in dioceses and religious orders, along with the formation of young people, teenagers, and children, is important. Indeed, if it is true that the chicks come home to roost in adulthood, when one enters a seminary, a religious community, into an affective relationship or a professional activity, it is also true that the chicks were formed in a previous stage. Therefore, the integral growth of a person must begin at a very early stage and can be a kind of prevention. In many religious or spiritual movements and communities, people, mostly without any training or qualifications for spiritual accompaniment, interfere in the lives of others and influence fundamental life decisions in a lasting way, and not always for the better. This does not cast into doubt that well trained spiritual companions and guides, founders, and superiors in communities and movements exist who are prepared and respect the boundaries of others. But this is not always the case. Therefore, only those who have the appropriate training and personal skills should be allowed to accompany others spiritually. In communities, support should also be provided by people from outside to furnish an objective perspective.

The issue of spiritual abuse, its dynamics and consequences, should be introduced into the basic training of seminarians and novices to make them aware of it from the very beginning, as they can be both potential victims and perpetrators. Even later, priests and members of religious congregations and communities should be required to attend regular training and ongoing formation on spiritual abuse as well as on possible prevention and intervention measures.[47] As with sexual abuse, this training should gradually be extended to all Church workers and be open to other interested parties.[48] In this way communities can be created that are able to combat abusive situations in which exchange, discussion, and resistance are welcome.[49]

Training should also be aimed at all laypeople in the service of the Church, since they can be primarily and secondarily affected by spiritual abuse but can also, in their roles as spiritual companions, pastoral caregivers, or founders of movements, be possible perpetrators. Training programs and prevention courses at all levels within dioceses, religious orders, communities, and movements are needed. Furthermore, these courses and trainings will help to create awareness. Important topics for reflection are healthy obedience, spiritual rights, spiritual self-determination, spiritual freedom, different ways of spiritual accompaniment, responsibility, trust, the use or abuse of power and authority, control and manipulation, boundary crossing, and closeness and distance to accompany in a healthy way.

Holistic Formation: An Italian Test Case

In 2019, the Italian Bishops' Conference (CEI) founded the *Servizio Nazionale per la Tutela dei Minori e delle Persone Vulnerabili* (SNTM), or the National Service for the Protection of Minors and Vulnerable Persons, whose goal is to prevent all forms of abuse in the Church through educational and informative paths. Since that time, the SNTM has published three documents that capture the culture of mediocrity as a source of abuse in the Church. In particular, the third document, *Formazione iniziale in tempo di abusi*, Initial Formation in Times of Abuse, published in 2021, addresses the theme of accompaniment and discernment. Worldwide, much attention has developed around the issue of sexual abuse in the Catholic Church; parallel to this, a certain sensitivity is beginning to mature around other forms of abuse, such as psychological or spiritual abuse. This renewed attention has allowed the Italian Church not only to think about a programmatic solution to the problem of abuse but also to initiate a process of self-reflection that would help to recognize the causes of the rise and spread of certain abusive practices. Focusing on the issue of "relationship," the document states:

> It is necessary, then, to pay attention in the time of first formation to those who somehow seem to avoid relationship, in the name of a misunderstood idea of spirituality, dangerously prevalent today in a certain generation of young people (who seem to defend themselves from relationship or seek only the virtual one), or in view of a perfection of an essentially individualistic kind (for which relationship is only an *accidens*); Just as it is necessary, on the other hand, to correct immediately a certain relational spontaneity, without reference criteria and in the end without meaning, where the relationship is in fact sought in order to put oneself at the center of the relationship with the other, to make use of it, without any more self-decentralizing and self-transcendent openness to the mystery. Then the abuse is already somehow in place.[50]

At the beginning of the document, the authors state how the document was intended as a proposal for a formative-didactic itinerary that brings into dialogue the necessary formation for the presbyterate and religious life and the scourge of abuse, which, in fact, shows that in some cases there has been a deterioration of the formation process, both on the human and spiritual level. For this reason, the pivot of reflection remains the integral growth of persons and their relational capacity (with self, God, and others). Furthermore, it remains open to three other themes: priestly identity, the issue of power, and the drama of abuse. The three themes of reflection are closely connected to each other, and this interconnection represents a deepening of the themes already announced in the *Ratio Fundamentalis Institutionis Sacerdotalis*, The Gift of the Priestly Vocation.

In fact, the issues of integral growth and priestly identity are not new. What is new is the ability to see how some themes have been misinterpreted in some formative practices and in the concreteness of priestly life. This is precisely the case with a certain confusion between priestly identity and power; over time, the boundary between power and authority has crumbled, reducing the function of authority, though exercised by the priest, to that of power. The latter, in fact, is a form of domination that tends to possess the other, denying both the person's dignity and originality and belying the beauty of the Christian message.[51] Also included in these forms of power are narcissism and clericalism, possible signs of low self-esteem and of an inadequate vision of self and presbyteral identity.[52] Formative pedagogy needs this analysis so that it can offer a path of spiritual and human growth designed to respond to the various challenges (including the reality of spiritual abuse) that ecclesial and civil realities present in the contemporary world. Integration is not just recomposing crazy splinters but means being centered in Christ, who does not erase our imperfections but shapes and molds our imperfections.

Nonabusive Accompaniment: An Illusion?

Can completely nonabusive behavior or abuse-free human relationships exist?[53] Are there any human relationships in which no power is exercised, in which there is never any harm, but in which the self-determination of the other is always and completely respected? Or is it an illusion? Do we not have to concede that every human mediation of God necessarily leaves traces of transgressions and abuse? These questions are not easy to answer. Most probably we must accept and admit that no preventive measure will completely eliminate the risk of spiritual abuse. Nevertheless, we know from the field of sexual abuse that prevention works to reduce the risk of abuse or, in cases where primary prevention was not possible, to intervene and to stop the abuse.

The first vital step is to recognize spiritual abuse, to break taboos, to raise awareness of and sensitivity to spiritual abuse on all levels—from Church leaders to the faithful, from experts in the field of abuse prevention to society at large, from those in accompaniment to those who accompany, from superiors or founders of religious communities or movements to their members. If there is a suspicion of undesirable developments, boundary violations, or even abuse, everyone near the situation should take a closer look and contribute to create a "culture of awareness." The creation of such a culture as well as the development, implementation, and evaluation of preventive measures (on different levels) can be done only with a common effort within the Church. Both internal and external experts from various nations, cultures, and disciplines—psychology, theology, spirituality, canon law, and pedagogy—must be included.

10

Healing After Spiritual Abuse

PEOPLE WHO HAVE experienced abuse of any kind often wonder whether there is a way out of their misery and suffering. To answer the question, "what happened to me?" requires an understanding of the dynamics of abuse as well as the various dimensions of its consequences. This requires information as well as social and professional support from outside. Only in this way can the long path to healing succeed.

Most of those affected by spiritual abuse say that the silence and lack of awareness that surrounds the issue allows it to continue and makes disclosure difficult. To create more awareness and sensitivity toward spiritual abuse and its consequences for individuals and communities is essential. Only then will primary and secondary victims of spiritual abuse be understood and helped. Survivors must be listened to and believed. Those people affected primarily or secondarily need access to professional help and protection from revictimization.[1] A second victimization often intensifies primary victimhood and results from the reactions of responsible persons to a victim's disclosure of the primary victimization through a lack of empathy, disbelief, minimizing, or cover-up. Victims often interpret such reactions as protection of the abuser.[2] Affected persons should have the opportunity and the right to get the professional advice and support they need, be it psychological, therapeutical, spiritual, legal, medical, or social, in order to deal with the abusive experience and to start a process of recovery and healing. If a whole community is affected by spiritual abuse, both individual and group support can be useful.[3]

Spiritual abuse infringes on the spiritual integrity of victims, their relationships with grace, and the social and ecclesial community. Because the consequences of spiritual abuse can be experienced differently, the recovery or healing process is individual for each person affected. Victims should neither put themselves under pressure nor let anyone else put pressure on them. Some victims may want to start the process quickly and go into detailed processing soon; others might still be too shaken by the traumatizing experience to jump into processing, and any further confrontation with the abuse could lead to even greater destabilization.[4] This is especially true if a person is still part of an abusive system (for example, still a member of the abusive community or still in the abusive accompaniment) and is not ready or able to confront the abuse itself or the abuser(s) without risking further mental, physical, or spiritual damage.

The people involved in the healing process may differ according to the consequences and the kind of help victims need or are looking for in order to recover and hopefully to heal the wounds the abuse has created. Often, they need help and support on various levels, such as on a professional level and on a more informal, social level (such as family members, friends, and so on). Our focus here will be on psychological/therapeutic help as well as on spiritual/pastoral interventions. One big problem is that so far only a few psychologists, psychotherapists, spiritual companions, or pastoral counselors are sensitive to the issue of spiritual abuse and experienced or trained—or at least basically prepared—for the accompaniment of individuals or communities affected by spiritual abuse.

Creating more awareness about the reality, the dynamics, and the impact of spiritual abuse is crucial. This topic needs to be included in initial and ongoing training of those who work in accompaniment or care. Otherwise, there is the risk, as has happened in the past, that victims will not be believed and taken seriously when talking to Church officials, spiritual companions, psychologists, counselors, or psychotherapists about the abusive experiences and the impact these experiences have had on them. When this happens, victims may get trapped in their abuse without a concrete possibility of healing. Moreover, when victims of spiritual abuse show symptoms linked to mental health issues or a mental disorder, a trained psychologist or psychotherapist should be involved. When a person is or seems to be traumatized by the spiritually abusive experience (see chapter 3), a clinician (such as a psychotherapist or psychiatrist) with a specialization in trauma-focused therapies or interventions should be included.

Psychological and/or Psychosocial Interventions Following Traumatic Experiences

Various types of psychological and psychosocial interventions following trauma are discussed in the literature.[5] These include: trauma-focused cognitive behavior therapy (TFCBT), cognitive behavior therapy (CBT), cognitive processing therapy (CPT), exposure therapies, stress management, eye movement desensitization and reprocessing (EMDR), as well as group therapy and community- or family-based interventions. Cognitive trauma–focused approaches strive to modify negative appraisals, to correct the autobiographical memory, and to eliminate problematic behavioral and cognitive strategies.[6] Exposure techniques aim to counteract anxiety-based avoidance behavior and to convey to the person a feeling of self-determination.[7]

According to various research studies, trauma-focused interventions seem to be the most promising and recommended treatment options for various types of traumas, targeting directly trauma-related memories, emotions, and thoughts and their respective meaning for the traumatized person.[8] A therapy that combines psychodynamic approaches to trauma with behavioral therapy methods is the so-called Multidimensional Psychodynamic Trauma Therapy (MPTT).[9] Another valid form of treatment, effective in post-traumatic stress disorder (PTSD), is EMDR.[10] EMDR focuses on traumatic memories and the reduction of PTSD- and trauma-associated symptoms. A positive aspect is the difference and variety in length that these approaches offer and their symptom-reducing effects.[11]

The various approaches mentioned briefly have proven to be effective trauma-focused interventions and may also favor so-called post-traumatic growth (PTG). PTG means not simply returning to a baseline after the experience of trauma but experiencing improvement and lasting positive changes such as in interpersonal relationships, awareness of personal strengths, and spirituality, which for some individuals can be profound.[12] Nevertheless, further research—especially with regard to spiritual trauma and PTSD as a result of spiritual abuse—is needed. As highlighted in chapters 2 and 3, other community or family members as well as people who are part of the social environment of the primary victims can suffer from witnessing the spiritual abuse and show similar consequences. Therefore, group therapy, family therapy, or couple therapy could offer further support. These approaches usually focus on resources and support from the environment as well as the establishment of a functional family system or couple relationship.[13]

If victims have not lost their faith or their relationship with God due to the abuse or they want to retrieve a lost or destroyed relationship with God and "find again" their personal faith, spiritual accompaniment is indicated. In many cases during their healing process, affected individuals need both psychological or therapeutic accompaniment and spiritual accompaniment. According to the specific needs of the affected person, this could be done contemporaneously or sequentially. A combination of both psychological/therapeutical and spiritual/pastoral elements is very promising. A process and environment that favor healing after spiritually abusive experiences require respectful practices such as nonjudgmentalism, kindness, compassion, healthy boundaries, and mutual respect.

Spiritual accompaniment, counseling, and psychotherapy work with what the accompanied person "brings in" (for example, issues that regard everyday life, relationships, experiences in life or faith, problems, crises, and new spiritual insights). Common to all these forms of accompaniment is the conviction that healing, clarification, and maturation take place in the interaction. In addition to areas that affect personality, self-esteem, freedom, and health, spiritual accompaniment aims to deepen the relationship with God and help the person to grow and mature spiritually. Spiritual accompaniment does not mean healing in a medical sense, but it does include healing aspects, takes place in a healing atmosphere, and, if necessary, addresses the salvation that God has given to human beings.

We can see the healing process at work in the Gospels. Jesus can heal the whole person, both physically and in relationship with God and others in the community. But in the healing process, it is significant that Jesus asks for the collaboration of the sick person (see for example Matt 15:21–28; Mark 6:53–56; 7:24–30). Healing is not imposed; it happens through the recognition of the wounded person's faith. There is no judgment on the quality of this faith; Jesus simply ascertains that the faith is there (see for example Mark 5:25–34).[14] Following are various aspects of the healing process for spiritual abuse that strive to retrieve God and re-access faith while combining elements of psychological and spiritual accompaniment and interventions. Many of these aspects have also been useful in healing from other forms of abuse (such as psychological or sexual abuse).

Stable and Safe Places

After abusive experiences in the context of spiritual accompaniment, those affected should take time before choosing or deciding about a new community or accompaniment. They should formulate personal values and criteria that are important for them in spiritual accompaniment. Without appropriate distance—in time and space—and deep reflection, there is a great danger of ending up again in abusive accompanying relationships, communities, or movements. This may mean that persons who have been spiritually abused might first need to withdraw completely from anything related to religion, spirituality, faith, God, or Church to avoid triggers and to take the distance they need from the unsafe place in which they experienced the abuse.

Similar to those affected by other forms of abuse or violence, victims of spiritual abuse need a safe enough place to ensure a separation from continued abuse and to experience recovery and healing. Such a safe place should meet certain criteria.[15] It should:

- allow those affected a safe physical and temporary distance from the abusive person(s) or the abusive community or system
- offer protection against situations, events, or persons that can reopen wounds
- be a listening place where people genuinely try to understand the affected person

- be a place where the love of God can be imparted to the wounded as needed.

Possibilities for regular exchange with other faithful Christians can be helpful as victims slowly find their way back to spiritual life, faith, and God. During the recovery process, the decision to go back into spiritual accompaniment or to choose another community or movement can favor this process and lead to positive outcomes. Nevertheless, it is crucial to choose the new spiritual companion or the new community or movement cautiously and to make sure that they are sensitive to and prepared to accompany and welcome a person who experienced spiritual abuse and whose "wounds are still bleeding."

Listening and Believing

Those affected by spiritual abuse need the opportunity to disclose and to tell their story. They need to talk about their experiences honestly and without embellishment without fear of being judged negatively or being called a liar—or even worse, a "nest polluter." They need people who are willing to listen to them, who know about the reality of spiritual abuse and its horrific consequences, and who believe them. Encouraging feedback from people who listen or who accompany them after the abusive experience is also important to provide orientation and once again to clarify and condemn the injustice that has occurred.[16] Affected people usually need this "ego strengthening" in order to be validated in their perception that "I'm not the only one who feels that what happened to me is wrong." An essential resilience factor after traumatic experiences is the support of a constant, safe, and understanding social environment. With the loving support of people close to them, those affected can rebuild some of the trust that they have lost.[17]

As in the case of sexual abuse, most victims of spiritual abuse are not concerned with personal benefits or a special punishment for the abuser but want the institutional Church and its leaders to recognize the injustice and their suffering. They want to regain their credibility, and they want justice.[18] Frequently, they hope for an admission of guilt or an apology on the part of the abuser and/or a member of the leadership of the Church. Being listened to and believed by a Church leader and not "only" by an "arbitrary" person can lay the cornerstone for the healing process.

Recognizing and Naming the Abuse

To move forward in the healing process, victims need to be able to state clearly what has happened to them and why this experience(s) can be described as abusive. Victims of spiritual abuse often have great difficulty in articulating the wrongs done to them or in articulating their thoughts and feelings. This is often the result of systematic cognitive and spiritual manipulation and the abusive use of specific terms, phrases, or theological contexts. Consequently, victims of spiritual abuse may feel unsettled, disillusioned, confused, ashamed, and intimidated.[19] Recognizing and naming the ideals and idols that have motivated and held together abusive relationships and systems requires human and spiritual maturity. This means also the willingness to let go of things that have previously provided security and support and to accept the uncertainty that may follow the process of naming and recognizing spiritually abusive relationships and accompaniment.[20] The path of healing is not easy, especially at the beginning. To recognize and name the abuse clearly is important for those affected in order to leave the confusion and illusion that has kept them in the abusive accompaniment, community, or movement and to make the healing processes possible. To grasp and process an experience, human beings need to clearly recognize and name the issue at some point. Evidence in the scriptures shows that Jesus was not afraid of clarity and openly proclaimed his anger against abusive actions (for example, see Matt 18:3). In doing so, he acknowledged the pain of the wounded and showed his respect for them.

Identifying Abusive Dynamics

Identifying abusive dynamics requires working through the experienced manipulation and understanding the consequences of this manipulation. This also includes an understanding of thought reform processes in order to grasp how and where the lies could effectively influence the person. Understanding this point helps many victims during the healing process to forgive themselves. A central question for many adult victims in this process can be: "Why did I stay in the abuse for so long?" The answers can be quite diverse and range from the contents and nature of the experienced influence on thinking, to personal ideals, attitudes, or motives, to special circumstances in one's personal life (such as crisis, illness, search for meaning), or to a certain kind of predisposition caused by other negative or abusive experiences in the past.[21]

Answering the questions of whether, how, and where the affected person may possibly have unconsciously "participated" in the abuse can also contribute to the healing process. Reasons might be idolatry (replacing God and fearing a human being more than God), wrongly lived subordination (confusion with subservience instead of taking on responsibility), enforcing the order or rules of the system, or showing inappropriate loyalty that protects the system and favors silence.[22] Even those who suffered much in abusive systems or types of accompaniments will one day understand how they themselves "contributed" to the preservation and cult of the founder, superior, or accompanying person. That in no way makes them accomplices. But understanding the extent to which they have participated in these relationships will enable them to avoid falling into the same traps in the future. And through this consciousness and knowledge, they regain their freedom of choice and their dignity and may be able to leave the position of victim behind.[23]

Looking Carefully at the Consequences

A famous saying states that "it is easier to get out of a cult than to get the cult out of you!" This saying is also true for many victims of spiritual abuse because its devastating effects often last a long time and continue to have an impact on relationships, professional life, and mental, physical, or spiritual health (see chapter 3). For one's own recovery, revealing the internalized lies and erroneous beliefs is important. Such lies may spring from false interpretations of the Holy Scriptures or other religious texts (abusive teachings), manipulated terms that have been given incorrect content, prophetic threats in the event of leaving the community or movement or stopping the accompaniment, or attitudes and goals that were considered desirable.

If serious physical health issues appear, the involvement of a physician can be required. Victims of spiritual abuse may also have to accept current physical limitations, as it was explained earlier in this volume, and sort out carefully what activities are appropriate in their current situation given their vulnerabilities and weaknesses in order to avoid overstraining themselves. These limits can be expanded in small and slow steps, always with the consideration of current strengths and vulnerabilities.

Self-care is also vital to the healing process. That includes learning to be gentle with oneself, taking care of oneself and one's soul, and shedding self-dominance, especially if a person is very performance-oriented. Balancing challenges, rest, and relaxation can be achieved by being attentive toward one's personal well-being ("What's good for me?" "What increases my well-being?"). Many victims of spiritual abuse must learn (again) to do something good for themselves and to take care of themselves because many of them have lived a rigid, self-criticizing and self-sacrificing lifestyle for a long time in which nice or beautiful things were not granted to them because the lifestyle did not allow time or space for them or because the abusive system did not provide for it.[24]

Many victims also need to learn to deal with physical needs in a healthy and appropriate manner: for example, getting sufficient hours of sleep, exercise, and relaxation and maintaining proper nutrition. This is especially important if physical and emotional needs were neglected. The perception and meeting of physical needs can be a prerequisite for holistic healing as well as for therapeutic or pastoral processing of painful experiences. Therefore, attention must be paid to the interaction of body, mind, and soul, and how they affect each other. Relaxation and breathing exercises can be of great benefit in the healing process, especially for people who come from a performance-oriented system or a performance-oriented accompaniment.[25] Affected people need to learn what promotes their relaxation (activities, sensations, smells, good food, company, and so on). Depending on the presence of possible mental disorders, special relaxation techniques can be learned and incorporated into psychotherapeutic accompaniment.

To survive after being wounded in a boundary-violating environment, victims must acquire skills to shape their lives in a meaningful and healing way. They must learn to trust and to take themselves and their personal needs seriously.[26] This includes understanding one's own situation and state of mind and seeking professional therapeutic help or counseling, if necessary, especially if mental health issues or mental disorders are present. In cases of spiritual abuse, the psychotherapist or counselor must not only understand the dynamics of spiritually abusive systems and the potential impact of spiritually abusive experiences but also have no prejudices against religion or faith.

One of the most damaging consequences of spiritual abuse is renewed insecurity and instability in the victim's perception of the here and now. People, comments, or situations can trigger renewed destabilization or even lead to a second victimization.[27] The processing of the triggers helps individuals affected by spiritual abuse to understand why certain situations provoke strong emotional or physical reactions in them and when they are more likely to occur. The question to be asked is, which internalized lies still need to be identified in order to get rid of the spiritual burden that has accumulated?[28] Similar to victims of other forms of abuse or violence, victims of spiritual abuse need to learn to deal with triggers and how to take care of themselves in such moments. Dealing with triggers means knowing what needs to be done if a trigger occurs and how to relax in the moment. In addition, triggering situations can also be useful, helping to access areas of the trauma that have not been processed yet.[29] This again is why sensitivity toward the issue and an understanding of spiritually abusive dynamics, be it on a professional or a nonprofessional level, are vital for the healing process.

Shaping New (and Old) Relationships

To retrieve the courage and confidence that makes it possible to relate to and trust others in a new and different way takes time. New trustful relationships can contribute positively to the healing process. Due to the experience(s) of the abuse of trust, new relationships should be built up with care and caution. Individuals affected by spiritual abuse first need to learn to trust (again) and should not expect their new friends and acquaintances to understand their experiences immediately. This can possibly happen later, when a stable basis for the relationship has been created and those affected feel secure enough to talk about their past. This also includes developing the skills to be able to sense with whom to share sensitive experiences. This is necessary to protect against incompetent or ignorant people who can open new wounds.[30] As outlined in chapter 3, people who are members of abusive communities or movements or who are accompanied by an abusive person frequently have lost or had to give up relationships with family members, friends, colleagues, or acquaintances for various reasons. Many of these people may have gone through a difficult time or been secondarily affected. Therefore, their emotions and suffering need to be taken seriously, and they should be gently included in the restoration of the relationship as part of the healing process.

Contact with other affected people who have ended the abusive accompaniment or who have left the abusive community or movement can be helpful. However, the question about whether and to what extent contact can or should be maintained with people who are still part of the abusive community or movement must be assessed carefully and on a case-by-case basis. Such contacts can represent a great emotional challenge for those who stopped the accompaniment or left the community or movement, making it difficult to achieve the necessary emotional distance.

Mourning Injuries and Losses

When victims of spiritual abuse realize that the community, the movement, or the spiritual companion they had sacrificed so much for were, in fact, idols that could not give life to them and intensify their relationship with God, it causes a profound shock to victims' faith and their purpose in life.[31] Added to this is the disappointment that the many promises that they had hoped and waited for will no longer be fulfilled. They go through a true mourning process with all the associated stages of shock, denial, anger, bargaining, depression and testing until they arrive at the point of the upward turn that allows for a process of reconstruction to begin. At the end of this process, there is acceptance and hope. "Blessed are those who mourn, for they will be comforted" (Matt 5:4).

To experience healing of deep emotional and spiritual wounds, people must perceive what has happened to them and what it has done to their lives. This is especially crucial when it comes to experiences such as spiritual abuse that have devastating consequences for their life, health, and faith. To recognize the losses and prepare oneself for a period of mourning, a time in which painful memories can become conscious and felt, is important. At the beginning, these memories may provoke sadness and possibly anger; later, other memories may change these feelings.[32] People affected by spiritual abuse need to understand that their devotion was not wrong, but it had been used against them. Therefore, their grief is justified, and their healing will be easier if they allow themselves to mourn.[33] Talking about the experience is part of the grieving process and helps victims to survive the injuries and losses without further negative impact on their health. Living out grief takes various forms. One person may cry or be angry, another could feel the pain and start to let it go, and still another could talk or pray. Scolding, missing former companions, recognizing and naming the abuse and getting to the heart of the matter, pouring out one's heart to God, or forgiving are all ways of mourning and expressing pain and suffering, hoping to feel better afterward.[34]

Finding Inner Freedom and Healing

In order to find again a place not only in life but also in the kingdom of God, a healthy confrontation with certain topics is a prerequisite to avoid having bad experiences again. Part of the healing process is gaining a healthy perspective and a biblical understanding of issues that used to be a risk or danger. That means, for example to learn about a "truly" Christian lifestyle, to learn to deal with ecclesial or communal services and structures, and to learn and understand how God intended these to be. It also means being open for an "inner" healing process as a gift from God, a sign of God's unconditional love and grace. Being open and ready to accept that inner healing may mean continuing to live with some physical or mental health issues, but it may also mean accepting the loss of the illness as secondary gain (psychologically speaking) and the fixation on a spirituality and a theology of the cross.[35]

However, if inner healing does not happen, spiritual exercises and accompaniment can help to find inner freedom and spiritual growth. Finding new inner freedom may initially create feelings of fear, anxiety, and resistance in victims of spiritual abuse because they were not allowed by their abuser or the abusive system to live in an autonomous and self-responsible way; they could not trust in their personal perceptions but instead depended on others. For this reason, the process of regaining inner freedom needs to proceed slowly and sensitively to give the affected persons the time needed to allow joy and appreciation of the newly gained freedom grow. In this way, the "miracle" of forgiveness and reconciliation may happen.[36]

Forgiveness and Reconciliation

Forgiveness in the context of abuse is a delicate topic. For many people affected by spiritual abuse, the forgiveness process represents a hurdle that seems insurmountable. Therefore, the process of forgiveness requires gentleness, patience, and sensitivity, and should always be carried out carefully and cautiously, if and when the affected person feels ready for it. Furthermore, it usually requires the completion of the above-mentioned steps.

Forgiveness does not mean trivializing what has happened, nor does it mean continuing to be dominated and abused. Forgiveness does not require being well disposed toward the abuser or the abusive community and does not mean diminishing the blame. Abusers are still responsible before God; any forgiveness does not waive their responsibility.[37] Consciously breaking ties that have arisen through the intimidation by those in power will be necessary. Often, physical, social, and temporal distance from the abuser (especially if remorse and any admission of the abuse is lacking) and the place where the abuse took place will be required.[38]

From a Christian perspective, the spiritual dimension of what happened also needs to be taken seriously. Often victims of spiritual abuse think that they are expected to forgive their abusers as soon as possible, freely paraphrasing Matthew 6:14–15, "Only those who forgive will be forgiven." But expecting forgiveness from the victim would be counterproductive as it creates spiritual pressure and harms victims again. Forgiveness cannot be forced. The experience of forgiveness takes time before the person can blossom again. It is itself the experience of a special encounter with God, who "judges no one" (see John 8:11).

Forgiving one's abuser is possible, but only if there is a real and honest sense of repentance and conversion. Often abusers deny or minimize their crime, so there is no sense of guilt and no repentance. Some abusers do express the desire to speak to their victims and ask them for forgiveness. Such an encounter can have a healing effect on both the victim and the abuser. But sometimes the victim is not ready for such an encounter, and sometimes the request for forgiveness by the abuser is not honest but more a formality. Therefore, discernment is needed to ascertain if the request for forgiveness is authentic and whether a victim feels ready to forgive.

Forgiveness happens by the grace of God. At some point, the soul of the wounded person may long for forgiveness and reconciliation. This wish may grow and mature slowly, bringing change to the victim's own history and the relationship with God.[39] The affected person will not ask anymore, "Why did God allow this? How could I endure this for such a long time?" but will be able to trust again—in God and in others, being aware of the risk of being hurt again in the future. In this sense, reconciliation can be understood as a deep acceptance of what has happened without denying the injustice or forgetting or diminishing the suffering. In short, forgiveness does not necessarily include reconciliation with the abuser or the abusive community, but reconciliation with oneself and with God.

An essential healing factor for those affected by spiritual abuse is to be able to forgive themselves and to stop blaming themselves for what has happened. The help and support of a professional can be crucial in this process. Furthermore, an essential step is to rediscover for themselves how God relates to them. God's indignation about the abuse and God's love and deep appreciation of the person are healing elements unlike anything else in the world. When and how affected persons (re)discover the heart of God on their healing journey is individual and depends also on the grace of God. To get rid of false, negative images of God, an exchange with other Christians who are shaped by positive images of God can be helpful; praying with others in a protected context can also help. Becoming more aware of the voice of God and believing in it is important. God is a benevolent God whose heart is especially for the wounded.[40] Therefore, forgiving oneself and reconciling with oneself and with God helps the affected person to be done with the abuser, to break or overcome the latent power that the abuser might continue to have, to move forward and one day be able to start a "new life," and to find peace and freedom. On this journey, forgiving is an important step toward healing and toward resurrection.

Spiritual abuse can have profoundly damaging effects over time. This is why the experience of Jesus on the cross can be helpful, Jesus who suffered not only with the victims but also for them.[41] His resurrection after his painful death on the cross can also become a source of strength and hope for those affected by spiritual abuse, in which destruction and evil lose their power and healing and good triumph. In this way, the logic of the cross and resurrection, fully understood, becomes a new way of relating and living. When we as Christians say we believe in the resurrection of the dead, it is not only for after death; we believe that it also applies for here and now on earth.[42] Thanks to forgiveness, we are capable of being "reborn" and starting over. Jesus alone saves, but he never saves alone.[43] All members of his body—the Church—are called to help to make this resurrection real.

Caring for Secondary Victims

Spiritual abuse often affects people from the social environment of the primary victims or the abuser through knowing about or witnessing the abuse or by experiencing and perceiving the impact it has on primary victims (see chapter 3). It may also happen that the abuser tries to manipulate or threaten other persons in the social environment of the primary victims. Therefore, secondary victims can develop symptoms that are similar to those of primarily affected individuals. Mental health issues and mental disorders as well as doubts in faith and accusations toward God who seems to be indifferent before the suffering of their dear ones can occur. So far little research has looked at the effects on the social environment of victims of spiritual abuse. Frequently, the abuse and the fight against it become the life's purpose for those primarily affected, but this can also be the case for those who are close to them. Further research in this area is needed to better understand the connection between primary and secondary spiritual victimization and the mutual influence in terms of the above illustrated healing process. Based on our personal and professional experience in listening to and working with primary and secondary victims, we can say that there is a strong mutual influence, and often the suffering increases or diminishes reciprocally. If one or more persons close to the primary victim suffer and express their suffering openly, this often leads to a rippling effect in the suffering of the primary victim. This is particularly important if the abuse happens in communities and movements. Ultimately, access to professional help (for example, counseling, psychotherapy, group therapy, pastoral care, spiritual accompaniment, and other remedies) should be provided to secondary victims too.[44] Whether to help them or to help the primary victim by avoiding an "exponentiating" effect of the abuse and by facilitating the healing process of their dear ones, secondary victims also need their own healing process.

Dignity as Children of God

From the perspective of spirituality, integrating the wounds of abuse, whatever they may be, is experienced as a gift of grace that reconciles, first and foremost, abused persons with themselves. Not surprisingly, the Greek term for *reconcile* (*apokatallassó*: see 1 Cor 1:20–22) means to return to a state prior to fragmentation, to a "unified" state in which people experience themselves entirely and again in communion with God. Individuals return to the starting point of their faith: being God's beloved children. Hidden in this concrete reality of faith is the identity "child of God," and the inheritance of the kingdom of God. Spiritual abuse and its wounds do not take away or annul this dignity. Abused persons remain members of the Church and are not only subjects of care and attention but also subjects of pastoral care, capable of caring for other people and for the journey of the Church in the world. Because of the special journey of faith they make in integrating their own wounds, they clarify in practice some fundamental elements of Christian faith and theology. As abused people integrate their wounds, their experience of integration can help the entire Church community on its path to truth. Such a testimonial of a flourishing path can help theologians and other Christians to flourish in an unknown renewal. For example, rather than demonizing human frailties, spiritual integration of wounds helps us to see such frailties as assets to be shared. Integration also facilitates the appreciation of personal experience without judging it, knowing that experience is the place where God sows his grace. Healing and integration can push theology and pastoral and spiritual care toward new frontiers, unexplored terrains in which the seeds of the Holy Spirit can be recognized.

Finally, the spiritual accompaniment of the wounded recognizes, along with the importance of divine adoption, the value of spiritual *kinship*: "We discover we are children of God at the moment that we discover we are brothers and sisters, children of the same Father. This is why it is essential to be *part of a journeying community*. We are not alone, we belong to a people, a nation, a city that is on the move, a church, a parish, this group…a community on the move."[45] So, spiritual healing of abuse reconciles victims with themselves and the Church community. The latter benefits because it is itself "reconciled," that is, brought back to a condition of "integration" that values being and walking as a community in which there are brothers and sisters along the way and not mere governing roles.

We can offer a simple example. If theologians discuss grace, redemption, and forgiveness from a rational reflection on these contents, abused persons who have spiritually integrated their wounds can show de facto how grace heals, how it makes forgiveness flourish, and how it enables reconciliation. Thus, the spiritual experience of the abused allows theologians to maintain a constant learner's attitude and to divest themselves of the shoes of the omniscient teacher. The abused who is wounded and healed facilitates a deeper understanding of theological and spiritual content and shows the deficits of pastoral reflections and actions. This new gaze represents a new and privileged vantage point from which the Church increasingly learns to inhabit geographical and existential frontiers.

Conclusion

The following summary might be helpful when responding to the disclosure of a story of spiritual abuse.

- Actively listen to the story.
- Be aware that the person might seem confused, and the story might not follow chronological order.
- Believe what the person is telling you and express that belief.
- Assure the person who discloses abuse that you value the person.

- Thank the person for trusting you and be clear about the boundaries of confidentiality.
- Do not judge or defend a person, a community, a congregation, a movement, or the Church.
- Do not minimize what the person is telling you.
- Do not force the person to name the abuse if the person is not yet ready to do so.
- Do not force the person to tell you details if the person is not willing to do so.
- Understand that the person may have ambivalent feelings and behavior toward the abuser(s).
- Take care if offering prayer or Scripture as a response to a disclosure of spiritual abuse.
- Do not rush the person to forgive or to reconcile; this is something that needs time and is given by God's grace.
- Allow the person to mourn.
- Look for help and exchange information, if needed, with experts in the field.
- Consider next steps carefully and avoid hasty actions (especially if the person is still part of the abusive relationship or system).
- Be aware of personal and professional competencies and limits.
- Be aware that God is stronger than we are.

11

A Chastened Vision for the Future

AT THIS POINT WE have crossed the swamp and shown enough courage to face the challenge of spiritual abuse. Throughout this journey, the idea that spiritual abuse is paradoxically a manifestation of humanity's continued longing for God remains firm. We have spoken of spiritual accompaniment, of grace and freedom as its constituent elements, recognized in abuse a deviation that shatters the individual and the Christian community, and proposed suggestions for the prevention of spiritual abuse and care of the abused. All these reflections have been further enriched by the wisdom of Christian spirituality. The religious experience of the first communities that arose in the encounter with the risen Christ has continued to nourish different forms of spirituality and theological reflections throughout the centuries. Despite their diversity, all of these have borne witness to the core message of the cross. All this gives rise to the desire, somewhere between reality and a dream, to imagine possible strategies and further avenues for reflection, so that every form of accompaniment, whether individual or community, may be as healthy as possible, listening to the Spirit who speaks to the heart of humanity and forges our freedom and interiority.

The wholesomeness of any accompaniment is measured by respect for the boundaries of the other and is aimed at the integral growth of the person, the realization of that person's fullest humanity, and the following of Christ, regardless of the state of life chosen. Ultimately, the growth of individuals facilitates and forms part of the integral growth of their faith community and, ultimately, of the universal Church.

The issue of healthy spiritual accompaniment challenges various professional figures who are involved at differing levels and capacities. Underlying questions are not only how to accompany and help the individual believer and the believing community to grow but also include theological questions that involve all Christians, with their charisms and personal resources. How do we build a global educational village with the decision-making processes that can generate a new Christian community and a new civil society? As Pope Francis noted, the need for this village arose to overcome the culture of waste and to recognize the dignity of human persons, understood and respected in their uniqueness.[1]

Returning to the issue of abuse and to a Church rediscovering its missionary drive *ad intra* and *ad extra*, we ask ourselves how each member of God's people, including those who experienced abuse can participate in this new community and what contribution they can make. From this question another one arises: since the issue of spiritual abuse is a theological affair, what role does theological reflection play in the redemptive processes of history? It is ultimately a question of understanding how to build a global educational village in which theological reflection can have space and act as a leaven for all the educational realities that have human beings and their growth at heart. Thus, we can avoid the multiplication of new practices that, a priori, exclude the life-giving action of grace in human history.[2]

If we look retrospectively at all that has been developed in the preceding pages, we can recognize a common thread. It is the mystery of God and humanity and their relationship. On the one hand, this has functioned as a compass and has allowed us to open horizons and discover the complex depths of spiritual accompaniment and its abuse, avoiding taking wrong turns. But on the other hand, this thread has allowed us to keep our feet on the ground and recognize how our proposals could not completely resolve the challenges of the relationship between humanity and God.

The Abused as Part of the Ecclesial Community

We have emphasized a relationship of reciprocity and complementarity that exists between the individual believer and the community of faith, by reason of being immersed in Christ through baptism. This baptismal identity also gives rise to the care that the individual baptized person should have for the Christian community and the care that the community should have for each baptized individual. It follows, therefore, that the principle of the believer's "inclusion" in the community of faith is provided solely by baptism.[3] While this perspective may be too restrictive for some, it is also powerful and liberating. It means, in fact, that despite our fragile humanity, we are not expelled from the community. This principle carries with it an even more important corollary: if by reason of baptism, no one is expelled from the ecclesial reality, then victims of abuse are and remain children of God, members of the local and universal Church.[4]

As violently as abuse can shatter an active and conscious cooperation with grace, the baptismal dignity of being God's beloved children (see Rom 1:6–7) can never be detached from the essence of humanity (see Rom 8:35–39).[5] This does not mean relativizing abuse but simply recognizing that God is stronger than humans and the evil they can enact. Overcoming the culture of rejection, which Pope Francis mentions in the encyclical *Fratelli Tutti*, means not only showing care and sensitivity toward the victims but also listening to and believing their stories.

Spiritual abuse brings suffering and possibly resentment. Sometimes there is a failure to integrate the wound. Nevertheless, these stories deserve to be welcomed and cherished, precisely so that the Church can continue to exercise its missionary drive. We are helped in this reflection by a crucial passage from the encyclical letter *Evangelii Gaudium*, in which Pope Francis refers to the poor and their necessary inclusion in society. Here he states:

> Each individual Christian and every community is called to be an instrument of God for the liberation and promotion of the poor, and for enabling them to be fully a part of society.

> This demands that we be docile and attentive to the cry of the poor and to come to their aid.... The Church has realized that the need to heed this plea is itself born of the liberating action of grace within each of us, and thus it is not a question of a mission reserved only to a few. (187)

In the following passage, the pope recalls how the preferential option for the poor is a theological category and not simply a philosophical, sociological, or cultural one. It is, in fact, a concrete exercise of Christian charity, shining forth God's mercy for his people.

> This is why I want a Church which is poor and for the poor. They have much to teach us. Not only do they share in the *sensus fidei*, but in their difficulties they know the suffering Christ. We need to let ourselves be evangelized by them. The new evangelization is an invitation to acknowledge the saving power at work in their lives and to put them at the center of the Church's pilgrim way. We are called to find Christ in them, to lend our voice to their causes, but also to be their friends, to listen to them, to speak for them and to embrace the mysterious wisdom which God wishes to share with us through them.... The poor person, when loved, "is esteemed as of great value," and this is what makes the authentic option for the poor differ from any other ideology. (*EG* 198–99)

The poor are not simply those who suffer the economic damage of a society. We know from biblical teachings that the "poor" represent a broad category, including, for example, widows, orphans, and foreigners (see Psalm 72; Luke 4:18).[6] Today, by virtue of the social changes that have taken place and those that are still occurring, the category is broadened to include other and different forms of "poverty" that, likewise, cry out because of the injustices that have been suffered.[7] For this reason, the category of "poor" can also include victims of abuse, regardless of the type of violence they have suffered and the wounds they carry. It is not a matter of pietism but of attention to the other whose beauty—anthropological and christological—remains intact. Nor is it an attempt to resolve the scourge of abuse at all costs, slipping into various forms of moralism and rigid legalisms. It is about living that contemplative love (see 1 Cor 13:4–8) modeled on God's *agape*[8] and ultimately not far removed from the Ignatian spirituality we find in *The Spiritual Exercises*. "This brings an inner knowledge which goes beyond the level of intellect into the interior of a person, penetrating to the mysteries of the heart and its deepest truths."[9]

Therefore, the first concrete commitment of the ecclesial community is to recognize in the abused a beloved and wounded member of the Church whose experience is to be treasured, both to prevent the repetition of abusive events and to strengthen the identity of a Church in mission. For this reason, reparative actions are important, insofar as they give the abused person time to blossom and rise again, without judging, without taking possession of their pain, and without imposing abstractly formulated models and time frames for healing. It is not simply a matter of new arrangements to be put into place, but of recognizing that healing itself is an event of grace that requires the active and open cooperation of the abused person. In this way, restorative action is transformed into redemptive action.

Toward a Healing Memory

The presence of the abused within the ecclesial community is a dynamic but extremely varied one. Not everyone will have the same perception of the trauma they experienced. Their experiences of healing also vary greatly in how long this process took and how it was realized. In fact, some individuals live in abusive dynamics without fully realizing it. Others, by receiving the grace of forgiveness, have managed, generally with the support of professional aid, to heal the memory of their trauma and have been able to integrate their wounds into their lives both psychologically and spiritually. Still others struggle with their fears, memories, and unfulfilled desires, in patient care for themselves. Generally, listening to their stories allows their memory to take shape and acquire dynamism, to become alive and no longer a dark and shadowy force in which to get stuck.

In *Fratelli Tutti*, Pope Francis reflects on the themes of fraternity and social friendship.

> In many parts of the world, there is a need for paths of peace to heal open wounds. There is also a need for peacemakers, men and women prepared to work boldly and creatively to initiate processes of healing and renewed encounter. (225)

At the very beginning of the encyclical, the pope recalls a person in need of healing, and he points out that healing does not cancel the wound, nor does it create a restoration that transports the person to the past prior to the trauma suffered. The past *must* necessarily remain untouched. This is not to imply an invitation to succumb to the evil suffered. It means not erasing the cross, which, in the Christian perspective, is the road that leads to resurrection. As Currie notes, "Reconciliation cannot simply entail a 're-writing of history'…and it cannot be demanded of an entire people all at once: for in the end, reconciliation and forgiveness—which is truly the ultimate goal—is, and must always be, a personal act."[10]

We are well aware of how delicate this theme is. It is somewhat reminiscent of the words of Paul, who, speaking to the Romans, said: "What then shall we say? Shall we persist in sin that grace may abound? Of course not!" (Rom 6:1). Like the apostle, we, too, affirm that we must not succumb to injustice or go inordinately seeking crosses in order to gain quicker access to the resurrection and redemption. We simply want to affirm that being reconciled with one's trauma and painful past implies acknowledging and accepting a cross that is never carried on one's own shoulders. In *Evangelii Gaudium*, Pope Francis states that the crucified Christ is a manifestation of God's love for all humanity. It is the glorious and risen cross that gives support and rebuilds dignity, even when the latter may seem to have been lost. Those who feel wounded and crucified are therefore encouraged to nurture the certainty of faith that Jesus is still with them on their cross, and that God, in Jesus, is not afraid of allowing himself to be crucified again, because this scourge becomes the road to resurrection and full life (268).

A woman who had suffered spiritual abuse and was struggling to integrate that abuse into the fabric of her believing existence related that the turning point in the healing process was an image that she received during a moment of prayer. The woman saw herself clearly on the cross and could feel the nails piercing her hands and feet. In the moment of most acute pain, she discovered that the crucified Christ was with her. He stood between the abused person and the abuser. His presence had not prevented the nails from piercing her hands, but it had prevented her death. Thus began her process of rebirth, lived in the perception of a Crucified One who had not disdained to ascend the cross again. This testimony is precisely that of a healed memory that has not cancelled the event nor forgotten the violence of the blows suffered but has been able to heal the wound. This experience of personal resurrection does not tear out a page of the past to write it anew and more beautifully. It allows new pages to be written for the future.

Precisely for this reason, one of the documents of the SNTM reflects on the magisterium of the abused. Although it does not place this magisterium alongside the ordinary magisterium of the pope and the bishops, it recognizes the inestimable value of the testimonies of those who have been able to sufficiently integrate abuse, both psychologically and spiritually.

> No one can convey the meaning of this drama like someone who has suffered abuse, and not only in terms of his or her personal experience, but also in terms of the abuse itself, the personality of the abuser, the dynamics of the abuse, and its dramatic consequences. Such teaching cannot be lacking in the years of spiritual formation and theological study. That is why it is important and highly appropriate to involve, listen to, and be able to open a dialogue, during the period of initial formation, with people who have survived the abuse, who have processed and integrated it sufficiently. This meeting/listening, which calls for delicacy and respect, and even before that a willingness to learn from another (especially from one who speaks from the "chair of suffering"), is necessary in order to understand how many and what wounds abuse causes and what traces it leaves in people's hearts and bodies. Even that of a deep and painful struggle with God and the Church, before which all those who work in the Church itself, and especially those in formation and discernment, must humbly allow themselves to be questioned. If ministry has dramatically become the place and instrument of the abuse that opened that wound, ministry itself can become the place and instrument to heal that wound. To listen to the victims is to meet "with the wounds of Christ." Their centrality, therefore, is primarily theological.[11]

Indeed, a special spirituality of the cross echoes in the victims' magisterium, which does not leave the person nailed to the rough wood of the cross but has a transformative power. A healed memory, in faith, bears witness to a healed and reconstituted humanity. Consequently, it allows the concrete exercise of that dialectic of the subject that reconciles the limits of its humanity with its capacity for self-transcendence. The spirituality of the cross, experienced by a survivor, facilitates the believing memory of the Risen Christ and the healing Christ. It represents the living memory of a God who overcomes death and oppression. In the light of this interweaving, it is possible to give due value to the practice of healing, which is sometimes misunderstood or insufficiently understood. Individual healings promote a healing of history, involving the entire Christian and social community, but this emphasis underestimates the importance of collective healing, as if it were simply and automatically the sum of individual healings.

> Interlinked with the memory of Easter, it [the memory of Christ the healer and exorcist] constitutes the basis of that promise of freedom and future restoration for the whole world that starts to become a reality in those liberating and restoring signs. With this key, the memory of the Christ that heals and expels demons cannot but be remembered as an invitation to churches to side with those who suffer and are treated unjustly and to commit themselves to a critical and transforming action that lives off the hope of resurrection, i.e., of the life in fullness that has been gifted to us in Christ, who stops, with his mercy, any power that destroys and kills.[12]

Indeed, these special teachings related to healing from abuse shine forth the merciful action of God who continues to create the face of humanity. Thus, victims of abuse are, in a special way, living images of that Creator God who asks humanity to share responsibility for creation and continued creation. Moreover, the importance of a praxis of healing also reshapes the way the Church understands itself. Before the "chair of suffering," the Church lays down the robes of a Church that teaches and assumes the attitude of a Church that learns to understand its mission, pastoral and theological, as a witness to a healed memory.

A Learning Church

From the living testimony of a life "resurrected" after abuse, the Church has much to learn. First, it recognizes that the pain inflicted on even one of its members causes pain to the entire community. For this reason, the Church should take responsibility for the healing of the entire ecclesial body. Ultimately, the Church is helped to discern its true identity and the biases it has consciously or unconsciously put in place.

Second, from the victims of abuse we can learn that there are different forms of suffering. In spiritual abuse, differing abuse strategies affect the individual's life in different ways. Alongside the perennial dark night of private suffering that generates isolation and victimization processes, there is also the transient, but equally dark night of suffering that leads to forgiveness and compassion for oneself and one's abuser. Generally, those who experience this second type of night have already passed through, not without effort and pain, the first night. They arrive at the second, not through personal intellectual effort, but thanks to the experience and immediate knowledge of a Jesus who heals and does not leave the sufferer alone. We could say, in this case, that the risen Christ is co-crucified with the victims of abuse.

Third, the Church learns from this model to live up to the signs of the times and not simply offer instructions; it learns to survive a world in crisis and a fragmented humanity. The Church, in fact, needs to experience for itself that redemptive spirituality of the cross that enables it to remain in tension between history and its limitations, on one hand, and God and God's unlimited power on the other. Only in this way is it possible not to flee history, mission, and authentic ecclesial identity. Echoing Doran's thought, we can say that the Church is that community of disciples who "replicate" the dynamics of God's incarnations. In this way, the Church is not represented by the community of the elect but by the community of those who follow Jesus, the Suffering Servant par excellence.

> The Church's participation in the specifically paschal dimension of "what Jesus did" is twofold. First—and this is what distinguishes the church's "place" in the economy of redemption from that of Jesus himself—the Christian is invited to acknowledge Jesus' suffering and death as his

> or her own *redemption.* But, second, the Christian is *then* invited as well to have some share in the historical catalytic agency of *that* suffering and death as its power mediates the transition from a prevailing situation to an alternative one, and to do so precisely by allowing there to become incarnate in his or her own person, as minister of the new covenant in the blood of Jesus, the very pattern or immanent intelligibility of Jesus's own redemptive self-offering.[13]

Fourth, the Church can learn from two incarnate and living models—the Suffering Servant Jesus and the many healed abused—the possibility of implementing actions that arise from the awareness that it is God who answers the "reality" of evil. In the face of abuse scandals, the Church, too, experiences a profound upheaval associated with extreme suffering. Emphasizing this perspective greatly reduces the risks of Pelagianism, which sometimes still snakes through many ecclesial and pastoral practices. Thus, we can focus on the praxis of the kingdom of God.

The mystery of humanity mirrors the mystery of God, and the former is allowed to participate in God's redemptive work through the constitutive structures of history. Thus, we can recognize that the autobiography of those who have integrated the wounds of abuse in faith is "transformation" that is brought about in the effective collaboration between the abused and grace and that, therefore, becomes a practical exercise of *sensus fidei*, which testifies and teaches how the response to abuse, while passing through the experience of the cross, becomes an *experientia lucis*. Then listening and understanding become not ends in themselves but push us, on a theological level, to a reworking in faith and to an ecclesial and social *praxis* that aims at the reconstruction of the torn humanity that concerns both the abused and the predator. What comes into play in these pages is not only the relationship between freedom and grace, but also the relationship between *fides qua* and *fides quae* and, more specifically, the identity and vocation of the theologian who, in the constant search for truth, indulges that natural process of communication of faith, insisting on the mystery of the incarnation.[14]

A Church that learns from those who have allowed themselves to be healed by grace affirms its prophetic, sacramental, and pastoral ministry, founded on active participation in the law of the cross of that

God who wants to break those chains that prevent humanity from an authentic contact with itself.

> The genuinely sacramental character of the church, insofar as the church is sign and instrument of the reconciling and healing grace of God in Jesus Christ and of the unity of humankind in its catholicity and cultural diversity, is here conceived, in the situation that truly is ours, as precisely proportional to the church's catalytic agency in bringing about this new law on earth. But the constitutive intelligibility of that catalytic agency remains what it has always been, in any and every situation, even when the universal mission of the church could not be conceived with the global explicitness that forces itself upon us today.[15]

And so, as we imagine practices that can redeem history, the importance and role of theology emerges ever stronger as an ecclesial service to humanity and history, listening to the signs of the times[16] and also to those redemptive practices that grace itself enacts in the life of a victim of abuse.

An Authentic Theology of the Cross

In light of all this, we understand that it is not possible to construct a theology, much less a theology of the cross, without it being rooted in the spirituality of the cross.

As proposed by Doran, the Church understands its pastoral and theological ministry as an incarnational exercise of the Suffering Servant. In particular, the fourth Song of the Suffering Servant (see Isa 52:13—53:13) seems to best direct the theology of the cross as it performs its service for the Church and society. Just as the servant participates, responsibly, in the divine redemptive action in history but instead of honor and glory receives contempt and mortification, theology needs to make the cross not the object of its reasoning but, rather, the stick with which to walk on the bumpy roads of humanity and history. As Doran notes,

> Let me conclude with the simple reminder that the Church, commissioned as it is to be the bearer of soteriological truth, will be faithful to its commission only to the extent that it embodies in its members, its communities, and its ministries the Law of the Cross through which the Servant of Yahweh fills up in his own body what is lacking in the sufferings of Christ, neither wavering nor being crushed until true justice is established on the earth. Such is the priestly vocation of the Church, and such alone is the fulfillment of presbyteral ministry.[17]

So, we return to the subject, first thematized by Luther and Ignatius and taken up again in recent times by Lonergan, that the only way to foster that process of self-appropriation of the theologian, called to mediate new meanings and that divine truth, is to take up the priestly, prophetic, and royal vocation of every baptized person.[18]

Conclusion

And now? And in the future? What can and should be done?

The present volume may offer help and support in taking care of emotional, spiritual, and intellectual reactions to the issue of spiritual abuse and its opposite: healthy spiritual accompaniment. Following the see-judge-act process as well as the holistic approach "head-heart-hands," this book has sought to affect and involve readers by letting them understand the roots of spiritual life and the reality of spiritual abuse and its related forms, viewing this new knowledge through the lens of the gospel, listening to the signs of times, acting to promote healthy spiritual accompaniment, and working to reverse human injustice, including spiritual abuses. Furthermore, this book can be understood as a communal invitation to open our horizons, to reflect and cooperate with others in being prophetic and creative in reacting to abusive spiritual practice and in accompanying people in their integral growth.

So far, only a few bishops' conferences, dioceses, congregations, communities, or movements have started to develop and implement measures to favor healthy accompaniment and to prevent spiritual abuse.

Thus, communal discernment is lacking, and much work remains. We can and must learn from our experiences and the errors of the past when dealing with issues of sexual abuse and apply what we learn to spiritual abuse. We can learn from those who have already started to deal with this issue and to develop preventive measures as well as from other helping and accompanying disciplines.

Spiritual abuse is complex, both in its origin and in its effects. The real answer to the complexity is to raise questions, the right ones. Everyone should ask, what can I personally do? How can I favor a "culture of awareness and sensitivity"? How can I help to prevent spiritual abuse and/or prepare for healthy accompaniment? How can I contribute to developing the kingdom of God in contemporary history and the world?

Those who accompany others spiritually may further ask, what are my attitudes in accompanying? Is there a risk I might manipulate others? Do I favor freedom and self-determination? Do I care enough about myself? Do I experience grace? What is my personal relationship with God? Is my spiritual accompaniment free from bias?

Theologians might raise similar questions. In which way do I develop my theological thought? Am I able to listen to the signs of the time? Am I willing to be challenged in the authentic proclamation of that promise of salvation made two thousand years ago? Do I care for my own inner life? How much weight do my spirituality and my baptismal vocation have in the exercise of my ministry as a theologian?

These questions can only be answered on an existential and personal level. But they are an excellent starting point for developing new horizons. The important step is to start to reflect, listening both to concrete realities and to the Word of God. Furthermore, one needs to be willing to get involved personally and to make a contribution—even a little one.

All of us are asked to bring more light into the darkness and into the lives of those who suffer, creating in this way a chain of lights and being vivid examples of living the gospel. All of us are called to be light for others, as is stated in Matthew 5:14–16:

> You are the light of the world. A city built on a hill cannot be hidden. No one after lighting a lamp puts it under the bushel basket, but on the lampstand, and it gives light to all in the house. In the same way, let your light shine before others, so

> that they may see your good works and give glory to your Father in heaven.

The hope is that this tiny light, which we have kindled by writing this book, may shed light on the reality of spiritual abuse and related issues. Only together, in a continuous, honest, and profound exchange and collaboration with other disciplines and with all states of life represented in the Catholic Church, will we be able to fight the phenomenon of spiritual abuse and favor healthy accompaniment.

By making more people aware of the issue of spiritual abuse and by training healthy spiritual accompanists, by promoting interdisciplinary, intercultural, interreligious, and international cooperation, and by involving experts, we will break the silence around the phenomenon of spiritual abuse. We must come to understand it better and to be able to counter it preventively. We need to ask the questions about how the Roman Catholic Church, as well as other Churches, religions, movements, and communities, should approach the issue of personal inner freedom and spiritual abuse in the future. In order for actions to follow words, the commitment of all members of the Church—priests, religious, and laypeople—is required. We should always remember that God has given us the answer to the problem of evil—the cross of Jesus, which smells of death but also of resurrection and redemption. Only in this way can healthy spiritual accompaniment be realized.

Notes

Preface

1. V. M. Fernández, *Intervista sull'abuso spirituale*, January 23, 2025, https://www.vatican.va/roman_curia/congregations/cfaith/fernandez/documents/rc_ddf_doc_20250123_fernandez-abuso-spirituale_it.html.

2. See R. Heyder, "Narrating and Remembrance in the Face of Abuse in the Church," *Religions* 13, no. 4 (2022): 1–12; R. Lennan, "Behind Scandal and Shame?: Ecclesiology and the Longing for a Transformed Church," *Theological Studies* 80, no. 3 (2019): 590–610; C. LeMasters, "Sexual Abuse in the Church 'Family,'" *Christianity and Crisis* 49 (1989): 394–95.

3. A. Vasiliauskaitė, "The Anthropological Crisis of the XXI Century: The Expression and the Church's Response to Its Forms in Catholic Schools," *The Person and the Challenges* 12, no. 2 (2022): 73.

4. Vasiliauskaitė, "The Anthropological Crisis," 76.

5. Pope Francis, *Discorso ai partecipanti all'assemblea plenaria della Congregazione per la Dottrina della fede*, January 30, 2020, https://www.vatican.va/content/francesco/it/speeches/2020/january/documents/papa-francesco_20200130_plenaria-cfaith.html. Translation is ours.

6. Pope Francis, General Audience, "Spiritual Accompaniment," January 4, 2023, https://www.vatican.va/content/francesco/en/audiences/2023/documents/20230104-udienza-generale.html.

7. Pope Francis, Message of the Holy Father to Participants in the International Conference "'Adamo, dove sei?' La questione antropologica oggi" on the Occasion of the Fiftieth Anniversary of the Founding of the

Institute of Psychology of the Pontifical Gregorian University, May 19, 2022, https://press.vatican.va/content/salastampa/en/bollettino/pubblico/2022/05/19/220519e.html.

8. Pope John XXIII, Encyclical on Christianity and Social Progress *Mater et Magistra*, May 15, 1961, §236, https://www.vatican.va/content/john-xxiii/en/encyclicals/documents/hf_j-xxiii_enc_15051961_mater.html.

9. See J. Sands, "Introducing Cardinal Cardijn's See–Judge–Act as an Interdisciplinary Method to Move Theory into Practice," *Religions* 129, no. 9 (2018): 1–10.

10. See S. De Vito, "'Scandalo di pochi, mediocrità di molti.' Sulle dinamiche di guarigione ecclesiale dagli abusi a partire da Rm 6,1–14," *Gregorianum* 103, no. 2 (2022): 287–307.

11. See Pope Francis, "Message for the 2022 World Day of Prayer for Vocations," May 8, 2022, https://www.vatican.va/content/francesco/en/messages/vocations/documents/20220508-messaggio-59-gm-vocazioni.html.

12. Pope Francis, "Message for the 2022 World Day of Prayer for Vocations."

13. Pope Francis, Encyclical Letter on Fraternity and Social Friendship *Fratelli Tutti,* October 3, 2020, chapter 1, "Dark Clouds over a Closed World," https://www.vatican.va/content/francesco/en/encyclicals/documents/papa-francesco_20201003_enciclica-fratelli-tutti.html.

Chapter I

1. K. A. Fuchs, and A. Deodato, "Vulnerabilità: aspetti personali e sistemici," *Tredimensioni. Psicologia, Spiritualità, Formazione* 21, no. 3 (2024): 255–69; G. Goulding, "Mediazione e autorità: l'esercizio dell'autorità spirituale," in *Autorità e mediazione. Le relazioni asimmetriche nella Chiesa*, ed. I. Vigorelli, J. Pujol, and F. Insa (EDS 2023): 48–53.

2. A. S. Denney, K. R. Kerley, and N. G. Gross, "Child Sexual Abuse in Protestant Christian Congregations: A Descriptive Analysis of Offense and Offender Characteristics," *Religions* 9, no. 1 (2016): 27.

3. R. Downen, L. Olsen, and J. Tedesco, "Abuse of Faith: Investigation Reveals 700 Victims of Southern Baptist Sexual Abuse over 20 Years," *Houston Chronicle* (February 10, 2019), https://www.chron

.com/news/investigations/article/Investigation-reveals-700-victims-of-Southern-13591612.php.

4. S. Pulliam Bailey, "Southern Baptists Vote Overwhelmingly to Amend Their Constitution to Address Sex Abuse," *Washington Post* (June 11, 2019), https://www.washingtonpost.com/religion/2019/06/11/southern-baptists-vote-overwhelmingly-amend-their-constitution-address-sex-abuse/.

5. W. Schaupp, "Spiritueller Missbrauch: Eine theologisch-ethische Analyse, in Grauzonen in Kirche und Gesellschaft," in *Geistiger Missbrauch*, ed. G. Hörting (LIT Verlag, 2021), 76.

6. L. Oakley and K. Kinmond, *Breaking the Silence on Spiritual Abuse* (Palgrave Macmillan, 2013), 7–10.

7. The Evangelical Church in Germany (Evangelische Kirche in Deutschland, abbreviated EKD) is a federation of twenty United, Lutheran, and Reformed (Calvinist) Protestant regional churches and denominations in Germany and collectively encompasses the majority of Protestants in that country.

8. Forschungsverband Forum, eds., "Forschung zur Aufarbeitung von sexualisierter Gewalt und anderen Missbrauchsformen in der Evangelischen Kirche und Diakonie in Deutschland," 2024, https://www.forum-studie.de/.

9. A. Denney, "Child Sex Abusers in Protestant Christian Churches: An Offender Typology," *CrimRxiv* (October 25, 2021), https://doi.org/10.21428/cb6ab371.e3e20c48.

10. K. A. Fuchs, "Wenn Körper und Seele leiden. Eine psychologische Perspektive des geistlichen Missbrauchs," in *Grauzonen in Kirche und Gesellschaft: Geistiger Missbrauch*, ed. G. Hörting (LIT Verlag, 2021), 13–28.

11. D. Johnson and J. Van Vonderen, *The Subtle Power of Spiritual Abuse—Recognizing and Escaping Spiritual Manipulation and False Spiritual Authority within the Church* (Bethany House, 1991), 20.

12. K. Kluitmann, "Was ist geistlicher Missbrauch? Grenzen, Formen, Alarmsignale, Hilfen. Manuskript zum Statement bei der DOK-Mitgliederversammlung in Vallendar," https://www.orden.de/dokumente/4._Aktuelles/Themen/Missbrauch/ok_innenseiten_ok_2_2019_kluitmann.pdf.

13. K. Mertes, "Vorwort," in *Spiritueller Missbrauch in der katholischen Kirche,* ed. Doris Wagner (Verlag Herder, 2019), 5–12.

14. Doris Reisinger née Doris Wagner, *Spiritueller Missbrauch in der katholischen Kirche* (Verlag Herder, 2019), 79.

15. L. Oakley and J. Humphreys, *Escaping the Maze of Spiritual Abuse: Creating Healthy Christian Cultures* (SPCK, 2019), 31.

16. Oakley and Humphreys, *Escaping the Maze of Spiritual Abuse*, 31.

17. Oakley, and Humphreys, *Escaping the Maze of Spiritual Abuse*, 31.

18. H.-P. Röhr, *Narzissmus—Das innere Gefängnis* (dtv Sachbuch, 2014).

19. R. Heyder and U. Leimgruber, "Spiritueller und sexueller Missbrauch an erwachsenen Frauen. Was aus den Berichten von Betroffenen zu lernen ist," in *Erzählen als Widerstand: Berichte über spirituellen und sexuellen Missbrauch an erwachsenen Frauen in der katholischen Kirche,* ed. B. Haslbeck, R. Heyder, U. Leimgruber, and D. Sandherr-Klemp (Kindle, 2020), pos. 2849.

20. K. A. Fuchs, "Abusi di potere, di coscienza e spirituali—di che cosa parliamo?" Talk given at the conference "La fiducia tradita. Gli abusi di potere, di coscienza e spirituali all'interno della Chiesa," organized by the Servizio Tutela Minori della Diocesi di Trento (November 10, 2023), Vigilianum, Trento, Italy, https://www.youtube.com/watch?v=BmpuLpqKd9o; K. A. Fuchs, "Cuando se transgreden los límites 'en Su nombre.' Una introducción a la realidad del abuso espiritual," *Humanitas. Revista de Antropología y Cultura Cristiana*, 29, no. 108 (2024): 437.

21. Mertes, "Vorwort," 5–12.

22. I. Tempelmann, *Geistlicher Missbrauch. Auswege aus frommer Gewalt* (R. Brockhaus, 2007), 42–97; K. Mertes, "Geistlicher Machtmissbrauch," *Geist und Leben. Zeitschrift für christliche Spiritualität* 90, no. 3 (2017): 249–59; K. Mertes, "Hilfe, die Schaden anrichtet: Geistlicher Missbrauch in der katholischen Kirche," *Theologisches Feuilleton*, March 13, 2017, https://www.feinschwarz.net/hilfe-die-schaden-anrichtet-geistlicher-missbrauch-in-der-katholischen-kirche/; Fuchs, "Cuando se transgreden los límites 'en Su nombre,'" 432–47.

23. Mertes, "Geistlicher Machtmissbrauch," 249–59; Mertes, "Hilfe, die Schaden anrichtet."

24. Fuchs, "Cuando se transgreden los límites 'en Su nombre,'" 442.

25. B. Haslbeck, R. Heyder, U. Leimgruber, and D. Sandherr-Klemp, *Erzählen als Widerstand: Berichte über spirituellen und sexuellen*

Missbrauch an erwachsenen Frauen in der katholischen Kirche (Kindle, 2020), pos. 2889.

26. Haslbeck et al., *Erzählen als Widerstand*, pos. 2889.

27. H. A. Schulz, "Geistlicher Missbrauch als Idolatrie," in *Grauzonen in Kirche und Gesellschaft. Geistiger Missbrauch,* ed. G. Hörting (LIT Verlag, 2021), 63–68.

28. Schulz, "Geistlicher Missbrauch als Idolatrie," 63–68.

29. Schulz, "Geistlicher Missbrauch als Idolatrie," 68–71.

30. Schulz, "Geistlicher Missbrauch als Idolatrie," 71.

31. Wagner, *Spiritueller Missbrauch in der katholischen Kirche*, 79–96; D. J. Ward, "The Lived Experience of Spiritual Abuse," *Mental Health, Religion and Culture*, no. 14 (2011): 899–915.

32. Wagner, *Spiritueller Missbrauch in der katholischen Kirche*, 79–96.

33. Ward, "The Lived Experience of Spiritual Abuse," 899–915.

34. Ward, "The Lived Experience of Spiritual Abuse," 906.

35. Wagner, *Spiritueller Missbrauch in der katholischen Kirche*, 79–96.

36. Mertes, "Vorwort"; Kluitmann, "Was ist geistlicher Missbrauch?"

37. N. Luhman, *Soziale Systeme. Grundriß einer allgemeinen Theorie* (Suhrkamp, 1984).

38. M. Wijlens, "Die Finsternis aufbrechen. Kirchenrechtliche Überlegungen zum geistlichen Missbrauch für kirchliches Leitungspersonal," in *Grauzonen in Kirche und Gesellschaft. Geistiger Missbrauch,* ed. G. Hörting (LIT Verlag, 2021), 124.

39. G. Werner, "Specifically Catholic: At the Intersection of Power, Maleness, Holiness, and Sexualized Violence," *Journal of the European Society of Women in Theological Research*, no. 27 (2019): 147–74.

40. B. Haslbeck, R. Heyder, U. Leimgruber, and D. Sandherr-Klemp, eds., *Erzählen als Widerstand: Berichte über spirituellen und sexuellen Missbrauch an erwachsenen Frauen in der katholischen Kirche* (Kindle, 2020).

41. S. Lang, "Ich fühle mich bis heute nicht wohl als Frau," in *Erzählen als Widerstand: Berichte über spirituellen und sexuellen Missbrauch an erwachsenen Frauen in der katholischen Kirche,* ed. B. Haslbeck, R. Heyder, U. Leimgruber, and D. Sandherr-Klemp (Kindle, 2020), pos. 1669. Translation is ours.

42. K. Weißenfels, "Zum Schweigen gebracht und kaltgestellt," in *Erzählen als Widerstand: Berichte über spirituellen und sexuellen Missbrauch an erwachsenen Frauen in der katholischen Kirche,* ed. B. Haslbeck, R. Heyder, U. Leimgruber, and D. Sandherr-Klemp (Kindle, 2020), pos. 2561–69.

43. B. Kranemann, "Liturgische Bildung als Missbrauchsprävention. Liturgie—gefährliche oder hilfreiche 'Seelenführerin'?," in *Herder Thema: Gefährliche Seelenführer? Geistiger und geistlicher Missbrauch,* ed. H. Timmerevers and T. Arnold (Verlag Herder, 2020), 37.

44. "When it began to get dark in the evenings, the rebaptizers would run through the streets and shout, 'Confess and repent! God is going to punish you!'" cf. H. Gresbeck, *False Prophets and Preachers: Henry Gresbeck's Account of the Anabaptist Kingdom of Münster* (Truman State University Press, 2016), 52, 113–24.

45. BBC, "Colonia Dignidad: Germany to Compensate Chile Commune Victims," May 18, 2019, https://www.bbc.com/news/world-latin-america-48318295.

46. The Christ Community *(Christusgemeinschaft)* is a religious community particularly active in the area of the German Catholic diocese of Osnabrück. Cf. TAZ, "Missbrauchsvorwurf: Ein Bischof räumt auf," November 17, 2010, https://taz.de/Missbrauchsvorwurf/!5132062/.

47. J. Berry, "Money Paved Way for Maciel's Influence in the Vatican," *National Catholic Reporter,* April 6, 2010, https://www.ncronline.org/money-paved-way-maciels-influence-vatican; J. Berry, "How Fr. Maciel Built His Empire," *National Catholic Reporter,* April 12, 2010, https://www.ncronline.org/news/accountability/how-fr-maciel-built-his-empire. Note: The authors only explicitly mention cases where the canonical and/or civil process is already concluded. They are aware that there are many other ongoing processes that have not yet been concluded or reached judgment.

48. Study Commission, *Control and Abuse, An Investigation on Thomas Philippe, Jean Vanier and L'Arche* (January 2023), https://commissiondetude-jeanvanier.org/commissiondetudeindependante2023-empriseetabus/wp-content/uploads/2023/01/Report_Control-and-Abuse_EN.pdf.

49. A summary of the final report can be downloaded on the following website: https://www.larche.org.uk/news/inquiry-statement.

50. Mertes, "Vorwort," 5–12.

51. Kluitmann, "Was ist geistlicher Missbrauch?"; Haslbeck et al., *Erzählen als Widerstand.*

52. B. Donohue, H. Hill, and T. Maier-Paarlberg, "Domestic Violence," in *Encyclopedia of Stress*, 2nd ed., ed. G. Fink (Academic Press, 2007), 848–52, https://doi.org/10.1016/B978-012373947-6.00129-X.

53. Save the Children, "Violenza psicologica da partner intimo: cos'è e come si manifesta," https://www.savethechildren.it/blog-notizie/violenza-psicologica-da-partner-intimo-cos-e-come-si-manifesta.

54. Donohue, Hill, and Maier-Paarlberg, "Domestic Violence," 848–52.

55. Save the Children, "Violenza psicologica da partner intimo."

56. L. Oakley and J. Humphreys, *Escaping the Maze of Spiritual Abuse*, 31.

57. Servizio Nazionale per la Tutela dei Minori e delle Persone Vulnerabili (SNTM), *La formazione iniziale in tempo di abusi* (2021), 56; D. Cito, "Brevi annotazioni canonistiche sul concetto di abuso di potere e di coscienza," *Tredimensioni. Psicologia, Spiritualità, Formazione* 17, no. 3 (2020): 302–12.

58. Original text: "È una forma di violazione dell'intimità altrui, consistente nell'induzione nell'altro del proprio modo di giudicare e dei propri criteri di discernimento, o della propria sensibilità morale (e penitenziale)." SNTM, *La formazione iniziale in tempo di abusi*, 56.

59. J. Häuselmann and F. Insa, "Abuse of Power, Spiritual Abuse, and Abuse of Conscience: Similarities and Differences," 1–10. Official English translation of the article "Abuso di potere, abuso spirituale e abuso di coscienza: Somiglianze e differenze, *Tredimensioni. Psicologia, Spiritualità, Formazione* 20, no. 1 (2023): 42–53. Downloadable from: https://www.isfo.it/files/File/Spagnolo/Hauselmann-Insa23.pdf.

60. Häuselmann and Insa, "Abuse of Power, Spiritual Abuse, and Abuse of Conscience," 7–10.

61. K. A. Fuchs, "Cuando se transgreden los límites 'en Su nombre,'" 442; K. A. Fuchs. "Abuso spirituale e abuso di coscienza: Una realtà sfidante con conseguenze spesso gravi," in *La tutela dei minori e degli adulti vulnerabili nella Chiesa italiana – 3, Prevenzione e formazione nella vita consacrata,* ed. A. Cencini, A. Deodato, and L. Sabbarese (Edizioni San Paolo, 2025), 249–319.

Chapter 2

1. N. Madge, *Abuse and Survival: A Fact File* (The Prince's Trust-Action, 1997), 14.

2. For example, the "Regulation for Dealing with Sexual Abuse of Minors and of Vulnerable Adults by Clergy and Other Church Staff" of the German Bishops' Conference underlines that a special relationship of power and/or dependency can also be given or arise in the pastoral context (no. 1.4).

3. R. Heller, "Die andere Seite. Psychologische Aspekte bei Bezichtigten und (potentiellen)Tätern," in *Grauzonen in Kirche und Gesellschaft. Geistiger Missbrauch*, ed. G. Hörting (LIT Verlag, 2021), 51.

4. Code of Canon Law, cc. 129–44, https://www.vatican.va/archive/cod-iuris-canonici/eng/documents/cic_lib1-cann129-144_en.html.

5. H. Samonigg, "Sobald ein Machtgefälle entsteht, besteht das Risiko, dass Macht missbraucht wird," in *Grauzonen in Kirche und Gesellschaft. Geistiger Missbrauch*, ed. G. Hörting (LIT Verlag, 2021), 15–16.

6. H. Keul, "Macht ausüben, aber nicht missbrauchen,“ *futur2 Magazin* 2 (2019), https://www.futur2.org/article/macht-ausueben-aber-nicht-missbrauchen/; K. A. Fuchs and A. Deodato, "Vulnerabilità: aspetti personali e sistemici," *Tredimensioni. Psicologia, Spiritualità, Formazione* 21, no. 3 (2024): 255–69.

7. K. A. Fuchs, "Cuando se transgreden los límites 'en Su nombre.' Una introducción a la realidad del abuso espiritual," *Humanitas. Revista de Antropología y Cultura Cristiana*, 29, no. 108 (2024): 433–34.

8. Fuchs, "Cuando se transgreden los límites 'en Su nombre,'" 433–34.

9. L. Oakley and J. Humphreys, *Escaping the Maze of Spiritual Abuse: Creating Healthy Christian Cultures* (SPCK, 2019), 25.

10. W. Schaupp, "Spiritueller Missbrauch: Eine theologisch-ethische Analyse," in *Grauzonen in Kirche und Gesellschaft. Geistiger Missbrauch*, ed. G. Hörting (LIT Verlag, 2021), 87–88.

11. Cf. Code of Canon Law, c. 240 §1; c. 630; c. 991.

12. K. Mertes, "Geistlicher Machtmissbrauch," *Geist und Leben. Zeitschrift für christliche Spiritualität* 90, no. 3 (2017): 249–59; K. Mertes, "Hilfe, die Schaden anrichtet: Geistlicher Missbrauch in

der katholischen Kirche," Theologisches Feuilleton, March 13, 2017, https://www.feinschwarz.net/hilfe-die-schaden-anrichtet-geistlicher-missbrauch-in-der-katholischen-kirche/.

13. D. J. Ward, "The Lived Experience of Spiritual Abuse," *Mental Health, Religion and Culture* 14 (2011): 906.

14. B. Kranemann, "Liturgische Bildung als Missbrauchsprävention. Liturgie—gefährliche oder hilfreiche 'Seelenführerin?,'" in *Herder Thema: Gefährliche Seelenführer? Geistiger und geistlicher Missbrauch,* ed. H. Timmerevers and T. Arnold (Verlag Herder, 2020), 35–38.

15. Diocese of Osnabrück, "Arbeitsgrundlagen geistlicher Missbrauch."

16. E. Adler, "Dafür sind wir nicht zuständig," in *Erzählen als Widerstand: Berichte über spirituellen und sexuellen Missbrauch an erwachsenen Frauen in der katholischen Kirche*, ed. B. Haslbeck, R. Heyder, U. Leimgruber, and D. Sandherr-Klemp (Kindle, 2020), pos. 351.

17. Diocese of Osnabrück, "Arbeitsgrundlagen geistlicher Missbrauch."

18. B. Haslbeck, "Warum haben die Frauen nicht nein gesagt? Psychotraumatologische und systemische Einsichten," in *Erzählen als Widerstand: Berichte über spirituellen und sexuellen Missbrauch an erwachsenen Frauen in der katholischen Kirche*, ed. B. Haslbeck, R. Heyder, U. Leimgruber, and D. Sandherr-Klemp (Kindle, 2020), pos. 3285.

19. G. Klug, "Geistige Übergriffe. Systemische Verlockung und individuelle Schwäche," in *Grauzonen in Kirche und Gesellschaft. Geistiger Missbrauch,* ed. G. Hörting (LIT Verlag, 2021), 39.

20. Klug, "Geistige Übergriffe," 39.

21. K. A. Fuchs, "Charakteristika und Dimensionen geistlichen Missbrauchs—Eine unterschätzte Gefahr mit gravierenden Folgen," in *Herder Thema. Sonderpublikation. Gefährliche Seelenführer—Geistiger und geistlicher Missbrauch*, ed. H. Timmerevers, and T. Arnold (Verlag Herder, 2020), 24.

22. K. Kluitmann, "Was ist geistlicher Missbrauch? Grenzen, Formen, Alarmsignale, Hilfen. Manuskript zum Statement bei der DOK-Mitgliederversammlung in Vallendar," https://www.orden.de/dokumente/4._Aktuelles/Themen/Missbrauch/ok_innenseiten_ok_2_2019_kluitmann.pdf; K. A. Fuchs. "Abuso spirituale e abuso di coscienza: Una realtà sfidante con conseguenze spesso gravi," in *La tutela dei minori e degli adulti vulnerabili nella Chiesa italiana – 3, Prevenzione e formazione nella vita*

consacrata, ed. A. Cencini, A. Deodato, and L. Sabbarese (Edizioni San Paolo, 2025), 296–304.

23. Kluitmann, "Was ist geistlicher Missbrauch?"

24. R. Heyder and U. Leimgruber, "Spiritueller und sexueller Missbrauch an erwachsenen Frauen. Was aus den Berichten von Betroffenen zu lernen ist," in *Erzählen als Widerstand: Berichte über spirituellen und sexuellen Missbrauch an erwachsenen Frauen in der katholischen Kirche*, ed. B. Haslbeck, R. Heyder, U. Leimgruber, and D. Sandherr-Klemp (Kindle, 2020), pos. 2850; Kluitmann, "Was ist geistlicher Missbrauch?"

25. Kluitmann, "Was ist geistlicher Missbrauch?"; D. Wagner, *Spiritueller Missbrauch in der katholischen Kirche* (Verlag Herder, 2019); Fuchs, "Abuso spirituale e abuso di coscienza: Una realtà sfidante con conseguenze spesso gravi," 295–303.

26. Cf. Travailleuses missionnaires—Esclaves au nom de Dieu, https://www.gemppi.org/sectes-et-mouvances/profils-religieux/travailleuses-missionnaires-esclaves-au-nom-de-dieu/.

27. In November 2021, the bishop of Münster, Dr. Felix Genn, dissolved the association of faithful "Totus Tuus New Evangelization" in the diocese. After serious deficiencies in the spiritual treatment and accompaniment of members of the community came to light, an initial investigation phase was followed by an almost two-year accompanied discussion and review process for the community that ended with a final report in November 2020. This overall process was evaluated, and after detailed consultation, the next step was to discuss which decision should be made as the leaders of the association were not willing to recognize these serious deficiencies and remedy them.

28. Fuchs, "Abuso spirituale e abuso di coscienza: Una realtà sfidante con conseguenze spesso gravi," 295–303.

29. Cf. K. A. Fuchs, "Verwundete Kinderseelen. Sexueller Missbrauch und seine teils verheerenden Auswirkungen," in *Sexualisierte Gewalt gegen Kinder. Hintergründe—Zusammenhänge—Erklärungen*, ed. P. Kerschke-Risch (Kohlhammer, 2022), 49–50.

30. Fuchs. "Abuso spirituale e abuso di coscienza: Una realtà sfidante con conseguenze spesso gravi," 295–303.

31. Cf. G. Hörting, *Grauzonen in Kirche und Gesellschaft. Geistiger Missbrauch* (LIT Verlag, 2021).

32. K. A. Fuchs and A. Deodato, "Vulnerabilità: aspetti personali

e sistemici," *Tredimensioni. Psicologia, Spiritualità, Formazione* 21, no. 3 (2024): 255–69.

33. Klug, "Geistige Übergriffe," 37.

34. Klug, "Geistige Übergriffe," 37.

35. Oakley and Humphreys, *Escaping the Maze of Spiritual Abuse*, 31.

36. Klug, "Geistige Übergriffe," 34.

37. Klug, "Geistige Übergriffe," 34.

38. Klug, "Geistige Übergriffe," 34.

39. Fuchs and Deodato, "Vulnerabilità: aspetti personali e sistemici," 255–269; H. Keul, "Vulnerability, Vulnerance and Resilience—Spiritual Abuse and Sexual Violence in New Spiritual Communities," *Religions* 13, no. 5 (2022): 425. https://doi.org/10.3390/rel13050425.

40. Oakley and Humphreys, *Escaping the Maze of Spiritual Abuse*, 42.

41. Schulz, "Geistlicher Missbrauch als Idolatrie," 67.

42. Fuchs and Deodato, "Vulnerabilità: aspetti personali e sistemici," 255–69.

43. K. Mertes, "Vorwort," in *Spiritueller Missbrauch in der katholischen Kirche*, ed. Doris Wagner (Verlag Herder, 2019), 12.

44. This does not mean that all charismatic leaders or charismatic leadership are always and automatically abusive.

45. The Diocese of Münster in Germany has made available a catalog with various signs and indicators. https://www.bistum-muenster.de/fileadmin/user_upload/Website/Downloads/Rat-Hilfe/2018-05-Checkliste-kritische-Anzeichen.pdf; Schaupp, "Spiritueller Missbrauch. Eine theologisch-ethische Analyse," 92–93; G. Ronzoni, "L'abuso spirituale. Riconoscerlo per prevenirlo," in *La tutela dei minori e degli adulti vulnerabili nella Chiesa italiana – 3, Prevenzione e formazione nella vita consacrata,* ed. A. Cencini, A. Deodato, and L. Sabbarese (Edizioni San Paolo, 2025), 321–44.

46. Cf. Catalog of the Diocese of Münster, https://www.bistum-muenster.de/fileadmin/user_upload/Website/Downloads/Rat-Hilfe/2018-05-Checkliste-kritische-Anzeichen.pdf.

47. Schaupp, "Spiritueller Missbrauch. Eine theologisch-ethische Analyse," 92–93.

48. M. Hogg and G. Vaugh, "Leadership and Group Decision-Making," in *Social Psychology*, ed. M. Hogg and G. Vaugh (Pearson International Content, 2017), 338.

49. Hogg and Vaugh, "Leadership and Group Decision-Making," 338.

50. Hogg and Vaugh, "Leadership and Group Decision-Making," 338.

Chapter 3

1. K. A. Fuchs, "Charakteristika und Dimensionen geistlichen Missbrauchs—Eine unterschätzte Gefahr mit gravierenden Folgen," in *Herder Thema. Sonderpublikation. Gefährliche Seelenführer—Geistiger und geistlicher Missbrauch*, ed. H. Timmerevers and T. Arnold (Verlag Herder, 2020), 24–25.

2. "Resilience is a strength present during development. However, resilience also applies to adults and to their functioning after trauma." Cf. E. M. Altmaier, "Resilience," in *Promoting Positive Processes after Trauma*, ed. E. M. Altmaier (Elsevier Academic Press, 2019), 55.

3. Altmaier, "Resilience," 56–57.

4. L. Kong, M. Fang, T. Ma, G. Li, F. Yang, Q. Meng, Y. Li, and P. Li, "Positive Affect Mediates the Relationships between Resilience, Social Support and Posttraumatic Growth of Women with Infertility," *Psychology, Health and Medicine* 23 (2018): 707–16.

5. C. L. Park, J. M. Currier, J. I. Harris, and J. M. Slattery, *Trauma, Meaning, and Spirituality: Translating Research into Clinical Practice* (APA, 2017), 185–99.

6. K. A. Fuchs. "Abuso spirituale e abuso di coscienza: Una realtà sfidante con conseguenze spesso gravi," in *La tutela dei minori e degli adulti vulnerabili nella Chiesa italiana – 3, Prevenzione e formazione nella vita consacrata,* ed. A. Cencini, A. Deodato, and L. Sabbarese (Edizioni San Paolo, 2025), 304–7.

7. K. I. Pargament, N. A. Murray-Swank, and A. Mahoney, "Problem and Solution: The Spiritual Dimension of Clergy Sexual Abuse and Its Impact on Survivors," *Journal of Child Sexual Abuse* 17 (2008): 398.

8. K. A. Fuchs, "Wenn Körper und Seele leiden. Eine psychologische Perspektive des geistlichen Missbrauchs," in *Grauzonen in Kirche und Gesellschaft. Geistiger Missbrauch*, ed. G. Hörting (LIT Verlag, 2021), 24–26.

9. Fuchs. "Abuso spirituale e abuso di coscienza: Una realtà sfidante con conseguenze spesso gravi," 306–15.

10. Cf. D. Finkelhor and A. Browne, "Initial and Long-Term Effects: A Conceptual Framework," in *A Sourcebook on Child Sexual Abuse*, ed. D. Finkelhor (Sage, 1997); D. R. Wilson, "Health Consequences of Childhood Sexual Abuse," *Perspectives in Psychiatric Care* 46 (2010): 56–64; R. McElvaney, "Disclosure of Child Sexual Abuse: Delays, Non-Disclosure and Partial Disclosure: What the Research Tells Us and Implications for Practice," *Child Abuse Review* 24 (2015): 159–69; V. Schönbucher, T. Maier, M. Mohler-Kuo, U. Schnyder, and M. Landolt, "Disclosure of Child Sexual Abuse by Adolescents: A Qualitative In-Depth Study," *Journal of Interpersonal Violence* 27 (2012): 3486–513.

11. Cf. I. Tempelmann, *Geistlicher Missbrauch. Auswege aus frommer Gewalt* (R. Brockhaus, 2007), 242–92; Fuchs. "Abuso spirituale e abuso di coscienza: Una realtà sfidante con conseguenze spesso gravi," 306–15.

12. Cf. Tempelmann, *Geistlicher Missbrauch*, 242–92; L. Oakley and J. Humphreys, *Escaping the Maze of Spiritual Abuse: Creating Healthy Christian Cultures* (SPCK, 2019).; Fuchs, "Wenn Körper und Seele leiden," 13–28.

13. H. A. Schulz, "Geistlicher Missbrauch als Idolatrie," in *Grauzonen in Kirche und Gesellschaft. Geistiger Missbrauch*, ed. G. Hörting (LIT Verlag, 2021), 63–68.

14. Fuchs. "Abuso spirituale e abuso di coscienza: Una realtà sfidante con conseguenze spesso gravi," 306–15.

15. Fuchs. "Abuso spirituale e abuso di coscienza: Una realtà sfidante con conseguenze spesso gravi," 306–15.

16. Fuchs, "Wenn Körper und Seele leiden," 16–17; Fuchs, "Charakteristika und Dimensionen geistlichen Missbrauchs," 24–25; Tempelmann, *Geistlicher Missbrauch*, 242–92.

17. For further information, see APA, *Diagnostic and Statistical Manual of Mental Disorders*, 5th ed. (APA, 2022), 301–10; National Institute of Mental Health, https://www.nimh.nih.gov/health/topics/post-traumatic-stress-disorder-ptsd.

18. World Health Organization, *International Classification of Diseases for Mortality and Morbidity Statistics*, 11th ed. (2018a), https://icd.who.int/browse11/l-m/en; J. L. Herman, "Complex PTSD:

A Syndrome in Survivors of Prolonged and Repeated Trauma," *Journal of Traumatic Stress* 5 (1992b): 377–91.

19. Cf. B. A. van der Kolk, *The Body Keeps the Score: Brain, Mind, and Body in the Healing of Trauma* (Viking, 2014), 237.

20. APA, *Diagnostic and Statistical Manual of Mental Disorders*, 191, 309–12; Fuchs. "Abuso spirituale e abuso di coscienza: Una realtà sfidante con conseguenze spesso gravi," 306–15.

21. See W. B. Cannon, *Bodily Changes in Pain, Hunger, Fear and Rage: An Account of Recent Researches into the Function of Emotional Excitement* (Appleton and Co., 1915); A. Löw, M. Weymar, and A. O. Hamm, "When Threat Is Near, Get Out of Here: Dynamics of Defensive Behavior during Freezing and Active Avoidance," *Psychological Science*, 26 (2015): 1706–16.

22. See E. M. Altmaier, "An Introduction to Trauma," in *Promoting Positive Processes after Trauma*, ed. E. M. Altmaier (Elsevier Academic Press, 2019), 6–7; P. Walker, *Complex PTSD: From Surviving to Thriving* (Azure Coyote Publishing, 2013); Löw, Weymar, and Hamm, "When Threat Is Near, Get Out of Here," 1706–16.

23. M. Huber, *Trauma und die Folgen. Trauma und Traumabehandlung Teil 1* (Junfermann Druck and Service GmbH and Co. KG, 2020), 53.

24. APA, *Diagnostic and Statistical Manual of Mental Disorders*, defines depersonalization and derealization as follows: "Depersonalization: Experiences of unreality, detachment, or being an outside observer with respect to one's thoughts, feelings, sensations, body, or actions (e.g., perceptual alterations, distorted sense of time, unreal or absent self, emotional and/or physical numbing). 2. Derealization: Experiences of unreality or detachment with respect to surroundings (e.g., individuals or objects are experienced as unreal, dreamlike, foggy, lifeless, or visually distorted)" (344).

25. B. Haslbeck, "Warum haben die Frauen nicht nein gesagt? Psychotraumatologische und systemische Einsichten," in *Erzählen als Widerstand: Berichte über spirituellen und sexuellen Missbrauch an erwachsenen Frauen in der katholischen Kirche*, ed. B. Haslbeck, R. Heyder, U. Leimgruber, and D. Sandherr-Klemp (Kindle, 2020), pos. 3285.

26. Haslbeck, "Warum haben die Frauen nicht nein gesagt?," pos. 3285.

27. Haslbeck, “Warum haben die Frauen nicht nein gesagt?,” pos. 3339.

28. Haslbeck, “Warum haben die Frauen nicht nein gesagt?,” pos. 3291.

29. Haslbeck, “Warum haben die Frauen nicht nein gesagt?,” pos. 3311.

30. Haslbeck, “Warum haben die Frauen nicht nein gesagt?,” pos. 3311.

31. Walker, *Complex PTSD: From Surviving to Thriving*, 129–44.

32. APA, *Diagnostic and Statistical Manual of Mental Disorders*, 216–17, 302–19; B. J. Sadock, V. A. Sadock, and P. Ruiz, *Synopsis of Psychiatry* (Lippincott Williams and Wilkins, 2015), 437–45.

33. A. C. McFarlane, “The Long-Term Costs of Traumatic Stress: Intertwined Physical and Psychological Consequences,” *World Psychiatry* 9, no. 1 (2010): 3–8.

34. McFarlane, “The Long-Term Costs of Traumatic Stress,” 6.

35. Fuchs, “Charakteristika und Dimensionen geistlichen Missbrauchs,” 24–25; Fuchs, “Abuso spirituale e abuso di coscienza: Una realtà sfidante con conseguenze spesso gravi,” 306–15.

36. Fuchs. “Abuso spirituale e abuso di coscienza: Una realtà sfidante con conseguenze spesso gravi,” 306–15.

37. M. Wiljens, “Die Finsternis aufbrechen. Kirchenrechtliche Überlegungen zum geistlichen Missbrauch für kirchliches Leitungspersonal,” in *Grauzonen in Kirche und Gesellschaft. Geistiger Missbrauch*, ed. G. Hörting (LIT Verlag, 2021), 136–37; Fuchs, “Abuso spirituale e abuso di coscienza: Una realtà sfidante con conseguenze spesso gravi,” 306–15.

38. K. A. Fuchs and S. De Vito, *Comprendere la realtà degli abusi spirituali, Versione integrale*, Movimento dei Focolari in Svizzera: Che cosa è l’abuso spirituale, 2022, 8–9, https://movimento-focolari.ch/seite/cosa-e-labuso-spirituale.

Chapter 4

1. See F. Jalics, *Lerner wir beten: Eine Anleitung, mit Gotta ins Gespräch zu kommen* (Echter Verlag, 1996).

2. See D. Mansfield, "Spiritual Accompaniment and Discernment," in *The Way* 47, no. 1 (2008): 155–64.

3. H. Ospino, "Theological Horizons for a Pedagogy of Accompaniment," in *Religious Education* 105, no. 4 (2010): 413–29.

4. D. Lonford and J. Megill, "Idolatry, Indifference, and the Scientific Study of Religion: Two New Human Arguments," *Religious Studies* 56, no. 4 (2020): 488–508.

5. Pope Francis, General Audience, June 5, 2013, https://www.vatican.va/content/francesco/en/audiences/2013/documents/papa-francesco_20130605_udienza-generale.html.

6. S. De Vito, *Ecco! Ti racconto un'esperienza di Dio* (Tau Editrice, forthcoming).

7. See R. M. Doran, *Theology and Dialectics of History* (University of Toronto Press, 1990), 112.

8. See S. De Vito, "El abuso espiritual como *bias* teológico. Destroza El rostro de Dios y del hombre," in *Abuso de podere en la Iglesia. Una prepuesta interdisciplinare*, ed. V. Ferrer Usó (Tirant Humanidades, 2025), 293–308.

9. We will return to the figure of Saint Ignatius in more detail in the next chapter, where we will highlight the contents of his spirituality and his ecclesiology.

10. See G. J. Günter, "*Sentire cum Ecclesia*," *La Civiltà Cattolica* 144, no. 3429 (May 1, 1993): 227–37.

11. G. E. Ganss, "Thinking with the Church: The Spirit of St. Ignatius's Rules," *The Way* (1973): 74.

12. See S. De Vito, "Reconciliation Process in the Letter to the Colossians: A Response to Abuse Crises," in *Salvation in a Crises-Ridden World: An Intercultural-Biblical Response*, ed. N. Gatti, F. Gmainer-Pranzl and B. Kowalski (Brill, 2025), forthcoming.

13. See A. Witwer, "Geistlicher Missbrauch. Eine 'Vergewaltigung' der göttlichen Tugenden. Missbrauch von Glaube, Hoffnung und Liebe," in *Grauzonen in Kirche und Gesellschaft. Geistiger Missbrauch*, ed. G. Hörting (LIT Verlag, 2021), 97–98.

14. F. Genn, "Dokumentation des Eröffnungsvortrags der Tagung 'Gefährliche Seelenführer. Theologische Aspekte des "Geistlichen Missbrauchs,"'" in *Herder Thema: Gefährliche Seelenführer? Geistiger und geistlicher Missbrauch*, ed. H. Timmerevers and T. Arnold (Verlag Herder, 2020), 11–13.

15. Witwer, "Geistlicher Missbrauch," 99.

16. F. Genn, "Dokumentation des Eröffnungsvortrags der Tagung 'Gefährliche Seelenführer. Theologische Aspekte des "Geistlichen Missbrauchs,"'" 11–13.

17. Witwer, "Geistlicher Missbrauch," 99.

18. Genn, "Dokumentation des Eröffnungsvortrags der Tagung 'Gefährliche Seelenführer. Theologische Aspekte des "Geistlichen Missbrauchs,"'" 11–13.

19. Witwer, "Geistlicher Missbrauch," 99.

20. Witwer, "Geistlicher Missbrauch," 100.

21. See J. E. Joullié, A. M. Gould, R. Spillane, and S. Luck, "The Language of Power and Authority in Leadership," *The Leadership Quarterly* 32, no, 4 (2021): 101491; F.C. Luneburg, "Power and Leadership: An Influence Process," *International Journal of Management, Business, and Administration* 15 (2012): 1–9.

22. See P. P. Bellini, "The Role of Authoritativeness in Educational Relationships: A Theoretical Reflection," *Italian Journal of Sociology of Education* 10 (2018): 90.

23. See Bellini, "The Role of Authoritativeness," 90–91. F. Tuccari, "Autorità," *Enciclopedia dei Ragazzi* (2005).

24. L. Oakley and J. Humphreys, *Escaping the Maze of Spiritual Abuse: Creating Healthy Christian Cultures* (SPCK, 2019), 27–29.

25. W. Schaupp, "Spiritueller Missbrauch. Eine theologisch-ethische Analyse," in *Grauzonen in Kirche und Gesellschaft. Geistiger Missbrauch*, ed. G. Hörting (LIT Verlag, 2021), 83.

Chapter 5

1. Congregation for the Doctrine of the Faith, *Instruction Donum Veritatis on the Ecclesial Vocation of the Theologian*, May 24, 1990, §1, https://www.vatican.va/roman_curia/congregations/cfaith/documents/rc_con_cfaith_doc_19900524_theologian-vocation_en.html.

2. G. Greshake, *Libertà donata. Introduzione alla dottrina della grazia* (Brescia: Queriniana, 2002), 37. Translation is ours.

3. Greshake, *Libertà donata*, 39. Translation is ours.

4. See S. Curtis, "Will and Grace: The Essence of Pelagian

Debate," in *Journal of Asian Evangelical Theology* 20, no. 2 (2016): 55–73.

5. See A. H. M. Evans, "Augustine and Pelagius as a Cameo of the Dilemma between Original Sin and Free Will," in *Scriptura* 120, no. 1 (2021): 1–12.

6. Greshake, *Libertà donata*, 64. Translation is ours.

7. See R. C. Kaczor, "Thomas Aquinas on Gratitude to God," *Religions* 13, no. 8 (2022): 1–14.

8. See D. Spezzano, "'Those He Predestined He Also Called' (Romans 8:30): Aquinas on the Liberating Grace of Conversion," *Journal of Moral Theology* 10 (2021): 67–83.

9. See Hubertus Blaumeiser, "Dal cuore della Rivelazione al centro della vita. Dimensioni di fondo della teologia di Martin Lutero," *Nuova Umanità* 21, nos. 3–4 (1999): 387–403.

10. Devotio moderna is a spiritual renewal movement of the fourteenth and fifteenth centuries, which advocated an intimate and subjective religiosity, as opposed to medieval-style collective piety. See K. Goudriaan, "Empowerment through Reading, Writing and Example: The Devotio Moderna," in *Cambridge History of Christianity IV: Christianity in Western Europe c. 1100–c. 1500*, ed. M. Rubin and W. Simons (Cambridge University, 2009), 405–19.

11. See Timothy J. Wengert, "Peace, Peace...Cross, Cross. Reflections on How Martin Luther Relates the Theology of the Cross to Suffering," *Lutheran Quarterly* 33, no. 3 (2019): 304–23.

12. See Johann Heinz, "Martin Luther and His Theology in German Catholic Interpretation before and after Vatican II," *Andrews University Seminary Studies* 26, no. 3 (Season 1988): 253–65.

13. George L. Murphy, "The Theology of the Cross and God's Work in the World," in *Zygon* 33, no. 2 (1998): 224.

14. H. Orchard, "The Creature and the Sovereign Self: The Anthropology of the Spiritual Exercises and Contemporary Spiritual Narcissism," *The Way* 1 (2020): 12.

15. B.J.F. Lonergan, *Method in Theology* (University of Toronto Press, 2017), 101–2.

16. Lonergan, *Method in Theology*, 102.

17. See R. M. Doran, "Lonergan's Philosophical and Theological Anthropology as a Catholic Humanism," *Salesianum* 79 (2017): 17–37.

18. See S. De Vito, "'Scandalo di pochi, mediocrità di molti': Sulle

dinamiche di guarigione ecclesiale dagli abusi a partire da Rm 6:1–14," *Gregorianum* 103, no. 2 (2022): 295–99.

19. P. D. Murray, "*Ecclesia et Pontifice*: On Delivering on the Ecclesiological Implications of *Evangelii Gaudium*," *Ecclesiology* 12 (2016): 25.

20. See G. E. De Mauro, "Modern Psychology and Ancient Heresy: The Rebirth of Pelagianism," *The Catholic Social Science Review* 4 (1999): 205–15; K. Martin, "The Individual and Society in Psychotherapy: Reflections from Anthropology," *European Journal of Psychotherapy & Counselling* (2025): 1–16; K. Seelay, "History in the Psyche, Particles in the Self: The Case Z," in *Psychotherapy, Anthropology and the Work of Culture*, ed. K. Martin (Routledge, 2019), 106–20.

21. See T. Healy, "The Challenge of Self-Transcendence," in *A Journey to Freedom: An Interdisciplinary Approach to the Anthropology of Formation*, ed. F. Imoda (Peeters, 2000), 70–114.

22. In this case, we speak of a three-dimensional anthropological vision.

23. See F. Imoda, "Spiritual Exercises of Ignatius of Loyola and Psychology," *Studies in Spirituality* 1 (1991): 206.

Chapter 6

1. See N. Vest, ed., *Tending the Holy: Spiritual Direction across Traditions* (Morehouse, 2003); P. Sheldrake, "Spirituality in History," Τέλειος/*Teleios* 1, no. 2 (2021): 3–17.

2. See G. Zevini, "'Ti guido per la strada su cui devi andare.' Icone bibliche di accompagnamento spirituale,"*Quaderni di Spiritualità Salesiana* 1, Nuova Serie-2 (2004): 11–28.

3. See G. H. Ettlinger, "Church Fathers and Desert Mothers: Male and Female in the Early Church," *America* 164 (May 25, 1991): 558–56; M. Plekon, "Merton's Monastic Renewal and the Desert Mothers and Fathers," *The American Benedictine Review* 73, no. 4 (2022): 390–413.

4. See C. Lane, "Jesus and the Cross-Centered Spirituality of the Reformation and Later Protestantism," *Religions* 14, no. 6 (2023): 1–10; A. Peirats and G. Ruben, "Meditation and Contemplation: Word and Image at the Service of Medieval Spirituality," *Religions* 14, no. 2 (2023): 1–20;

S. Chan, "'Sin and Grace' or 'Grace and Sin'?: Implications for Christian Spirituality," *Evangelical Review of Theology* 48, no. 2 (2024): 126–38.

5. See G. Greshake, *Chiesa, dove vai? Guardare al futuro in prospettiva real-utopista* (Queriniana, 2023), 27–71.

6. See G. Dames, "Exploring Attributes for an Authentic Christian Spirituality in an Age of Growing Secularization and Skepticism: A Practical Theological Reflection," *Stellenbosch Theological Journal* 9, no. 2 (2023): 1–27.

7. S. M. Schneiders, "Religion versus Spirituality: A Contemporary Conundrum," *Spiritus* 3, no. 2 (2003):168.

8. S. Selvam, "The Unnamed Companion on the Road: Spiritual Accompaniment in the Context of Youth Ministry," *The Journal of Youth Ministry* 11, no. 2 (2013): 43.

9. See M. Lavra, "Dirigere o accompagnare?" *Appunti di spiritualità* 35 (1993): 64.

10. T. McGuinness, "The Way of Accompaniment," *The Way Supplement* 104 (November 2002): 104.

11. Selvam, "The Unnamed Companion," 44.

12. See J.-B., Lecuit, "Le Spirituel et Le Psychique: Sans confusion ni séparation: Repères pour l'accompagnement spirituel," *Teresianum* 72, no. 1 (2021): 95–126.

13. See F. Jalics, *Die Geistliche Begleitung im Evangelium* (Echter Verlag, 2012).

14. M. Schneiders, "Religion versus Spirituality," 168.

15. See J. Hauselmann and F. Insa, "Abuso di potere, abuso spirituale e abuso di coscienza. Somiglianze e differenze," *Tre dimensioni. Psicologia. Spiritualità. Formazione* 20 (2023): 46–47.

16. See F. X. Lawlor, "The Doctrine of Grace in the Spiritual Exercises," *Theological Studies* 3 (1942): 513–21.

17. See M. Rotsaert, "Ignatian Spirituality: Some Changes in Vision and Practise," *The Way* 55, no. 4 (2016): 121–23.

18. See M. Rotsaert, *De Loyola au Vatican. Idées reçues sur les jésuites* (Le Cavalier Blue, 2013), 7.

19. J. N. Tylendia, ed., *A Pilgrim's Journey: The Autobiography of Ignatius of Loyola* (Ignatius Press, 2001), §6.8.

20. All quotations from *The Spiritual Exercises* are taken from: Ignatius of Loyola, *The Spiritual Exercises of St. Ignatius: Based on Studies in the Language of the Autograph* (Loyola Press, 2019). In the body text, we will refer to it with the expression "Exx."

21. See Tylendia, *A Pilgrim's Journey*, 68, 30.

22. See Philip Endean, "Ignazio di Loyola e Lutero," *La Civiltà Cattolica* 167, no. 3974 (2013): 140–50; David C. Steinmetz, "Luther and Loyola," *Interpretation* 47, no. 1 (1993): 5–14.

23. P. R. Sauer, "Reassessing Luther and Ignatius," *Lutheran Forum* 47, no. 3 (2013): 13.

24. The name *Society of Jesus* states that the new group has its core in Jesus Christ and not in Ignatius of Loyola. Further, the noun *Jesuit*, employed to refer to the new religious order, was also used in the Middle Ages with the meaning "a good Christian." See Rotsaert, *De Loyola au Vatican*, 7–8.

25. See M. Rotsaert, *Esercizi spirituali di sant'Ignazio. Storia, contenuto, metodo, finalità* (Edizioni San Paolo, 2005), 61–62.

26. Tylendia, *A Pilgrim's Journey*, §25.26.

27. M. Rotsaert, "Ignatian Spirituality: Some Changes in Vision and Practise," *The Way* 55, no. 4 (2016): 119.

28. In the *Constitutions (*1538), Ignatius stated that every novice joining the Society of Jesus must spend a month making the "exercises." John O' Malley, *The Jesuits: A History from Ignatius to the Present* (Rowman & Littlefield, 2014), 17.

29. See T. O'Reilly, "Melchor Cano and the Spirituality of St. Ignatius Loyola: *Censura y parecer contra el Insituto de los Padres Jesuitas*," *Journal of Jesuit Studies* 4 (2017): 365–94.

30. See Rotsaert, "Ignatian Spirituality: Some Changes in Vision and Practise," 119.

31. See Rotsaert, *Esercizi spirituali di sant'Ignazio*, 22–25.

32. See Ç. Roblero Cum, "Spiritual Exercises and Abuse of Conscience: A Process of Liberation from Submission and Affective Manipulation," *The Way* 60, no. 4 (2021): 23–32.

33. See W. A. Barry and Robert G. Doherty, *Contemplative in Action: The Jesuit Way* (Paulist Press, 2002), 9–11.

34. L. Deam, *3000 Miles to Jesus: Pilgrimage as a Way of Life for Spiritual Seekers* (Broadleaf Books, 2021), 97–98.

35. Deam, *3000 Miles to Jesus*, 93.

36. H. Orchard, "The Creature and the Sovereign Self: The Anthropology of Spiritual Exercises and Contemporary Spiritual Narcissism," *The Way* 59, no. 1 (2020): 14.

37. Orchard, "The Creature and the Sovereign Self," 12.

38. Orchard, "The Creature and the Sovereign Self," 19.

39. See J. Sheppard, "See, Judge, Act and Ignatian Spirituality," *The Way* 56, no. 1 (January 2017): 102–11; A. S. Costa, "Times of Ignatian Election: The Wisdom of the Directories," *The Way* 42, no. 4 (October 2003): 73–88.

40. L. Deam, *3000 Miles to Jesus*, 97–98.

41. M. Giuliani, "St. Ignatius Embracing the Future," *The Way* 58, no. 1 (2019): 45.

42. Giuliani, "St. Ignatius Embracing the Future," 47.

43. Giuliani, "St. Ignatius Embracing the Future," 50.

44. G. Aschenbrenner, "Becoming Whom We Contemplate," *The Way Supplement* 52 (1985): 39.

45. Aschenbrenner, "Becoming Whom We Contemplate," 42.

Chapter 7

1. The word *karismata* suggests the participation of all Christians in God's grace (see Rom 12:6). See James Breed, "The Church as the 'Body of Christ': A Pauline Analogy," *Theological Review* 6, no. 2 (1985): 9–32.

2. See Albert Vanhoye, *I carismi nel Nuovo Testamento* (Gregorian Press, 2011), 77–88.

3. For example, Spiritual Directors International, "Guidelines for Ethical Conduct," 2014, https://www.sdiworld.org/sites/default/files/publications/Guidelines%20Revised%202014-proof1-2.pdf.

4. For example, the Exerzitien-Forum Schweiz (Forum for Retreat in Switzerland), the Arbeitsgemeinschaft deutscher Diözesen für Exerzitien und Spiritualität (Working Group of German Dioceses for Retreats and Spirituality).

5. See *AL*; Pope Francis, Post-synodal Apostolic Exhortation to Young People and to the Entire People of God *Christus Vivit* (March 25, 2019), §§137–61, https://www.vatican.va/content/francesco/en/apost_exhortations/documents/papa-francesco_esortazione-ap_20190325_christus-vivit.html; Dicastery of Laity, Family and Life, *Catechumenal Pathways for Married Life*, 2022, http://www.laityfamilylife.va/content/dam/laityfamilylife/amoris-laetitia/OrientamentiCatecumenatomatrimoniale/Catechumenal%20Pathways_ENG.pdf.

6. K. A. Fuchs, "Nähe und Distanz in Begleitbeziehungen: Wovon

sprechen wir? Grundlegende Einführung in die Thematik," talk given at the conference *Heilsam oder unheilvoll? Tagung zum Umgang mit Nähe und Distanz in geistlicher Begleitung, Seelsorge und Beratung* (Lasalle-Haus Bad Schönbrunn, Switzerland, March 20, 2022); K. A. Fuchs, "Der Umgang mit Nähe und Distanz als ein wichtiger Baustein der Präventionsarbeit" (September 2019), Seminar St. Beat—Für kirchliche Berufe im Bistum Basel, https://stbeat.ch/wp-content/uploads/2019/09/Artikel-von-Dr.-Katharina-Fuchs.pdf.

7. Fuchs, "Nähe und Distanz in Begleitbeziehungen: Wovon sprechen wir?"

8. H. Thiersch, "Nähe und Distanz in der Sozialen Arbeit," in *Nähe und Distanz. Ein Spannungsfeld pädagogischer Professionalität*, ed. M. Dörr (Beltz, 2019), 42.

9. W. Helsper and S. Reh, "Nähe, Diffusität und Asymmetrie in pädagogischen Interaktionen," in *Sexualisierte Gewalt, Macht und Pädagogik*, ed. W. Thole, M. Baader, W. Helsper, M. Kappeler, M. Leuzinger-Bohleber, S. Reh, U. Sielert, and C. Thompson (Verlag Barbara Budrich, 2012), 274.

10. Thiersch, "Nähe und Distanz in der Sozialen Arbeit," 45. Translation is ours.

11. Helsper and Reh, "Nähe, Diffusität und Asymmetrie in pädagogischen Interaktionen," 274.

12. Thiersch, "Nähe und Distanz in der Sozialen Arbeit," 44.

13. Fuchs, "Nähe und Distanz in Begleitbeziehungen: Wovon sprechen wir?"

14. Thiersch, "Nähe und Distanz in der Sozialen Arbeit," 48.

15. See Mary Clyde, "Faith, Hope, and Charity," *Dialogue* 27, no. 2 (1994): 227–34; Kevin Leidich, "Every Increase in Hope, Faith, and Charity: Understanding Ignatian Consolation," *The Way* 61, no. 2 (2022): 55–64.

16. Fuchs, "Nähe und Distanz in Begleitbeziehungen: Wovon sprechen wir?"

17. K. A. Fuchs, "Herausforderungen von Nähe und Distanz im multikulturellen Kontext," talk given at the conference *Heilsam oder unheilvoll? Tagung zum Umgang mit Nähe und Distanz in geistlicher Begleitung, Seelsorge und Beratung* (Lasalle-Haus Bad Schönbrunn, Switzerland, March 21, 2022).

18. Fuchs, "Der Umgang mit Nähe und Distanz als ein wichtiger Baustein der Präventionsarbeit."

19. W. Müller, "Heilsame Nähe und Distanz: Was gilt es zu beachten? Voraussetzungen und Möglichkeiten," talk given at the conference *Heilsam oder unheilvoll? Tagung zum Umgang mit Nähe und Distanz in geistlicher Begleitung, Seelsorge und Beratung* (Lasalle-Haus Bad Schönbrunn, Switzerland, March 21, 2022).

20. Fuchs, "Herausforderungen von Nähe und Distanz im multikulturellen Kontext."

21. Thiersch, "Nähe und Distanz in der Sozialen Arbeit," 42–51.

22. Fuchs, "Herausforderungen von Nähe und Distanz im multikulturellen Kontext."

23. Fuchs, "Nähe und Distanz in Begleitbeziehungen: Wovon sprechen wir?"

24. Cf. M. Heiner, *Professionalität in der sozialen Arbeit: theoretische Konzepte, Modelle und empirische Perspektiven* (Kohlhammer, 2004), 155–68; M. Heiner, *Kompetent handeln in der Sozialen Arbeit* (Ernst Reinhardt Verlag, 2010), 9–20, 54.

25. Cf. Heiner, *Professionalität in der sozialen Arbeit*, 155–68; Heiner, *Kompetent handeln in der Sozialen Arbeit*, 9–20, 54.

26. Cf. Heiner, *Professionalität in der sozialen Arbeit*, 155–68; Heiner, *Kompetent handeln in der Sozialen Arbeit*, 9–20, 54.

27. Cf. Heiner, *Professionalität in der sozialen Arbeit*, 155–68; Heiner, *Kompetent handeln in der Sozialen Arbeit*, 12, 54.

28. H. A. Schulz, "Bei euch soll es nicht so sein! Wie in der Praxis Missbrauch vermeiden?," talk given at the conference *Heilsam oder unheilvoll? Tagung zum Umgang mit Nähe und Distanz in geistlicher Begleitung, Seelsorge und Beratung* (Lasalle-Haus Bad Schönbrunn, Switzerland, March 22, 2022).

29. K. A. Fuchs, "Emotions, Emotion Regulation, and Self-Care in the Field of Safeguarding Minors," in *Sexual Abuse of Minors: Theology, Care and Prevention*, CCP Series 1, ed. K. Demasure, K. A. Fuchs, and H. Zollner (Peeters, 2018), 217–20.

30. See James Hanvery, "Frontiers of the Spirit," *The Way* 60 (2021): 93–108.

31. APA, "Ethical Principles of Psychologists and Code of Conduct" (2017), https://www.apa.org/ethics/code.

32. APA, "Ethical Principles of Psychologists and Code of Conduct."

33. APA, "Ethical Principles of Psychologists and Code of Conduct."

34. APA, "Ethical Principles of Psychologists and Code of Conduct."

35. M. Duffy, "Confidentiality," in *The Ethical and Professional Practice of Counselling and Psychotherapy*, ed. L. Sperry (Pearson Education, 2007), 94.

36. Duffy, "Confidentiality," 94.

37. APA, "Ethical Principles of Psychologists and Code of Conduct."

38. APA, "Ethical Principles of Psychologists and Code of Conduct."

39. APA, "Ethical Principles of Psychologists and Code of Conduct."

40. APA, "Ethical Principles of Psychologists and Code of Conduct."

41. APA, "Ethical Principles of Psychologists and Code of Conduct."

42. APA, "Ethical Principles of Psychologists and Code of Conduct."

43. APA, "Ethical Principles of Psychologists and Code of Conduct."

44. APA, "Ethical Principles of Psychologists and Code of Conduct."

45. APA, "Ethical Principles of Psychologists and Code of Conduct."

46. APA, "Ethical Principles of Psychologists and Code of Conduct."

47. APA, "Ethical Principles of Psychologists and Code of Conduct."

48. APA, "Ethical Principles of Psychologists and Code of Conduct."

49. APA, "Ethical Principles of Psychologists and Code of Conduct."

50. APA, "Ethical Principles of Psychologists and Code of Conduct."

51. APA, "Ethical Principles of Psychologists and Code of Conduct."

52. G. P. Koocher and P. Keith Spiegel, "On Being Ethical," in *Ethics in Psychology: Professional Standards and Cases*, ed. G. P. Koocher and P. Keith Spiegel (Oxford University Press, 2016), 150.

53. Koocher and Spiegel, "On Being Ethical," 153.
54. Duffy, "Confidentiality," 106.
55. Duffy, "Confidentiality," 106.
56. Duffy, "Confidentiality," 93.
57. Duffy, "Confidentiality," 101–5.
58. Duffy, "Confidentiality," 94–96.
59. Schulz, "Bei euch soll es nicht so sein!"
60. M. Kollig, "Gott und die Krise. Freiheit als Paradigma geistlicher Begleitung, " in *Herder Thema. Sonderpublikation. Gefährliche Seelenführer—Geistiger und geistlicher Missbrauch*, ed. H. Timmerevers and T. Arnold (Verlag Herder, 2020), 59–61.
61. Kollig, "Gott und die Krise. Freiheit als Paradigma geistlicher Begleitung," 59–61.
62. Kollig, "Gott und die Krise. Freiheit als Paradigma geistlicher Begleitung," 61.
63. Schulz, "Bei euch soll es nicht so sein!"
64. Schulz, "Bei euch soll es nicht so sein!"
65. Fuchs, "Nähe und Distanz in Begleitbeziehungen: Wovon sprechen wir?"
66. Schulz, "Bei euch soll es nicht so sein!"
67. K. A. Fuchs, "Emotions, Emotion Regulation, and Self-Care in the Field of Safeguarding Minors," 217–20.
68. Fuchs, "Nähe und Distanz in Begleitbeziehungen: Wovon sprechen wir?"; Schulz, "Bei euch soll es nicht so sein!"
69. See A. Buhler, "Where Is God in This? Discerning God's Presence in Spiritual Direction," *Vision* 21, no. 1 (2020): 36–41.
70. Cf. K. A. Fuchs, "Wenn Körper und Seele leiden. Eine psychologische Perspektive des geistlichen Missbrauchs," in *Grauzonen in Kirche und Gesellschaft. Geistiger Missbrauch*, ed. G. Hörting (LIT Verlag, 2021), 26–28.
71. S. Hoffmann, "Erfahrungsbericht und Präventionsempfehlungen. Geistlichen Missbrauch verhindern," in *Herder Thema. Sonderpublikation. Gefährliche Seelenführer—Geistiger und geistlicher Missbrauch*, ed. H. Timmerevers and T. Arnold (Verlag Herder, 2020), 20.
72. Pope Francis, Letter to the Pilgrim People of God in Chile, May 31, 2018, §4, https://www.vatican.va/content/francesco/es/letters/2018/documents/papa-francesco_20180531_lettera-popolodidio-cile.html.

73. C. M. Martini, *Il frutto dello Spirito nella vita quotidiana* (Gribaudi, 1980), 47–59.

Chapter 8

1. M. Aletti, "Processi psicologici e accompagnamento spirituale. Specificità e interazioni," in *Accompagnamento spirituale e intervento psicologico: interpretazioni,* ed. F. G. Brambilla, M. Aletti, M. I. Angelini, and A. Montanari (Edizioni Glossa Srl, 2008), 14.

2. D.-S. Browing, "La psicologia può evitare la religione? Dovrebbe farlo?," in *Antropologia interdisciplinare e formazione,* ed. F. Imoda (EDB, 1997), 57–74.

3. Pope Francis, "Message of the Holy Father to Participants in the International Conference "'Adamo, dove sei?' La questione antropologica oggi," on the Occasion of the Fiftieth Anniversary of the Founding of the Institute of Psychology of the Pontifical Gregorian University," May 19, 2022, https://press.vatican.va/content/salastampa/en/bollettino/pubblico/2022/05/19/220519e.html.

4. S. De Vito and K. A. Fuchs, "Psychology and Theology in Dialogue: The Challenge of Integral Maturation in Formation for the Priesthood," in *For a Fundamental Theology of the Priesthood*, ed. M. Ouellet, vol. 2, *Additional Perspectives* (Paulist Press, 2023), 515–53.

5. Pope Francis, Apostolic Constitution on Ecclesiastical Universities and Faculties *Veritatis Gaudium* (January 29, 2018), https://www.vatican.va/content/francesco/en/apost_constitutions/documents/papa-francesco_costituzione-ap_20171208_veritatis-gaudium.html; Congregation for the Clergy, The Gift of Priestly Vocation *Ratio Fundamentalis Institutionis Sacerdotalis* (December 8, 2016), https://www.clerus.va/content/dam/clerus/documenti/ratio-2026/Ratio-EN-2017-01-03.pdf.

6. Humboldt-Universität zu Berlin, Juristische Fakultät, Wissenschaft, Inter- /Transdisziplinarität, December 8, 2016, https://www.rewi.hu-berlin.de/de/lf/ls/bae/wissen/intertransdisziplinaritaet/index.html.

7. See *Ratio Fundamentalis*, §§146–47.

8. See *Ratio Fundamentalis*, §§190–96.

9. See Congregation for Catholic Education, *Guidelines for the Use of Psychology in the Admission and Formation of Candidates for the Priesthood*, June 29, 2008, https://www.vatican.va/roman_curia/

congregations/ccatheduc/documents/rc_con_ccatheduc_doc_20080628_orientamenti_en.html.

10. See Pope John Paul II, Post-synodal Apostolic Exhortation on the Formation of Priests in the Circumstances of the Present Day *Pastores Dabo Vobis* (March 25, 1992), https://www.vatican.va/content/john-paul-ii/en/apost_exhortations/documents/hf_jp-ii_exh_25031992_pastores-dabo-vobis.html.

11. *Guidelines for the Use of Psychology*, §2.

12. Thomas Aquinas, *Scriptum super Sententiis* (Fordham University Press, 1980).

13. J. W. Stroud, "*Instinctus* and the Gifts of the Holy Spirit: Explaining the Development in St. Thomas's Teaching on the Gifts of the Holy Spirit," *Journal of Moral Theology* 8, no. 2 (2019): 65.

14. *Guidelines for the Use of Psychology*, §5.

15. Since June 2022, Dicastery for the Clergy. After the reform of the Curia in 2022, based on the Constitution *Praedicate Evangelium,* the Congregations and Pontifical Councils that existed until then have been transformed into dicasteries, all at the same level and with an identical structure.

16. Conferenza Episcopale Triventino, "Presentazione della nuova Ratio per la formazione dei seminaristi n occasione della riunione Conferenza Episcopale Triveneto 24 ottobre 2017," *Rivista della Diocesi di Vicenza,* no. 4 (2017): 258–60.

17. S. Lassi, K. A. Fuchs, and H. Zollner, "Formazione e Prevenzione. Confrontare i differenti approcci di formazione umana e valutazione psicologica nei Seminari: un ulteriore passo verso il safeguarding in Europa," *Vivens Homo* 28, no. 1 (2017): 190–200.

18. De Vito and Fuchs, "Psychology and Theology in Dialogue," 515–53.

19. De Vito and Fuchs, "Psychology and Theology in Dialogue," 515–53.

20. "Pastoraltheologie—Pastoralpsychologie—Public Care," University of Graz, Institute for Pastoral Theology, https://pastoraltheologie.uni-graz.at/de/institut/.

21. For example, the School of Theology at Boston University offers courses in the field of pastoral theology and psychology of religion, https://www.bu.edu/academics/sth/courses/pastoral-psychology-and-psychology-of-religion/.

22. Website of the journal *Pastoral Psychology*: https://www.springer.com/journal/11089.

23. De Vito and Fuchs, "Psychology and Theology in Dialogue," 515–53.

24. D. M. Wulff, "Psychology of Religion," in *Encyclopedia of Psychology and Religion*, ed. D. A. Leeming, K. Madden, and S. Marian (Springer, 2010), 732–35.

25. Wulff, "Psychology of Religion," 732–35; "Psicologia della Religione," Università Cattolica del Sacro Cuore, Istituto di Psicologia, https://dipartimenti.unicatt.it/psicologia-unita-di-ricerca-psicologia-della-religione; "What Is Practical Theology?," University of Vienna, Department of Practical Theology and Psychology of Religion, https://etfpt.univie.ac.at/en/practical-theology/.

26. R. A. Piedmont and T. A. Wilkins, "Spirituality, Religiousness, and Personality: Theoretical Foundations and Empirical Applications," in *APA Handbook of Psychology, Religion and Spirituality*, vol. 1, ed. K. I. Paragament, J. J. Exline, and J. W. Jones (APA, 2013), 173–86.; J. Meindl and A. Bucher, "Gibt es eine spirituelle Persönlichkeit? Eine differentialpsychologische Studie," *Wege zum Menschen* 67 (2015): 228–38.

27. F. Imoda, "Psichiatria, psicologia e teologia: un dialogo critico," in *Associazione Italiana Psicologi e Psichiatri Cattolici* (AIPPC), ed. Atti del i Convegno Nazionale "Gli dei morti sono diventati malattie" (March 4–5, 2000), https://www.toninocantelmi.it/gli-dei-morti-son-diventati-malattie/.

28. F. Imoda, "Psichiatria, psicologia e teologia: un dialogo critico," https://www.toninocantelmi.it/gli-dei-morti-son-diventati-malattie/. Translation is ours.

29. L. Sperry, "Multicultural, Relational, and Spiritual Issues in Ethics," in *The Ethical and Professional Practice of Counseling and Psychotherapy*, ed. L. Sperry (Pearson, 2007), 45–51.

30. Sperry, "Multicultural, Relational, and Spiritual Issues in Ethics," 47.

31. Sperry, "Multicultural, Relational, and Spiritual Issues in Ethics," 46–47.

32. C. S. Cashwell and R. E. Watts, "The New ASERVIC Competencies for Addressing Spiritual and Religious Issues in Counseling," *Counseling and Values* 55, no. 1 (2010), 1–5. The complete list is

available under https://onlinelibrary.wiley.com/doi/10.1002/j.2161-007X.2010.tb00018.x.

33. L. Sperry, "Varieties of Religious and Spiritual Treatment: Spirituality Oriented Psychotherapy and Beyond," *Spirituality and Clinical Practice* 3, no. 1 (2016): 2.

34. Sperry, "Varieties of Religious and Spiritual Treatment," 2.

35. L. Sperry, "Spiritually Sensitive Psychotherapy: An Impending Paradigm Shift in Theory and Practice," in *The Oxford Handbook of Psychology of Spirituality,* ed. L. Miller (Oxford University Press, 2012), 223–33.

36. Sperry, "Varieties of Religious and Spiritual Treatment," 2. As the authors stated in the preface of this volume, they have decided to use the terms *spiritual accompaniment* to highlight the interplay between the companion, the person being accompanied, and God. This term keeps the focus on the person being accompanied and the path that God takes with the person. Thus, they have taken the liberty of adapting the table by adding the term *spiritual accompaniment* to it.

37. H. Koenig, *Spirituality in Patient Care: Why, How, When, and What*, 3rd ed. (Templeton Press, 2013), 75.

38. Sperry, "Varieties of Religious and Spiritual Treatment," 1.

39. Sperry, "Varieties of Religious and Spiritual Treatment," 1.

40. S. Guarinelli, *Coinvolgersi. Teologia e psicologia delle relazioni pastorali difficili* (Àncora Editrice, 2022), 30.

41. Guarinelli, *Coinvolgersi*, 30.

42. Guarinelli, *Coinvolgersi*, 31.

43. Guarinelli, *Coinvolgersi*, 31–32.

44. Guarinelli, *Coinvolgersi*, 32.

45. Guarinelli, *Coinvolgersi*, 33.

46. Pontifical Gregorian University, Collegium Maximum Institute of Psychology, "Profile of the Institute of Psychology," https://www.unigre.it/en/psychology/profile/.

47. L. M. Rulla, *Anthropology of Christian Vocation*, vol. 1, *Interdisciplinary Bases* (Gregorian Biblical Press, 2004); L. M. Rulla, J. Ridick, and F. Imoda, *Anthropology of Christian Vocation*, vol. 2, *Existential Confirmation* (Gregorian Biblical Press, 1989).

48. B. Lonergan, *Method in Theology* (Toronto University Press, 2017), 99.

Chapter 9

1. The Diocese of Münster in Germany has made available a catalog with various signs and indicators: https://www.bistum-muenster.de/fileadmin/user_upload/Website/Downloads/Rat-Hilfe/2018-05-Checkliste-kritische-Anzeichen.pdf; W. Schaupp, "Spiritueller Missbrauch. Eine theologisch-ethische Analyse," in *Grauzonen in Kirche und Gesellschaft. Geistiger Missbrauch*, ed. G. Hörting (LIT Verlag, 2021), 92–93.

2. See C. Martini and R. Arnandez, *Letting God Free Us: Meditations on Ignatian Spiritual Exercises* (New City Press, 1993), J. J. English, *Spiritual Freedom: From an Experience of the Ignatian Exercises to the Art of Spiritual Guidance* (Loyola House, 1995).

3. A. Witwer, "Geistlicher Missbrauch. Eine 'Vergewaltigung' der göttlichen Tugenden. Missbrauch von Glaube, Hoffnung und Liebe," in *Grauzonen in Kirche und Gesellschaft. Geistiger Missbrauch,* ed. G. Hörting (LIT Verlag, 2021), 101–2.

4. M. Kollig, "Gott und die Krise. Freiheit als Paradigma geistlicher Begleitung," in *Herder Thema. Sonderpublikation. Gefährliche Seelenführer—Geistiger und geistlicher Missbrauch*, ed. H. Timmerevers and T. Arnold (Verlag Herder, 2020), 59.

5. Kollig, "Gott und die Krise. Freiheit als Paradigma geistlicher Begleitung," 59.

6. R. Heyder and U. Leimgruber, "Spiritueller und sexueller Missbrauch an erwachsenen Frauen. Was aus den Berichten von Betroffenen zu lernen ist," in *Erzählen als Widerstand: Berichte über spirituellen und sexuellen Missbrauch an erwachsenen Frauen in der katholischen Kirche*, ed. B. Haslbeck, R. Heyder, U. Leimgruber, and D. Sandherr-Klemp (Kindle, 2020), pos. 2784.

7. R. Haller, "Die andere Seite. Psychologische Aspekte bei Bezichtigten und (potentiellen) Tätern," in *Grauzonen in Kirche und Gesellschaft. Geistiger Missbrauch*, ed. G. Hörting (LIT Verlag, 2021), 51–53.

8. Haller, "Die andere Seite. Psychologische Aspekte bei Bezichtigten und (potentiellen) Tätern," 51–53.

9. Haller, "Die andere Seite. Psychologische Aspekte bei Bezichtigten und (potentiellen) Tätern," 51–53.

10. Heyder and Leimgruber, "Spiritueller und sexueller Missbrauch an erwachsenen Frauen," pos. 2935.

11. Heyder and Leimgruber, "Spiritueller und sexueller Missbrauch an erwachsenen Frauen," pos. 2942.

12. See S. De Vito, "'To God Be the Glory, to Us Be the Shame.' Rebuilding the Ecclesial Community," *ET-Studies* 13, no. 2 (2022): 329–45.

13. G. Hörting, "Geistlicher Missbrauch als Thema der Kanonistik. Rechtspolitische Schlussfolgerungen im kirchlichen Recht," in *Herder Thema. Sonderpublikation. Gefährliche Seelenführer—Geistiger und geistlicher Missbrauch*, ed. H. Timmerevers and T. Arnold (Verlag Herder, 2020), 53.

14. K. Demasure, K. A. Fuchs, and H. Zollner, *Sexual Abuse of Minors: Theology, Care and Prevention*, CCP Series 1 (Peeters, 2018).

15. See G. Whelan, "John Courtney Murray and 'The Contemporary Clash between Classicism and Historical Consciousness,'" *Gregorianum* 97, no. 3 (2016): 471–93.

16. W. Schaupp, "Spiritueller Missbrauch. Eine theologisch-ethische Analyse," 93.

17. H. König, "Wenn Gottes Wort entweiht wird und sich zuletzt doch als heilsam erweist. Die Rolle der Heiligen Schrift in Missbrauchskontexten," in *Erzählen als Widerstand: Berichte über spirituellen und sexuellen Missbrauch an erwachsenen Frauen in der katholischen Kirche*, ed. B. Haslbeck, R. Heyder, U. Leimgruber, and D. Sandherr-Klemp (Kindle, 2020), pos. 3544–3633.

18. Schaupp, "Spiritueller Missbrauch. Eine theologisch-ethische Analyse," 89.

19. Pope John Paul II, Apostolic Letter on the Dignity and Vocation of Women *Mulieris Dignitatem* (August 15, 1988), §10, https://www.vatican.va/content/john-paul-ii/en/apost_letters/1988/documents/hf_jp-ii_apl_19880815_mulieris-dignitatem.html.

20. The author of the Letter to the Ephesians sees no contradiction between an exhortation formulated in this way and the words: "Wives, be subject to your husbands, as to the Lord. For the husband is the head of the wife" (5:22–23). The author knows that this way of speaking, so profoundly rooted in the customs and religious tradition of the time, is to be understood and carried out in a new way: as a "mutual subjection out of reverence for Christ" (see Eph 5:21). See Martin Troy, "Performing the Head Role: Man Is the head of Woman (1Cor 11:3 and Eph 5:23)," *Biblical Research* 57 (2012): 69–80; Daria Spezzano, "'Be Imitators of God'

Eph 5:1: Aquinas on Charity and Satisfaction," *Nova et vetera* 15, no. 2 (2017): 615–51.

21. See Study Commission, *Control and Abuse, An Investigation on Thomas Philippe, Jean Vanier and L'Arche* (January 2023), 109–11, https://commissiondetude-jeanvanier.org/commissiondetudeindependante2023-empriseetabus/wp-content/uploads/2023/01/Report_Control-and-Abuse_EN.pdf.

22. M. Leb, "Freiheit durch Vergebung," in *Erzählen als Widerstand: Berichte über spirituellen und sexuellen Missbrauch an erwachsenen Frauen in der katholischen Kirche*, ed. B. Haslbeck, R. Heyder, U. Leimgruber, and D. Sandherr-Klemp (Kindle, 2020), pos. 1875.

23. S. Butenkemper, "Was ist mir da passiert?," in *Herder Thema. Sonderpublikation. Gefährliche Seelenführer—Geistiger und geistlicher Missbrauch*, ed. H. Timmerevers and T. Arnold (Verlag Herder, 2020), 17.

24. Butenkemper, "Was ist mir da passiert?" 17.

25. Butenkemper, "Was ist mir da passiert?" 17.

26. Pope Francis, *Motu Proprio Vos Estis Lux Mundi* (March 25, 2023), https://www.vatican.va/content/francesco/en/motu_proprio/documents/20230325-motu-proprio-vos-estis-lux-mundi-aggiornato.html.

27. Hörting, "Geistlicher Missbrauch als Thema der Kanonistik. Rechtspolitische Schlussfolgerungen im kirchlichen Recht," 53.

28. Diocese of Osnabrück, "Checkliste zur Bewertung geistlichen Missbrauchs." Available under https://bistum-osnabrueck.de/wp content/uploads/2017/01/principle-paper-spiritual-abuse-102020.pdf.

29. M. Wiljens, "Die Finsternis aufbrechen. Kirchenrechtliche Überlegungen zum Geistlichen Missbrauch für kirchliches Leitungspersonal," in *Grauzonen in Kirche und Gesellschaft. Geistiger Missbrauch*, ed. G. Hörting (LIT Verlag, 2021), 133.

30. Wiljens, "Die Finsternis aufbrechen. Kirchenrechtliche Überlegungen zum Geistlichen Missbrauch für kirchliches Leitungspersonal," 133.

31. M. Graulich, "Das Kirchenrecht als Prävention gegen geistigen Missbrauch," in *Grauzonen in Kirche und Gesellschaft. Geistiger Missbrauch*, ed. G. Hörting (LIT Verlag, 2021), 120.

32. Dicastery for the Doctrine of the Faith, "Foglio" for the Audience—False Mysticism and Spiritual Abuse, November 22, 2024,

https://www.vatican.va/roman_curia/congregations/cfaith/documents/rc_ddf_doc_20241122_falso-misticismo-e-abuso-spirituale_en.html.

33. Graulich, "Das Kirchenrecht als Prävention gegen geistigen Missbrauch," 120.

34. Code of Canon Law, c. 1389 §1.

35. Code of Canon Law, c. 1389 §2.

36. For example: Cf. Code of Canon Law, c. 240; c. 630; c. 991.

37. Code of Canon Law, c. 983 §1. "The sacramental seal is inviolable; therefore it is absolutely forbidden for a confessor to betray in any way a penitent in words or in any manner and for any reason."

38. Code of Canon Law, c. 1387; c. 1388 §1.

39. Hörting, "Geistlicher Missbrauch als Thema der Kanonistik. Rechtspolitische Schlussfolgerungen im kirchlichen Recht."

40. Code of Canon Law, c. 1339.

41. Code of Canon Law, c. 1340 §1.

42. Hörting, "Geistlicher Missbrauch als Thema der Kanonistik. Rechtspolitische Schlussfolgerungen im kirchlichen Recht," 53.

43. Graulich, "Das Kirchenrecht als Prävention gegen geistigen Missbrauch," 114–16, 120.

44. Code of Canon Law, c. 578. "All must observe faithfully the mind and designs of the founders regarding the nature, purpose, spirit, and character of an institute, which have been sanctioned by competent ecclesiastical authority, and its sound traditions, all of which constitute the patrimony of the same institute."

45. Code of Canon Law, c. 587 §1.

46. Graulich, "Das Kirchenrecht als Prävention gegen geistigen Missbrauch," 120.

47. K. A. Fuchs. "Abuso spirituale e abuso di coscienza: Una realtà sfidante con conseguenze spesso gravi," in *La tutela dei minori e degli adulti vulnerabili nella Chiesa italiana— 3, Prevenzione e formazione nella vita consacrata,* ed. A. Cencini, A. Deodato, and L. Sabbarese (Edizioni San Paolo, 2025), 249–319.

48. S. Hoffmann, "Erfahrungsbericht und Präventionsempfehlungen. Geistlichen Missbrauch verhindern," in *Herder Thema. Sonderpublikation. Gefährliche Seelenführer—Geistiger und geistlicher Missbrauch*, ed. H. Timmerevers and T. Arnold (Verlag Herder, 2020), 20.

49. "Dejémonos ayudar y ayudemos a generar una sociedad donde la cultura del abuso no encuentre espacio para perpetuarse." Pope Francis, "Letter to the Pilgrim People of God in Chile," May 31, 2018, §4, https://

www.vatican.va/content/francesco/es/letters/2018/documents/papa-francesco_20180531_lettera-popolodidio-cile.html.

50. SNTM, *La formazione iniziale in tempo di abusi* (2021), 32.

51. See SNTM, *La formazione iniziale in tempo di abusi*, 25–27.

52. See SNTM, *La formazione iniziale in tempo di abusi*, 27–29.

53. Schaupp, "Spiritueller Missbrauch Eine theologisch-ethische Analyse," 81.

Chapter 10

1. K. A. Fuchs, "Charakteristika und Dimensionen geistlichen Missbrauchs—Eine unterschätzte Gefahr mit gravierenden Folgen," in *Herder Thema. Sonderpublikation. Gefährliche Seelenführer—Geistiger und geistlicher Missbrauch*, ed. H. Timmerevers and T. Arnold (Verlag Herder, 2020), 25.

2. R. Heyder and U. Leimgruber, "Spiritueller und sexueller Missbrauch an erwachsenen Frauen. Was aus den Berichten von Betroffenen zu lernen ist," in *Erzählen als Widerstand: Berichte über spirituellen und sexuellen Missbrauch an erwachsenen Frauen in der katholischen Kirche*, ed. B. Haslbeck, R. Heyder, U. Leimgruber, and D. Sandherr-Klemp (Kindle, 2020), pos. 2865.

3. For further information, see R. Enroth, *Recovering from Churches That Abuse* (Zondervan, 1994).; M. D. Langone, *Recovery from Cults—Help for Victims of Psychological and Spiritual Abuse* (W. W. Norton, 1995); I. Tempelmann, *Geistlicher Missbrauch. Auswege aus frommer Gewalt* (R. Brockhaus, 2007); D. Wagner, *Spiritueller Missbrauch in der katholischen Kirche* (Verlag Herder, 2019).

4. Tempelmann, *Geistlicher Missbrauch. Auswege aus frommer Gewalt*, 298–99.

5. E. Kügler, "Interview: Missbrauch und Institution," *Buddhismus Aktuell*, no. 2 (2022): 62–65. For example, M. Cloitre, "Effective Psychotherapies for Posttraumatic Stress Disorder: A Review and Critique," *CNS Spectrums* 14, no. 1, Suppl. 1 (2009): 32–43; L. E. Watkins, K. R. Sprang, and B. O. Rothbaum, "Treating PTSD: A Review of Evidence-Based Psychotherapy Interventions," *Frontiers in Behavioral Neuroscience* 12 (2018): 258.

6. A. Ehlers and D. M. Clark, "A Cognitive Model of Posttrau-

matic Stress Disorder," *Behaviour Research and Therapy* 38, no. 4 (2000): 319–45.

7. J. D. Ford, D. J. Grasso, J. D. Elhai, and C. A. Courtois, "Treatment of Adults with PTSD," in *Posttraumatic Stress Disorder: Scientific and Professional Dimensions*, ed. J. D. Ford, D. J. Grasso, J. D. Elhai, and C. A. Courtois (Elsevier Academic Press, 2015), 299–366.

8. APA, "Clinical Practice Guideline for the Treatment of Posttraumatic Stress Disorder (PTSD) in Adults" (2017), https://www.apa.org/ptsd-guideline.

9. G. Fischer, *Mehrdimensionale Psychodynamische Traumatherapie MPTT. Manual zur Behandlung psychotraumatischer Störungen* (Heidelberg: Asanger, 2000).

10. Cf. A. Valiente-Gómez, A. Moreno-Alcázar, D. Treen, C. Cedrón, F. Colom, V. Pérez, and B. L. Amann, "EMDR beyond PTSD: A Systematic Literature Review," *Frontiers in Psychology* 8 (2017): 1668.

11. Ford et al., "Treatment of Adults with PTSD," 299–366; Watkins et al., "Treating PTSD: A Review of Evidence-Based Psychotherapy Interventions," 258.

12. E. M. Altmaier, "Meaning in life," in *Promoting Positive Processes after Trauma*, ed. E. M. Altmaier (Elsevier Academic Press, 2019), 81, 134; R. G. Tedeschi and L. G. Calhoun, "Target Article: 'Posttraumatic Growth: Conceptual Foundations and Empirical Evidence,'" *Psychological Inquiry* 15 (2004): 1–18.

13. D. Riggs, C. Monson, S. Glynn, and J. Canterino, "Couple and Family Therapy for Adults," in *Effective Treatments for PTSD*, ed. E. B. Foa, T. M. Keane, M. J. Friedman, and J. A. Cohen (Guilford Press, 2008), 458–78.

14. See V. S. Paythress, *The Miracles of Jesus: How the Saviour's Mighty Acts Serve as Signs of Redemption* (Crossway Books, 2016).

15. Tempelmann, *Geistlicher Missbrauch. Auswege aus frommer Gewalt*, 299; G. Jenkinson, *Walking Free from the Trauma of Coercive, Cultic and Spiritual Abuse: A Workbook for Recovery and Growth* (Routledge, 2023), 29–32.

16. Tempelmann, *Geistlicher Missbrauch. Auswege aus frommer Gewalt*, 301–3.

17. Tempelmann, *Geistlicher Missbrauch. Auswege aus frommer Gewalt*, 303.

18. Heyder and Leimgruber, "Spiritueller und sexueller Miss-

brauch an erwachsenen Frauen. Was aus den Berichten von Betroffenen zu lernen ist," pos. 3037.

19. Heyder and Leimgruber, "Spiritueller und sexueller Missbrauch an erwachsenen Frauen. Was aus den Berichten von Betroffenen zu lernen ist," pos. 3115.

20. Tempelmann, *Geistlicher Missbrauch. Auswege aus frommer Gewalt*, 300–301; H. A. Schulz, "Geistlicher Missbrauch als Idolatrie," in *Grauzonen in Kirche und Gesellschaft. Geistiger Missbrauch*, ed. G. Hörting (LIT Verlag, 2021), 71–74.

21. Tempelmann, *Geistlicher Missbrauch. Auswege aus frommer Gewalt*, 303.; H. A. Schulz, "Geistlicher Missbrauch als Idolatrie," 71; B. Haslbeck, "Warum haben die Frauen nicht nein gesagt? Psychotraumatologische und systemische Einsichten," in *Erzählen als Widerstand: Berichte über spirituellen und sexuellen Missbrauch an erwachsenen Frauen in der katholischen Kirche*, ed. B. Haslbeck, R. Heyder, U. Leimgruber, and D. Sandherr-Klemp (Kindle, 2020), pos. 3285.

22. Tempelmann, *Geistlicher Missbrauch. Auswege aus frommer Gewalt*, 304.

23. Schulz, "Geistlicher Missbrauch als Idolatrie," 72.

24. Tempelmann, *Geistlicher Missbrauch. Auswege aus frommer Gewalt*, 325–30.

25. Tempelmann, *Geistlicher Missbrauch. Auswege aus frommer Gewalt*, 325–30.

26. Tempelmann, *Geistlicher Missbrauch. Auswege aus frommer Gewalt*, 325–30.

27. Heyder, and Leimgruber, "Spiritueller und sexueller Missbrauch an erwachsenen Frauen. Was aus den Berichten von Betroffenen zu lernen ist," pos. 2865.

28. Tempelmann, *Geistlicher Missbrauch. Auswege aus frommer Gewalt*, 325–30; G. Jenkinson, *Walking Free from the Trauma of Coercive, Cultic and Spiritual Abuse: A Workbook for Recovery and Growth*, 134.

29. G. Jenkinson, *Walking Free from the Trauma of Coercive, Cultic and Spiritual Abuse*, 152–55.

30. Tempelmann, *Geistlicher Missbrauch. Auswege aus frommer Gewalt*, 320–31.

31. Schulz, "Geistlicher Missbrauch als Idolatrie," 71–74.

32. Tempelmann, *Geistlicher Missbrauch. Auswege aus frommer Gewalt*, 306–15.

33. J. L. Tobias and J. Lalich, *Captive Hearts—Captive Minds. Freedom and Recovery from Cults and Abusive Relationships* (Hunter House, 1994), 123.

34. Tempelmann, *Geistlicher Missbrauch. Auswege aus frommer Gewalt*, 306–15.

35. H. A. Schulz, *Durch Nebel hindurch. Aus ignatianischer Sicht geistlichen Missbrauch erkennen und überwinden* (Kindle, 2022), pos. 1909–28.

36. Schulz, *Durch Nebel hindurch. Aus ignatianischer Sicht geistlichen Missbrauch erkennen und überwinden*, pos. 540.

37. Tempelmann, *Geistlicher Missbrauch. Auswege aus frommer Gewalt*, 318–20.

38. Tempelmann, *Geistlicher Missbrauch. Auswege aus frommer Gewalt*, 318–20.

39. Schulz, *Durch Nebel hindurch. Aus ignatianischer Sicht geistlichen Missbrauch erkennen und überwinden*, pos. 1508.

40. Tempelmann, *Geistlicher Missbrauch. Auswege aus frommer Gewalt*, 320–22.

41. J. Corkery, "Toward an Understanding of Salvation That Could Be 'Salvific' for Survivors of Sexual Abuse in the Church: An Exploration of the Notion of the Representation in Joseph Ratzinger's Soteriology," in *Sexual Abuse of Minors: Theology, Care and Prevention*, CCP Series 1, ed. K. Demasure, K. A. Fuchs, and H. Zollner (Peeters, 2018), 25.

42. S. De Vito, "'Scandalo di pochi, mediocrità di molti.' Sulle dinamiche di guarigione ecclesiale dagli abusi a partire da Rm 6,1–14," *Gregorianum* 103, no. 2 (2022): 295–99.

43. Corkery, "Toward an Understanding of Salvation That Could Be 'Salvific,'" 32.

44. K. A. Fuchs, "Verwundete Kinderseelen. Sexueller Missbrauch und seine teils verheerenden Auswirkungen," in *Sexualisierte Gewalt gegen Kinder. Hintergründe—Zusammenhänge—Erklärungen*, ed. P. Kerschke-Risch (Kohlhammer, 2022), 49–50.

45. Pope Francis, General Audience (January 4, 2023), https://www.vatican.va/content/francesco/en/audiences/2023/documents/20230104-udienza-generale.html.

Chapter II

1. See Pope Francis, General Audience (June 5, 2013), https://www.vatican.va/content/francesco/en/audiences/2013/documents/papa-francesco_20130605_udienza-generale.html.

2. See R. M. Doran, "Suffering Servanthood and the Scale of Values," in *Lonergan Workshop*, vol. 4, ed. Fred Lawrence (Scholar Press, 1983), 41–65; G. A. Dames, "Pastoral Care and Counselling in Current Time: Relevance and Context of Care," *HTS Theological Studies* 81, no. 1 (2025): 1–11.

3. "Being Church means being God's people, in accordance with the great plan of his fatherly love. This means that we are to be God's leaven in the midst of humanity. It means proclaiming and bringing God's salvation into our world, which often goes astray and needs to be encouraged, given hope and strengthened on the way. The Church must be a place of mercy freely given, where everyone can feel welcomed, loved, forgiven and encouraged to live the good life of the Gospel" (*EG* 114).

4. See Koos S. Tamminga, *Receiving the Gifts of Every Member: A Practical Ecclesiological Case Study on Inclusion and the Church* (Summum Academic Publication, 2020).

5. Stephen A. Cummins, "Divine Life and Corporate Christology: God, Messiah Jesus, and the Covenant Community in Paul," in *The Messiah in the Old and New Testament*, ed. Craig A. Evans (Eerdmans, 2007): 190–209.

6. W. Houston, "The King's Preferential Option for the Poor: Rhetoric, Ideology and Ethics in Psalm 72," *Biblical Interpretation* 7 (1999): 341–67; O. A. Adewale, "Narratological Reading of Poverty-Related Parables (Lk 12:13–21; 14:15–24; 16:19–31)," *HTS Theological Studies* 77, no. 1 (2021): 1–10; B. Worthington, "The Identity of the Poor in Luke 4:18, Jesus' Mission, and the Mission of the Church," *Criswell Theological Review* 19, no. 2 (2022): 23–44.

7. See Eva Marie Lumas, "It Takes a Whole Village to…Do Just about Everything! Embracing a Preferential Option for the Poor," *New Theological Review* 24, no. 2 (2011): 72–84.

8. See G. O'Collins, "Love as a Verb (1 Cor 13:4–8a)," *The Expository Times* 131, no. 5 (2020): 205–8.

9. Q. Paxman, "When His Eyes Were Opened a Little: The Role of Noticing in the Spiritual Exercises," *The Way* 61, no. 2 (2022): 28.

10. L. Currie, "Healing Memory: A Bonaventurian Response to Pope Francis' *Fratelli Tutti*," *Religions* 13 (2022): 2.

11. SNTM, *La formazione iniziale in tempo di abusi. Sussidio per formatori al presbiterato e alla vita consacrata e ai giovani in formazione* (SNTM, 2021): 85–86, https://tutelaminori.chiesacattolica.it/un-sussidio-formativo-per-i-candidati-agli-ordini-sacri. Translation is ours.

12. E. Estévez López, "Transformative Spirituality and Mission as Healing and Reconciliation," *International Review of Mission* 98, no. 2 (2009): 286.

13. R. M. Doran, *Theology and Dialectics of History* (University of Toronto Press, 1990), 121–22.

14. See S. De Vito, "'Il Magistero delle vittime' per una teologia dell'abuso: Il contro-esodo di Noemi nel libro di Rut," *Annales Theologici* 37 (2023): 169–98.

15. Doran, *Theology and Dialectics of History*, 125.

16. See M. Uwineza, *Risen from the Ashes. Theology as Autobiography in Post-Genocide Rwanda* (Paulines, 2022).

17. Doran, "Suffering Servanthood and the Scale of Values," 65.

18. See Doran, *Theology and Dialectics of History*, 161–69.

Selected Bibliography

Altmaier, E. M. *Promoting Positive Processes after Trauma*. Elsevier, 2019.

American Psychological Association. *Ethical Principles of Psychologists and Code of Conduct*. 2017. https://www.apa.org/ethics/code/ethics-code-2017.pdf.

Aschenbrenner, G. "Becoming Whom We Contemplate." *The Way Supplement* 52 (1985): 32–40.

Barry, W. A., and R. G. Doherty. *Contemplative in Action: The Jesuit Way*. Paulist Press, 2002.

Buhler, A. "Where Is God in This? Discerning God's Presence in Spiritual Direction." *Vision* 21, no. 1 (2020): 36–41.

Cencini, A., A. Deodato, and L. Sabbarese, eds. *La tutela dei minori e degli adulti vulnerabili nella Chiesa italiana—3, Prevenzione e formazione nella vita consacrata.* Edizioni San Paolo, 2025.

Chan, S. "'Sin and Grace' or 'Grace and Sin'?: Implications for Christian Spirituality." *Evangelical Review of Theology* 48, no. 2 (2024): 126–38.

Cito, D. "Brevi annotazioni canonistiche sul concetto di abuso di potere e di coscienza." *Tredimensioni. Psicologia, Spiritualità, Formazione* 17, no. 3 (2020): 302–12.

Clyde, M. "Faith, Hope, and Charity." *Dialogue* 27, no. 2 (1994): 227–34.

Congregation for the Clergy. *Ratio Fundamentalis Institutionis Sacerdotalis* [The Gift of the Priestly Vocation]. December 8, 2016. https://www.clerus.va/content/dam/clerus/documenti/ratio-2026/Ratio-EN-2017-01-03.pdf.

Congregation for the Doctrine of Faith. *Donum Veritatis* [On the Ecclesial Vocation of the Theologian]. May 24, 1990. https://www.vatican.va/roman_curia/congregations/cfaith/documents/rc_con_cfaith_doc_19900524_theologian-vocation_en.html.

Costa, A. S. "Times of Ignatian Election. The Wisdom of the Directories." *The Way* 42, no. 4 (October 2003): 73–88.

Cummins, S. A. "Divine Life and Corporate Christology: God, Messiah Jesus, and the Covenant Community in Paul." In *The Messiah in the Old and New Testament*. Edited by S. E. Porter. McMaster New Testament Studies. Eerdmans, 2007.

Curtis, S. "Will and Grace: The Essence of Pelagian Debate." *Journal of Asian Evangelical Theology* 20, no. 2 (2016): 55–73.

Dames, G. "Exploring Attributes for an Authentic Christian Spirituality in an Age of Growing Secularization and Skepticism: A Practical Theological Reflection." *Stellenbosch Theological Journal* 9, no. 2 (2023): 1–27.

Deam, L. *3000 Miles to Jesus: Pilgrimage as a Way of Life for Spiritual Seekers*. Broadliff Books, 2021.

Demasure, K., K. A. Fuchs, and H. Zollner, eds. *Sexual Abuse of Minors: Theology, Care and Prevention.* CCP Series 1. Peeters, 2018.

De Mauro, G. E., "Modern Psychology and Ancient Heresy: The Rebirth of Pelagianism." *The Catholic Social Science Review* 4 (1999): 205–15.

Denney A. "Child Sex Abusers in Protestant Christian Churches: An Offender Typology." *CrimRxiv*, October 25, 2021. https://doi.org/10.21428/cb6ab371.e3e20c48.

Denney, A. S., K. R. Kerley, and N. G. Gross. "Child Sexual Abuse in Protestant Christian Congregations: A Descriptive Analysis of Offense and Offender Characteristics." *Religions* 9, no. 1 (2016): 27.

De Vito, S. *Ecco! Ti racconto un'esperienza di Dio*. Tau Editrice, 2025. (forthcoming)

———. "El abuso espiritual como bias teológico. Destroza El rostro de Dios y del hombre," in *Abuso de podere en la Iglesia. Una prepuesta interdisciplinare*. Edited by V. Ferrer Usó. Tirant Humanidades, 2025 (forthcoming).

———. "Il Magistero delle vittime per una teologia dell'abuso. Il contro-esodo di Noemi nel Libro di Rut." *Annales Theologici* 37, no. 1 (2023): 169–98.

———. "Pastoral Care and Counselling in current time: Relevance and Context of Care." *HTS Theological Studies* 81, no. 1 (2025): 1–11.

———. "Reconciliation Process in the Letter to the Colossians: A Response to Abuse Crises." *Salvation in a Crises-Ridden World: An Intercultural-Biblical Response*. Edited by N. Gatti, F. Gmainer-Pranzl and B. Kowalski. Brill, 2025 (forthcoming).

———. "'Scandalo di pochi, mediocrità di molti.' Sulle dinamiche di guarigione ecclesiale a partire da Rm 6,1–14." *Gregorianum* 103, no. 2 (2022): 287–307.

De Vito, S., and K. A. Fuchs. "Psychology and Theology in Dialogue: The Challenge of Integral Maturation in Formation for the Priesthood." *For a Fundamental Theology of the Priesthood, Additional Perspectives*, vol. 2. Edited by M. Ouellet. Paulist Press, 2023.

Dörr, M., ed. *Nähe und Distanz. Ein Spannungsfeld pädagogischer Professionalität*. Beltz, 2019.

Enroth, R. *Recovering from Churches that Abuse*. Zondervan, 1994.

Estévez López, E. "Transformative Spirituality and Mission as Healing and Reconciliation." *International Review of Mission* 98, no. 2 (2009): 283–301.

Ettlinger, G. H. "Church Fathers and Desert Mothers: Male and Female in the Early Church." *America* 164 (May 25, 1991): 558–66.

Ford, J. D., D. J. Grasso, J. D. Elhai, and C. A. Courtois, eds. "Treatment of Adults with PTSD." *Posttraumatic Stress Disorder: Scientific and Professional Dimensions*. Elsevier, 2015.

Francis, Pope. *Amoris Laetitia* [On Love in the Family]. March 19, 2016. https://www.vatican.va/content/dam/francesco/pdf/apost_exhortations/documents/papa-francesco_esortazione-ap_20160319_amoris-laetitia_en.pdf.

———. *Evangelii Gaudium* [The Joy of the Gospel]. November 24, 2013. https://www.vatican.va/content/francesco/en/apost_exhortations/documents/papa-francesco_esortazione-ap_20131124_evangelii-gaudium.html.

———. *Fratelli Tutti* [On Fraternity and Social Relationship]. October 3, 2020. https://www.vatican.va/content/francesco/en/encyclicals/documents/papa-francesco_20201003_enciclica-fratelli-tutti.html.

———. General Audience. January 4, 2023. https://www.vatican.va/content/francesco/en/audiences/2023/documents/20230104-udienza-generale.html.

———. General Audience. June 5, 2013. https://www.vatican.va/content/francesco/en/audiences/2013/documents/papa-francesco_20130605_udienza-generale.html.

———. Letter to the Pilgrim People of God in Chile. May 31, 2018. https://www.vatican.va/content/francesco/es/letters/2018/documents/papa-francesco_20180531_lettera-popolodidio-cile.html.

———. Message to Participants in the International Conference "'Adamo, dove sei?' La questione antropologica oggi" [On the Occasion of the Fiftieth Anniversary of the Founding of the Institute of Psychology of the Pontifical Gregorian University]. May 14, 2022. https://www.vatican.va/content/francesco/en/messages/pont-messages/2022/documents/20220514-messaggio-convegno-adamo.html.

———. *Motu Proprio Vos Estis Lux Mundi.* March 25, 2023. https://www.vatican.va/content/francesco/en/motu_proprio/documents/20230325-motu-proprio-vos-estis-lux-mundi-aggiornato.html.

———. *Veritatis Gaudium* [On Ecclesiastical Universities and Faculties]. January 29, 2018. https://www.vatican.va/content/francesco/en/apost_constitutions/documents/papa-francesco_costituzione-ap_20171208_veritatis-gaudium.html.

Fuchs, K. A. "Abuso spirituale e abuso di coscienza: Una realtà sfidante con conseguenze spesso gravi," in *La tutela dei minori e degli adulti vulnerabili nella Chiesa italiana – 3, Prevenzione e formazione nella vita consacrata*. Edited by A. Cencini, A. Deodato, and L. Sabbarese. Edizioni San Paolo, 2025, 249–319.

———. "Cuando se transgreden los límites 'en Su nombre.' Una introducción a la realidad del abuso espiritual," *Humanitas. Revista de Antropología y Cultura Cristiana* 29, no. 108 (2024): 432–47.

———. "Emotions, Emotion Regulation, and Self-Care in the Field of Safeguarding Minors." *Sexual Abuse of Minors: Theology, Care and Prevention*. CCP Series 1. Edited by K. Demasure, K. A. Fuchs, and H. Zollner. Peeters, 2018.

———. "Verwundete Kinderseelen. Sexueller Missbrauch und seine teils verheerenden Auswirkungen." *Sexualisierte Gewalt gegen*

Kinder. Hintergründe—Zusammenhänge—Erklärungen. Edited by P. Kerschke-Risch. Kohlhammer, 2022, 40–52.

———. "Wenn Körper und Seele leiden. Eine psychologische Perspektive des geistlichen Missbrauchs." *Grauzonen in Kirche und Gesellschaft. Geistiger Missbrauch.* Edited by G. Hörting. LIT Verlag, 2021, 13–28.

Fuchs, K. A., and A. Deodato. "Vulnerabilità: aspetti personali e sistemici." *Tredimensioni. Psicologia, Spiritualità, Formazione* 21, no. 3 (2024): 255–69.

Fuchs, K. A., and S. De Vito. *Comprendere la realtà degli abusi spirituali, Versione integrale.* Movimento dei Focolari in Svizzera: Che cosa è l'abuso spirituale. 2022. https://www.fokolar-bewegung.ch/it/seite/cosa-e-labuso-spirituale.

Ganss, G. E. "Thinking with the Church: The Spirit of St. Ignatius's Rules." *The Way* (Fall 1973): 71–82.

Giuliani, M. "St. Ignatius Embracing the Future." *The Way* 58, no. 1 (2019): 41–59.

Goudriaan, K. "Empowerment through Reading, Writing and Example: The *Devotio moderna*." *Cambridge History of Christianity.* Vol 4: *Christianity in Western Europe c. 1100–c. 1500.* Edited by M. Rubin and W. Simons. Cambridge University Press, 2009.

Greshake, G. *Chiesa dove vai? Guardare alla Chiesa in prospettiva real-utopista.* Queriniana, 2023.

———. *Libertà donata. Introduzione alla dottrina della grazia.* Brescia, Italy: Queriniana, 2002.

Günter, G. J. "*Sentire cum Ecclesia*." *La Civiltà Cattolica* 144, no. 3429 (May 1, 1993): 227–37.

Hanvery, J. "Frontiers of the Spirit." *The Way* 60 (2021): 93–108.

Haslbeck, B., R. Heyder, U. Leimgruber, and D. Sandherr-Klemp, eds. *Erzählen als Widerstand: Berichte über spirituellen und sexuellen Missbrauch an erwachsenen Frauen in der katholischen Kirche.* Aschendorff Verlag, 2020. Kindle.

Häuselmann, J., and F. Insa. "Abuse of Power, Spiritual Abuse, and Abuse of Conscience: Similarities and Differences," 1–10. Official English translation of the article "Abuso di potere, abuso spirituale e abuso di coscienza: Somiglianze e differenze, *Tredimensioni. Psicologia, Spiritualità, Formazione* 20, no. 1 (2023): 42–53. https://www.isfo.it/files/File/Spagnolo/Hauselmann-Insa23.pdf.

Healy, T. "The Challenge of Self-Transcendence." *A Journey to Freedom: An Interdisciplinary Approach to the Anthropology of Formation*. Edited by F. Imoda. Peeters, 2000.

Heiner, M. *Kompetent handeln in der Sozialen Arbeit*. Ernst Reinhardt Verlag, 2010.

———. *Professionalität in der sozialen Arbeit: Theoretische Konzepte, Modelle und empirische Perspektiven*. Kohlhammer, 2004.

Helsper, W., and S. Reh. "Nähe, Diffusität und Asymmetrie in pädagogischen Interaktionen." *Sexualisierte Gewalt, Macht und Pädagogik*. Edited by W. Thole, M. Baader, W. Helsper, M. Kappeler, M. Leuzinger-Bohleber, S. Reh, U. Sielert, and C. Thompson. Barbara Budrich Verlag, 2012.

Heyder, R. "Narrating and Remembrance in the Face of Abuse in the Church." *Religions* 13, no. 4 (2022): 1–12.

Hörting, G., ed. *Grauzonen in Kirche und Gesellschaft. Geistiger Missbrauch*. LIT Verlag, 2021.

Imoda, F. "Spiritual Exercises of Ignatius of Loyola and Psychology." *Studies in Spirituality* 1 (1991): 199–228.

Jalics, F. *Die Geistliche Begleitung im Evangelium*. Echter Verlag, 2012.

———. *Lerner wir beten: Eine Anleitung, mit Gotta ins Gespräch zu kommen*. Echter Verlag, 1996.

John XXIII, Pope. *Mater et Magistra* [On Christianity and Social Progress]. May 15, 1961. https://www.vatican.va/content/john-xxiii/en/encyclicals/documents/hf_j-xxiii_enc_15051961_mater.html.

John Paul II, Pope. *Catechism of the Catholic Church*, 2nd ed. United States Catholic Conference, 2011.

———. *Pastores Dabo Vobis* [On the Formation of Priests]. March 25, 1992. https://www.vatican.va/content/john-paul-ii/en/apost_exhortations/documents/hf_jp-ii_exh_25031992_pastores-dabo-vobis.html.

Johnson, D., and J. Van Vonderen. *The Subtle Power of Spiritual Abuse—Recognising and Escaping Spiritual Manipulation and False Spiritual Authority within the Church*. Bethany House, 1991.

Lane, C. "Jesus and the Cross-Centered Spirituality of the Reformation and Later Protestantism." *Religions* 14, no. 6 (2023): 1–10.

Langone, M. D. *Recovery from Cults—Help for Victims of Psychological and Spiritual Abuse*. W. W. Norton, 1995.

Lavra, M. "Dirigere o accompagnare?" *Appunti di spiritualità* 35 (1993): 59–66.

Lawlor, F. X. "The Doctrine of Grace in the Spiritual Exercises." *Theological Studies* 3 (1942): 513–21.

Lecuit, J.-B. "Le Spirituel et Le Psychique: Sans Confusion Ni Séparation: Repères pour l'accompagnement spirituel." *Teresianum* 72, no. 1 (2021): 95–126.

Lennan, R. "Behind Scandal and Shame?: Ecclesiology and the Longing for a Transformed Church." *Theological Studies* 80, no. 3 (2019): 590–610.

Lonford, D., and J. Megill. "Idolatry, Indifference, and the Scientific Study of Religion: Two New Human Arguments." *Religious Studies* 56, no. 4 (2020): 488–508.

López, E. "Transformative Spirituality and Mission as Healing and Reconciliation." *International Review of Mission* 98, no. 2 (2009): 283–301.

Lumas, E. M. "It Takes a Whole Village to…Do Just about Everything! Embracing a Preferential Option for the Poor." *New Theological Review* 24, no. 2 (2011): 72–84.

Mansfield, D. "Spiritual Accompaniment and Discernment." *The Way* 47, no. 1 (2008): 155–64.

McGuinness, T. "The Way of Accompaniment." *The Way*. Supplement 104 (November 2002): 96–107.

Mertes, K. "Geistlicher Machtmissbrauch." *Geist und Leben. Zeitschrift für christliche Spiritualität* 90, no. 3 (2017): 249–59.

Murphy, G. L. "The Theology of the Cross and God's Work in the World." *Zygon* 33, no. 2 (1998): 224.

Nijdam, M. J., C. van der Meer, M. van Zuiden, P. Dashtgard, D. Medema, Y. Qing, P. Zhutovsky, A. Bakker, and M. Olff. "Turning Wounds into Wisdom: Posttraumatic Growth over the Course of Two Types of Trauma-Focused Psychotherapy in Patients with PTSD." *Journal of Affective Disorders* 227 (2018): 424–31.

Oakley, L., and J. Humphreys. *Escaping the Maze of Spiritual Abuse: Creating Healthy Christian Cultures*. SPCK, 2019.

Oakley, L., and K. Kinmond. *Breaking the Silence on Spiritual Abuse*. Palgrave Macmillan, 2013.

O'Collins, G. "Love as a Verb (1 Cor 13: 4–8a)." *The Expository Times* 131, no. 5 (2020): 205–8.

Orchard, H. "The Creature and the Sovereign Self: The Anthropology of the Spiritual Exercises and Contemporary Spiritual Narcissism." *The Way* 1 (2020): 12.

Ospino, H. "Theological Horizons for a Pedagogy of Accompaniment." *Religious Education* 105, no. 4 (2010): 413–29.

Paul VI, Pope. *Dignitatis Humanae* [Declaration on Religious Freedom]. December 7, 1965. https://www.vatican.va/archive/hist_councils/ii_vatican_council/documents/vat-ii_decl_19651207_dignitatis-humanae_en.html.

———. *Gaudium et Spes* [On the Church the Modern World]. December 7, 1965. https://www.vatican.va/archive/hist_councils/ii_vatican_council/documents/vat-ii_const_19651207_gaudium-et-spes_en.html.

———. *Lumen Gentium* [Dogmatic Constitution on the Church]. November 21, 1964. https://www.vatican.va/archive/hist_councils/ii_vatican_council/documents/vat-ii_const_19641121_lumen-gentium_en.html.

Paxman, Q. "When His Eyes Were Opened a Little: The Role of Noticing in the Spiritual Exercises." *The Way* 61, no. 2 (2022): 27–41.

Peirats, A., and G. Ruben. "Meditation and Contemplation: Word and Image at the Service of Medieval Spirituality." *Religions* 14, no. 2 (2023): 1–20.

Piva, G. *Dignità e responsabilità. Un cammino di liberazione per tutt**. Il Pellegrino, 2024.

Plekon, M. "Merton's Monastic Renewal and the Desert Mothers and Fathers." *The American Benedictine Review* 73, no. 4 (2022): 390–413.

Ronzoni, G. "L'abuso spirituale. Riconoscerlo per prevenirlo," in *La tutela dei minori e degli adulti vulnerabili nella Chiesa italiana – 3, Prevenzione e formazione nella vita consacrata*. Edited by A. Cencini, A. Deodato, and L. Sabbarese. Edizioni San Paolo, 2025, 321–52.

Rotsaert, M. *De Loyola au Vatican. Idées reçues sur les jésuites*. Le Cavalier Blue, 2013.

———. *Esercizi spirituali di sant'Ignazio. Storia, contenuto, metodo, finalità*. Edizioni San Paolo, 2005.

———. "Ignatian Spirituality: Some Changes in Vision and Practise." *The Way* 55, no. 4 (2016): 118–27.

———. "Spiritual Discernment. The Horizon That Is God." *The Way* 58, no. 4 (October 2019): 99–110.

Sands, J. "Introducing Cardinal Cardijn's See–Judge–Act as an Interdisciplinary Method to Move Theory into Practice." *Religions* 129, no. 9 (2018): 1–10.

Schneiders, S. M. "Religion versus Spirituality: A Contemporary Conundrum." *Spiritus* 3, no. 2 (2003): 163–85.

Schulz, H. A. *Durch Nebel hindurch. Aus ignatianischer Sicht geistlichen Missbrauch erkennen und überwinden*. Echter Verlag.

Selvam, S. "The Unnamed Companion on the Road: Spiritual Accompaniment in the Context of Youth Ministry." *The Journal of Youth Ministry* 11, no. 2 (2013): 41–55.

Sheldrake, P. "Spirituality in History." Τέλειος/*Teleios* 1, no. 2 (2021): 3–17.

Sheppard, J. "See, Judge, Act and Ignatian Spirituality." *The Way* 56, no. 1 (January 2017): 102–11.

SNTM. *La formazione iniziale in tempo di abusi. Sussidio per formatori al presbiterato e alla vita consacrata e ai giovani in formazione*. SNTM, 2021.

Spezzano, D. "'Those He Predestined He Also Called' (Romans 8:30): Aquinas on the Liberating Grace of Conversion." *Journal of Moral Theology* 10 (2021): 67–83.

Tamminga, K. S. *Receiving the Gifts of Every Member: A Practical Ecclesiological Case Study on Inclusion and the Church*. Summum Academic, 2020.

Tempelmann, I. *Geistlicher Missbrauch. Auswege aus frommer Gewalt*. R. Brockhaus, 2007.

Timmerevers, H., and T. Arnold, eds. *Herder Thema. Sonderpublikation. Gefährliche Seelenführer—Geistiger und geistlicher Missbrauch*. Verlag Herder, 2020.

Tobias, J. L., and J. Lalich. *Captive Hearts—Captive Minds. Freedom and Recovery from Cults and Abusive Relationships*. Hunter House, 1994.

Vest, N., ed. *Tending the Holy: Spiritual Direction across Traditions*. Morehouse, 2003.

Vigorelli, I., J. Pujol, and F. Insa. *Le relazioni asimmetriche nella Chiesa*. Edusc, 2023.

Wagner, D. *Spiritueller Missbrauch in der katholischen Kirche*. Verlag Herder, 2019.

Ward, D. J. "The Lived Experience of Spiritual Abuse." *Mental Health, Religion and Culture* 14 (2011): 899–915.

Watkins, L. E., K. R. Sprang, and B. O. Rothbaum. "Treating PTSD: A Review of Evidence-Based Psychotherapy Interventions." *Frontiers in Behavioral Neuroscience* 12 (2018): 258.

Wengert, T. J. "Peace, Peace…Cross, Cross. Reflections on How Martin Luther Relates the Theology of the Cross to Suffering." *Lutheran Quarterly* 33, no. 3 (2019): 304–23.

Werner, G. "Specifically Catholic: At the Intersection of Power, Maleness, Holiness, and Sexualized Violence." *Journal of the European Society of Women in Theological Research*, no. 27 (2019): 147–74.

Zevini, G. "'Ti guido per la strada su cui devi andare.' Icone bibliche di accompagnamento spirituale." *Quaderni di Spiritualità Salesiana* 1, New Series 2 (2004): 11–28.